[handwritten: Emm]

[handwritten: I pray you ...]

LIFE DIRECTIONS:

RAISING HOPE, BUILDING PEACE

40 Years of Peers Inspiring Peers

Through Forgiving

[handwritten: of pioneers for the poor! Pray for our mission and know I'll remember you! F. John Phelps]

By Rev. John Phelps, C.Ss.R.

With co-founders
Sister Rosalie A. Esquerra, OP
Alexander and Judith MacDonald
and Father Alex Steinmiller, CP

www.lifedirections.org

[handwritten: Hope all is well at EWTN]

Copyright @ 2014 by Life Directions

Published in the United States by: Life Directions, a not-for-profit 501 (c) organization

All Photos and art are copyrighted

All rights reserved. No part of this book may be reproduced by any mechanical, photographic, or electronic process, or in the form of a photographic recording; nor may it be stored in a retrieval system, transmitted, or otherwise copied for public or private use-other than "fair use" as brief quotations embodied in articles and reviews-without prior written permission of the authors.

The opinions set forth herein are those of the authors, and do not necessarily express the views of Life Directions or any of its affiliates or associates.

Anniversary Edition, November 2013

Third Edition, June 2014

Printed in the United States

Cover and Interior Design by Lacey O'Connor

Additional editing, photo and design support: Christine Hathaway, Hannah Hillier with Dandelion

ADMIRATION FOR LIFE DIRECTIONS

"God sent me here for a reason - to be with and for the students least valued. That's what I love about Life Directions. Their heart is the same. Together we plant the seeds and watch them grow."

- Carol Williams, Agricultural Education Teacher, John Marshall Metropolitan High School

"As a teacher, I have personally seen students grow in maturity as a result of the Peer Motivation Program. The various aspects of Life Directions form a powerful combination to influence young people's lives in a positive way."

- Bruce Wojciechowski, Mathematics and Physics Teacher, Western International High School

"The founders of this more than forty year old effort have exhibited true grit, tenacity, imagination and resilience in entering difficult, at times forbidding, situations and establishing beachheads where lights have started to flicker on again. Life Directions has engaged young people often unwilling to be engaged and have watered and fertilized sprouting lives so that some greenery has begun to break the surface."

– Rev. Sebastian MacDonald, CP, Author & Professor of Moral Theology, Chicago IL

"Life Directions: Raising Hope, Building Peace..." is a passionate account of 40 years of transforming the ordinary into the extraordinary. It is a constant reminder of the path of peace that leads to graced outcomes in real life situations. It turns hoped for dreams into visible steps toward peace. Hope has new meaning in these pages of grace."

- Sr. Gail Trippett, CSJ – Principal, Resurrection Catholic School

Peace-Building Bed of Roses

Our children are the Springtime of our life
Our parents are the Summer of our living
Our grandparents are the Autumn of our loving
Our elders are the Winter of our love
As leaves lose their green and show their colors,
They give forth their warmth beneath the snow
To nurture the seeds of
The power of love
To overcome
The love of power
Remembering our past that empowers our future!

By Fr. John Phelps, C.Ss.R.

DEDICATION
FIND WISDOM AND ENJOY THE JOURNEY!

"When I get to heaven, I am going to ask God why He gave so much energy to children who do not appreciate it!" I remember my father saying this to me when we had a family gathering to celebrate their 40th Anniversary.

As we reflected on our journey and remembered the lessons learned, the place of grandparents led me to want to say, "If I make it to heaven, I am going to answer my dad by thanking mom and him for the wisdom I needed before I knew why."

We dedicate this book to the place of grandparents on the journey from fallen human nature to let go and let God show us the way to the truth that leads to life through forgiving. For those who have heard, "The truth will set you free," may I add a challenge, "It will either make your day or ruin the rest of your life." It all depends on our "response-ability."

There are three grandparents who were role models for Life Directions. They have all passed on and have met our maker. They are the following:

Alexander MacDonald, the father of eight children, whose wisdom and wit, along with his wife, Judith, worked wonders for so many years. He is the co-founder of nurturing young adults from eighteen to thirty-five years of age to be inspired through forgiving themselves and passing on its energy to their children.

James A. Hathaway, the judge who provided us with the way to build boundaries to be as wise as a serpent and as innocent as a dove. His second-nature way of walking in both the sacred and secular worlds continues to build the discipline of our dream— peers inspire their peers— letting those we serve do more and those who work with them do less.

Peter "Pete" Raskob, the funder, who taught us to be accountable to those who give us the resources for our work. His grandfather crafted the foundation whose mantra—to us—was "If you want peace, work for justice." Pete guided us to seed our mission for the next generation.

May the "grandchildren" be the beneficiaries of what these three men and those who loved them gently but firmly challenged us to be: faithful to our prayer—peace out of pain and hope out of despair—through the unconditional love that forgiving offers to those who do not know a way to a truth that sets us free.

AUTHOR'S NOTE

Life Directions: Raising Hope, Building Peace is a memoir based on the memories and recollections of the co-founders and long-time associates of Life Directions. In telling our story, we sought to protect the privacy of others by changing specific names or identities or simply using first names. Events and conversations are derived from our memories and extracted from our personal hand-written journals compiled over a 40-year period.

CHAPTERS AND PARABLES

INTRODUCTION
LESSONS LEARNED - A TIME FOR TELLING

"Did somebody die?"

This question was posed to me by the very first young person I met when I walked through the doors of Detroit's Western International High School. Apparently, the only time this young man had seen a priest was at a funeral. The year was 1973. Detroit, at the time, was known as the "Murder Capitol of America," with an average of one young death every eighteen hours, according to the news. The young man's question was a sign that I had started my journey in the right place.

I was following up on an opportunity given to me by my Provincial, Father Dan Lowery, to reach "into an unmet human need." That "need" was exemplified in the drastically high number of young people in Detroit who were killing each other and their futures. Detroit's Archbishop John Cardinal Dearden, the leader in our faith community, was encouraging us as we shared our dream to find a practical way of responding to the crisis of "kids killing kids."

Obviously, this mission would not work in the traditional church or private school structures. Young adults, especially those living in environments of poverty, were not present in our parishes and private schools by any great numbers. No, this "walk" had to begin in public schools where poverty and all its dysfunctional tentacles touch young people's lives and from which they leave and begin to live and die on the streets.

Without training or direction, Fr. Dan believed my "walking would create the path," with the Word of God as the map. Therefore, I walked into a public school where gangs, drugs, addictions, and violence were daily factors in young people's lives. That initial path led to what is known today as "Life Directions."

We celebrated our 40th anniversary on November 9, 2013. Some would call it a coincidence, a reversal of 9/11. We consider "coincidences" simply God's way of being anonymous. That night the gathering at Saint Anne's Shrine in Detroit opened us to discover that what we had gained went far beyond youth work. We were honored to celebrate with people we had inspired since 1973.

Annette was one of the hosts who shared with those in attendance how she was touched by focus: LIFE in 1974. Bill Kilburg, who you'll read more about, was carrying Donna, a paraplegic, up the stairs to the hall. He was there to thank us (and Donna) for his life-changing experience in 1981. Dr. Dave, now a pediatrician at Beaumont Hospital, enjoyed talking with David Fukuzawa, who takes part in the Kresge Foundation's work to invest in the challenge of rebuilding communities ravaged by generational cycles of poverty.

We thanked every person who heard of our celebration and made time to join us. Like the one leper who was cured and thanked Jesus (Luke 17:19), they came back to thank us. We had told their stories in the anniversary edition. Their stories opened our eyes to the healing that unconditional forgiving makes possible for life.

We began in 1973 as a response to injustices that happen to people who are deprived of quality education and all that happens because of it. This commitment led us to people who seemed trapped in the "wheel of self-defeat" but could be lifted by their peers who accept them just the way they are.

As companions on the journey of forgiving, the co-founders wanted to bring to others what had transformed our lives. Forgiving is a way to give the Power Greater Than Human a chance to do what only such energy can. We tell the stories of those who forgave themselves, as we learned to do ourselves. We share how remembering our need to receive forgiving ignited our desire to do the same to those who violate us.

This book is a reflection upon the experience of a small group of people seeking LIFE. It stands as a quiet reminder that life demands a community to make any one person's dream happen.

We want to encourage, through our story, people dedicated to wanting young people to thrive and we want to partner with them. We show the cause of violence from our experience as well as some of the reasons why young people make self-defeating choices. We are solution-focused and tell stories that are testimonials to what worked for them. By including all the ways we continue to search for Life in the midst of Death, we hope to encourage you to do the same. It is a quest for success as much as an unconditional commitment to being faithful to those for whom systems are not working.

Twenty-eight years after we began our work in Detroit, terrorists attacked the World Trade Center on September 11, 2001. The late Peter "Pete" Raskob, a senior board member of the Raskob Foundation, heard me explain some of the outcomes of the work of Life Directions while speaking in Tucson, Arizona.

"Wait," he said, responding to my comments. "Did I hear you say you can get to the cause of the kind of violence that destroyed the Twin Towers, killing more than 3,000 innocent people?"

On the day planes were deliberately flown into New York's Twin Towers, Pete was meeting with the leadership of Catholic Charities on the top floor of the Empire State Building. He told me it was built by his grandfather John J. Raskob, former businessman and head of the 1928 presidential campaign of Governor Al Smith, the first Catholic to run for President. John J. Raskob set up a foundation to work for justice for all God's children. His grandfather's foundation had given some support for the work of Life Directions in Tucson. They valued our work in public schools, as our priority was to develop a hunger for education among potential dropouts as a way to break the cycle of self-perpetuating poverty.

When extreme violence once again turned the Empire State Building into the tallest building in New York, Pete was inside looking down as the buildings fell into rubble. Our work gave him a ray of hope. He had seen the results of our mission in Sunnyside High School on the south side of Tucson. But now, to focus on the vision itself, he was open to hearing how we were asking to sustain the mission. He wanted to explore how our little effort has the potential to play a part in ridding the world of the root cause of violence.

In our forty years, we have gone beyond seeking the cause of violence, beyond ending school dropouts, beyond revitalizing cities, and beyond the towers. Why are we beyond it all? We believe because we have gone into the very souls of our children, young people and their parents, and young adults and their elders. We found in the Public Schools and on our "focus: LIFE" young adult retreats the effects of conditional love. Our story helps us celebrate how forgiving invites forgiving. It is the willingness to wait that is the wisdom that makes life grow. If and when forgiving is mutual, reconciliation happens. With reconciliation comes a joy that no one can take away.

Our work is the result of choosing life *together*. It is about each of us radiating joy in the knowledge that we are part of the solution. Our mission is to empower people to hope, to dream, and to have faith that there is a solution. It includes everyone.

We have seen such life for the past forty years! What a gift we have found. We are grateful to lift up this precious pearl that sparkles in the child within each of us. Then we can revitalize our community, make schools and churches work, and give peace a chance. Why? We believe because we are doing what we do for the sake of our children and our children's children.

We published a special "anniversary edition" of this book in November 2013. Knowing it was a work in progress, we set out to hear from people who knew us best but would also challenge us on what we wanted to present publicly. They asked questions such as: "What is it about your work and experience with youth and young adults that make you believe you have a lesson for all? What makes you qualified to speak?"

These questions invited us to discover what we-all by ourselves-would never have found. We are grateful to everyone who critiqued what we wrote. As we go public with our work, I am honored to respond to what we received.

We are responding to the inspiration from a Power Greater Than Human. To listen to God's will for the people to whom we are sent, is the spirit within which our journey has consistently sought to breathe. The breath of forgiving is the gift we found working among youth and young adults. It is a gift fashioned by grandparents to love and encourage their children and their children's children to forgive as they have been forgiven.

This is the way we were loved. We were blessed to find a way to awaken a hunger for such a love inside of the violence of Detroit. We found a way to respond that has touched lives beyond those we met. May the lessons we learned be a gift for those in sacred and secular settings—those who dare to love unconditionally. May our witness give some the courage to live the dream that someday all will be peace, all will be well. We believe it is time to share what we discovered.

We see ourselves as "first-responder peace-builders." We believe life continues in the face of tragedy. Most people rescue the casualties, run for cover and hunt the guilty. Our response is to be compassionate as we "breathe forgiving." We want to walk with the victims. We want to see the perpetrators as friends we want to forgive. We want to encourage each other to seek the *cause* of violence. We believe that in forgiving, we bring life to the world.

Among so many young people with whom we work, violence is a way of life. We were part of starting S.O.S.A.D., "Save Our Sons and Daughters", with Clementine Barfield in the 1980s. All the members were parents of children who had been killed. Breathing forgiving was integral to seeking a "Life Direction" for all those affected by the violence.

We start with life and the healing that revives the spirit in saying "I forgive." There is a time to get to the cause of violence. A desire to forgive positions us to seek to understand why a child of the Creator would destroy the life of another child.

We know that murder is as old as Cain and Abel. We want to do what Eve and Adam would have wanted to do: free their living son so that he might learn from his actions and work for peace. If we can get to the cause, maybe we can help the perpetrator awaken from his desire to kill; otherwise someday the one killing may lose his life in a similar way.

Every person has a parent. We all are interrelated in life. If I see my enemy as my brother or sister, would I not want to wake him or her up before it is too late?

I want to forgive because it is wrong to violate anyone, including myself. This gives me control of my decision. Wisdom is to go beyond knowledge to embrace the understanding that Solomon sought. Prevention is a patient process to educate through experience. We have discovered peers that have chosen to change their perception of the one who violated them. Their feelings evolved from wanting revenge to waiting for reconciliation. They are the "Peers to Inspire

Their Peers." When we choose to forgive before responding, our hope is to wake up the other. That is the challenge.

We have had no acts of violence in any programs. We are grateful and pray this continues to be true. We practice "breathing forgiving" as the first response to seeking peace.

To date, Life Directions has partnered with more than 165,000 youth and young adults (ages thirteen to thirty-five) and has operated in six cities: Detroit, Michigan; Chicago, Illinois; New Orleans, Louisiana; San Antonio, Texas; Tucson, Arizona; and Marion County, Oregon. Many of the young people we reach wholeheartedly embrace our ambitious vision of "Peers Inspiring Peers Through Forgiving."

Many of them choose to live the values and virtues that "make life grow." They want to inspire one person at a time, to cut the root cause of violence with the pruning knife that looks at life through forgiving. Many have mentored others over the years, transforming their lives for the better to positively impact communities throughout the country.

Life Directions was born as a response to violence that was leading to so many killings among young people. We started with a series of neighborhood discussions to discover the reasons behind senseless death and unspeakable violence. This led us to build sustainable programs and training. We needed a way to change patterns of violence into paradigms of forgiveness. If we had not focused on the cause, we believe there would have been more closures of churches and schools, the abandonment of homes, and the city's decay, leaving the children as the casualties of the "war on the value of life."

Our process centers on engaging the values that give direction to actions through forgiving, a word that has become meaningless and dismissed as a viable alternative to killing.

History is ripe with violence: thousands of years of conquering, plundering, exploiting, abusing, and misusing human life. Throughout the world, we are trapped in an endless cycle of combating violence with violence. Even though it does not work— has never worked—it seems most people cannot imagine another kind of world.

At the beginning of our journey, the co-founders believed our greatest gift was our imagination. We would use parables to encourage creativity. It would bring out of everyone a different meaning. We would discover insights and ways of living together that we may never have known. In this book, we end each chapter with a parable followed by open-ended questions. Life is a work-in-progress; we invite you to let your imagination open you to life that connects with the Power Greater Than Human. Then you can "let go and let God," however you know God, to lead you to the bridge for peace-building. We imagine a world beyond borders— boundless and timeless. We ask a complex but direct question, "Is there another way that works so we all can live together?"

It has taken us years of struggling within ourselves and with those with whom we work and whom we serve to believe the lesson given by the Master when He freely laid down His life. While nailed to the cross, His enemies laughed at Him, taunted Him, and pierced His flesh with a spear. He breathed forgiving, and nothing—not even death—took away His joy.

Every peace-building world leader—Buddha, Chief Joseph, Mahatma Gandhi, Martin Luther King Jr., Archbishop Oscar Romero, Mother Teresa of Calcutta and Benazir Bhutto—walked a path of pardoning as did Jesus. The Power Greater Than Human is recognized and acknowledged differently by world religions, but the path is the same. It is the way to see violence giving rise to peace-builders.

The human spirit is so resistant to forgiving. Most expect only God to do the forgiving. The Master preached forgiving. When He forgave, He was accused of blasphemy and was crucified. He turned right around and forgave his enemies from the cross. His last breath was "forgiving." When he came out of the grave, his first breath was "forgiving."

The decision to forgive challenges the human experience to the core. It is the fundamental option, the road less travelled and the way to be free. We encourage this spiritual value. It is throughout the Bible. It seems that most of us cannot bring forgiving into our relationships with one another. Most of us need role models, peers to inspire us and show us the path.

When two people decide to forgive one another, they are going to grow through a different kind of paradigm. They will create boundaries of respect and work to reverence their relationship. This is the core of our concept of "Peers Inspiring Peers Through Forgiving."

Let's not confuse the cliché "forgive and forget" with true forgiveness. The Master does not want us to *forget* those who trespass against us. Forgiving means that we are to remember what happened as forgiven. It is part of the process of Amazing Grace. He kept His nail marks when He rose.

We say, "I forgive you. I will not forget. Like the Master, I love you unconditionally." This means that sometimes we are going to love someone who does not love us back. What a contrary but powerful concept it is to love and forgive with no expectations!

When we grow in the discipline of forgiving, forgiveness happens. We come to see the real-life implications of the Master's truth expressed in our mantra, *"The enemy is the friend that I am forgiving."* If the enemy—be they in our homes, neighborhoods, or even across the ocean—receives our forgiveness and they want to reconcile with us, then forgiving invites mutual trust. Each of us moves toward a new paradigm and plans our own Life Direction as a peace-builder.

We have come to understand that violence is a symptom of a

disease and is the expression of "anorexia to values." Anorexia to values is one of the results of conditional love. When someone is born and raised without parents who love them unconditionally, it encourages anorexia to values. We do not believe we are responsible. We blame, shame, and defame others. We do not want to be with them and we call them our "enemy." Consider how the news is reported. The media takes one of those three verbs—blame, shame or defame—to tell the story. In our society we teach violence, conditional love, and anorexia to values, possibly without being aware.

Sadly this is the secular trinity—the news has been told this way for so long, yet we still use the word "news" to hide such an ancient way of remembering our history. Maybe that is why we repeat it.

We grow up and become adults under conditions that breed fear. Buried beneath that fear are feelings of hurt, rejection, and sadness: "I do not have what others have," or "I have been wronged" or "Other people are the source of the problems." Again: blame, shame, and defame. We may be unaware of the conditioning; it may not be our fault. We were born into an environment that encourages such anorexia to values. But we can be set free.

We may be conditioned to be an anorexic to values, but we can be drawn out of this through unconditional love, forgiveness of others, and surrender by letting go of one's agenda. Gandhi and Dr. King responded unconditionally to the ones who hated them. We can respond the same way with unconditional love through forgiving our enemies. It is a life-giving decision to surrender to the will of the Power Greater Than Human.

This action of forgiving is the first step for someone who has never experienced it to be given a choice to forgive rather than be violent. What follows is the first step in the beginning of our "walk by faith and not by sight." We have discovered in our walk toward reconciliation, a journey we chose for the joy that no one can take away (2 Corinthians 5:1-20). When I first heard the song, "We Are the World," I agreed that there is a choice we are making to save our own lives. Yes, we can all make a better day, not only for the next generation but for each other.

Our calling is based on the Master's example of giving unconditional love to those who are or who may become our enemies. Even if someone was born an anorexic to values, we practice the profound meaning of Isaiah 49:15, which reminds us that even if a mother (or father) would abandon her child, God will never forget that child. We want to remember to share the power of unconditional love.

There is a subtle way in which we avoid any possibility of the value of forgiving being received. It is couched in two major teachings that are almost Gospel truths the way they are declared. First, "If you have never done anything, you cannot teach me anything." Second, "You are from a different generation. Things are different now."

I was told both of these "facts" when I was thirty-one years old and beginning this work. I was told to get a toupee; because I was bald and that I was too old to relate to young people. I was told that I would be judged by my skin color, that I would be perceived as being prejudiced against them. They would judge my profession as a Catholic priest and that I would be incapable of understanding young people's human nature.

I will never forget being challenged that way in the multi-cultural Catholic high school where I began my ministry. It took time to reflect upon all these challenges. When my reflection opened me to see, I was free to move in a way that has empowered me to never look back.

I remember the comments of those Catholic high school students: "You cannot understand sex, since you have never done it. You cannot understand drugs, since you have never used them."

My response: "You say I cannot understand you, since I am too old. Did I hear you right?"

"Yes, you heard us," was their response. "So what do you have to say for yourself? Why are you still here?" they demanded.

"There is someone from whom you can never receive anything and a book from which you can learn nothing," I responded, "I would invite you to think about who is making money by encouraging you to have sex, drink and do drugs. The name of the person who has nothing to say to you is Jesus. He never sinned. The book that has His story is the Bible. You will probably touch one on a witness stand during a trial. Jesus is the one that I believe is sending me to you. Oh, and by the way, he rarely quoted the Bible. He just did it.

"Also, I assume you are not connected to your elders and never learned from the head coach of any sport. It is amazing how many people over 30 years of age make money off of you and have the power to decide if you go to school, have a job, or even live in this country.

"Before you respond, may I ask you to consider one thing? I am not making money off of you. The school does not pay me. So I will leave you to talk with each other. When I come back, let me know if you want me to stay. I am not Coach Carter from the movie that just came out, but I am a coach."

They invited me to stay.

It is all about remembering that our roots are the reason that branches bear fruit. The trunk of a tree is the target when we want to separate roots from branches. We see young adults from eighteen to thirty-five years of age as the parents of the group at risk. We center on that group to bring values and inclusive spirituality back to life. We focus on those over thirty-five years of age to sustain the mission of reconnecting the branches to the tree.

We, the five co-founders of Life Directions, encouraged each other to stay true to our commitment to get to the cause of spiritual anorexia. We were surrounded by the violent effects of anorexia. Leaders in both school-based and faith-based communities were constantly asking, "Why do young people drop out of school? Why do young adults leave the Church?"

But their question is not a *"why"* question. It is more of a *"how"* question. "How do we keep them or how do we get them back?" Most financially-supported people were focused on the problem of retention and looking at themselves as the solution. It would be a decision to focus on the "why" and to put aside wanting to know how to fix the problem. It would be a decision to surrender to the will of God that calls each person to be responsible for him or herself (Romans 14:12). Because of the primary value that each person is responsible for themselves, for us, the word "life" came to mean "out of death comes LIFE."

To ensure we followed the discipline of such a quest, we were very clear on the three-interdependent "quotients," to use an academic term. The most commonly used meaning had two letters "IQ"—the intellectual ability of the person. This would be ordinary language used by academics and referred to by most educators. Our "why" would not be found through our intellectual IQ alone.

The second quotient is the "EQ" – the Emotional IQ. This area of maturity is a determining factor with a direct impact on the decision to stay or leave, to continue or quit. We came up with a simple explanation of EQ. We asked each person to draw a picture frame. In the bottom left corner, we asked that they write the words "I see;" at the top left corner, write the words "I feel;" in the top right corner, "I do;" and in the bottom right corner, we asked that they write "I get." Based on my vision, how I see whatever is in the picture, I feel either negative or positive. If I follow my feelings, I'll do something negative or positive. If I do so I will receive a response similar to the response I have given.

The third quotient is the "SQ" – the Spiritual IQ. In this area lies the cause of anorexia. The focus is on "I see;" my vision is either near-sighted or far-sighted. All of us need to grow. We all begin as "fallen" or "broken." The human condition within a person is very complex and yet very simple. The complexity flows from the experience of conditional love when a person is growing up. What makes it simple is that God loves unconditionally. All that is needed is to submit to God's will for each of us. But to know God's will for us usually takes a spiritually mature person or group with whom to relate.

The awareness of my IQ, EQ and SQ, and those with whom I interact, reveals the opportunity to discover both the cause of self-defeating choices and the cure to a forgiving way of life. As we grow to encourage each other to see life as a gift, we want to be in harmony with the Power Greater Than Human.

The first few years of Life Directions were marked with struggle, sacrifice, setbacks, and nagging doubt. I am so grateful that we, the original co-founders--Rev. Alex Steinmiller, Sister Rosalie Esquerra, Alexander and Judith MacDonald, and myself--took the time to journal this amazing experience from its very inception.

Although I serve as our spokesperson here, the memories, voices, and reflections of my partners and our friends and supporters are integral to this story. This book is not just a celebration of our forty-year existence; it is an honest and frank recollection of "the walk" and the strategies, missteps, disappointments, and accomplishments along the way. In a way, our commitment to the purpose of our religious communities led us to what we are called to do. I am a Redemptorist. My community encourages us to seek ways to connect with the disconnected. Fr. Alex is a Passionist. His community is called to walk with people who go through the suffering that comes with breaking self-destructive patterns. Sister Rosalie, an

Adrian Dominican, challenges authority to face injustice to make life grow. When we met Alexander and Judith MacDonald, we met our complimentary "gift-for-others," the married way of loving. They were parents of six pre-teen children. They were willing to do what was needed to make a way for their own children, and other young people of all cultures and creeds, to live and learn to get along together. We all wanted to see their success as our succession plan--a way to ensure that the next generation will lead others to find their life direction without violence or premature death getting in the way.

We may have been "called" but, in the beginning, we managed by simply wandering around, experimenting, discovering, and trying all types of things. Some worked; others did not. We consider ourselves spiritual Thomas Edisons, looking for ways to find the light for Life that works in the darkness of violence. Before writing this book, we struggled to figure out what audience we should reach. Would it be the hundreds of thousands who have been touched by us or are familiar with Life Directions? Would it be faith-based organizations that are seeking ways to work with young people and are grappling with the issue of violence? Would it be the educational system, especially in struggling communities, trying to make school work for everyone? Or, would this book be for anyone seeking answers and solutions to the violence that consumes our world?

The answer, once again, was found in the story of our Master who did not pick or choose who should hear his message or follow his example. Our narrative is for anyone who will listen, especially anyone concerned about the challenges of our time—violence and hopelessness—for this is what seems to be defining the society that surrounds us.

For us, we see the people who are rooted in life-giving relationships as achievers needing training and development to inspire their less achieving peers who are not so rooted. We see people of great intelligence in the helping professions in schools, faith-based communities and community-based organizations with whom we collaborate. They are meeting so many needs that are created because of the lack of unconditional love by married couples to nurture and provide for their children. They are meeting needs but are not aware of the real need that is unmet, that is causing the issues that are on the surface. The real need is to wake up peers to inspire their peers to be self-responsible and balanced through building up healthy relationships.

The cry of the spiritual anorexic is to violate and be violated. Sex, drinking and drugs are the superficial ways to be violent. What is more substantive is to defame people, to gamble what is needed for people who trust us and, lastly, to physically or mentally destroy others. All these forms of addictions too often end in self-defeating and self-destructive violence against oneself, including suicide.

Many shake their heads and wonder why two college-aged brothers would devise pressure cooker bombs, timed to detonate at the finish line of the 2013 Boston Marathon killing three and injuring almost three hundred. What happened in a young man's life that made him shoot his own mother before traveling to an elementary school in Newtown, Connecticut, to gun down twenty children and six adults before taking his own life? What motivated the mass murders at a movie theater in Colorado or the Sikh Temple in Wisconsin?

These are some of our domestic tragedies. They do not include conflicts abroad or the one-on-one violent incidents that snuff out the lives of thousands, if not millions, more every year. All these events and atrocities—at home or abroad, on the battlefield, street corner or schoolyard—are all but violent symptoms of the greater disease of anorexia to values and anorexia to inclusive spirituality.

Pete Raskob was not the only one eager to hear more about our pathway to ridding the world of the cause of violence. Over the years, hundreds have asked me or the other Life Directions co-founders to put our story in writing for the general public. They want to know what can be learned from our journey. They want to read and reflect on our story and the wisdom we gained from forty years of service in public life.

Although each of us has shared our story in schools, on retreats, in public arenas, and in the material we have written, this is the first time our actual experiences and reflections have been compiled and presented publicly.

It is my desire that our work and words may serve as your personal beacon of light into the darkness of violence and despair. May these pages give you hope in the face of hopelessness, sustenance and inspiration when the struggle seems overwhelming. When you are convinced life is meaningless, when you are overwhelmed by negative statistics and the senselessness of homicides, I humbly pray that our story sparks *your* life direction.

As we wrote on the first page of our journal in 1973, "We pray its purpose is achieved; that it accomplishes but one task: to encourage. We wish this journal to be a source of encouragement for those whose faces are raw from the race and who are about to run into the unknown. Some are called to run the race. We pray you do so with faith and confidence. May you inherit the wind and set others free!"

— Rev. John Phelps, C.Ss.R.

CHAPTER ONE
RESTLESSNESS

"Where is God, Father?"

I was not prepared to answer the fireman's question, not at that time. With a gun in one hand and fire hose in the other, he challenged me to make sense out of a senseless situation. We hid behind a concrete barrier with violent chaos exploding around us. The year was 1967. Three days after I had arrived in Detroit for seminary training, riots broke out throughout the city.

I had just left St. Agnes Church, which is now closed, on 12th Street, which is now called Rosa Parks Boulevard. I jumped behind a wall. Smoke was everywhere. People were breaking windows, looting stores, and overturning cars. Troops with guns at the ready stormed the streets. A sniper took aim from a church steeple.

The Detroit riot was one of the worst in American history. The levels of frustration and despair were right there, in my face. Yet, I had no response to the fireman's question. Frozen in shock by what was unfolding around me, I could think of nothing to say.

Six years later I was ready to answer his question: "God is within those *He* sends."

In 1973, to the City of Detroit, I was one of those He sent.

I was experiencing a sense of restlessness in the early part of 1973. What I needed to learn was how to understand my restless spirit. I had read the confessions of a thirty-eight-year-old man in North Africa who had a mistress and a child but was unhappy. This man was intelligent and well employed, but there was something in him that was not satisfied. Then he found what it was; he made the connection. He continued to love the mother of his son, but he came to know a love stronger than human love. He fell in love with a Power Greater Than Human. He penned many books flowing from his transformation. His name was Augustine of Hippo. "My heart is restless until it rests in Thee," he wrote in the classic work *The Confessions of St. Augustine* (originally written around 400 A.D.).

Restlessness kept me unsettled until I would find what would ignite my passion. I wanted to find the cause of death, when it does not happen naturally. As a Redemptorist, part of my mission is to connect with those who have become disconnected—for whatever reason—from their faith communities. If they had been chosen to be Catholic Christian, then my task was to find out what happened that caused them to leave. If they had been chosen to be of another faith, I worked to awaken them to values, which touch everybody's life.

I worked with a group of priests and married couples in "Marriage Encounter," a movement for couples seeking to strengthen their marriage. In a way, I was living in three different worlds: neighborhood organizing, working in a Catholic high school, and being part of a team doing retreats for married people. I liked doing all three and I wondered if I could bring these experiences together. I wanted to reach people who had become disconnected from their faiths or schools. I was slowly becoming adept at the "how-to's" of this work, but there was still something missing: I seemed distant from the people I felt sent to serve.

There was a restlessness stirring inside. I was constantly aware of all the people who weren't going to church anywhere. At the same time, education in Detroit was facing challenges that were changing its entire system. People just could not afford to send their children to private schools. Tuition was costing more and more. Fewer and fewer people were looking to the Catholic school system as a viable option. Along with this challenge, the expectations of what a Catholic school system could do in the 1950s had changed drastically by the '70s.

More people found themselves turning to the public schools. With the influx of more students, the quality in those schools—especially in poverty areas—became more difficult to sustain. As young people "backed into" the public schools, a dual phenomenon began to happen: people moved out of Detroit, and the dropout rate began to increase among those who stayed in the city.

Two questions were coming to the forefront: What do people do who are in the city but want young people to achieve and succeed? What do we do for those "left behind," to help them to see themselves as a "gift for the world?"

I sensed in communities, like the one in which I lived, that we were having a systemic breakdown—for lack of a better description—in public life and an increasing values-conflict in private life.

After five years in ministry, I wanted time to reflect upon what I had experienced. The deaths of national leaders in 1968 (Martin Luther King, Jr. and Bobby Kennedy) and the impeachment proceedings over Watergate in 1973 were seen by me as symptoms of a deeper disease. The "noise" was too much. Alvin Toffler's *The Third Wave* identified the issues of "over-choice demand" needing to be faced. I wanted to listen to the "Sound of Silence." I wanted to live the question: "What is it All About, Alfie?" The songs of the '60s were on message. But what did they mean to me? Where was I being readied to be sent? What position on the "Enterprise" was a fit for me? I was looking for the "Jedidiah," the title given to

Solomon in the Hebrew Scriptures. I needed to step back to get a sense of my center in a world that was expanding its "war on values" and challenging so many at their very soul, especially the young.

I went on a special retreat down in Southern Missouri for the month of September in 1973. I wanted to understand what had happened in my life, as I lived among people of poverty. Through silence I hoped to find a way to discover what it meant to me. Young people were walking away from schools and churches. Parents were afraid for their children's futures. I wanted to step back from the struggle and find ways to awaken hope in myself and others.

When I returned, I wanted to engage people with the power of the knowledge that their lives are valuable. They do matter. I was especially focused on those living in poverty and surrounded by violence. I wanted to walk with people. I knew relationships would lead to the truth that comes to light as we know each other: our homes, families, jobs, education, faith — you name it. This truth will be the key to open the door to life with hope for everyone.

Sensing my restlessness, my Provincial, Fr. Dan Lowery, decided I should engage young people who were disconnected from church and were dropping out of school and into violence. My task, according to Fr. Lowery, was to find ways to "wake them up before it was too late."

I thought I needed training; Fr. Lowery disagreed: "Just do it!"

The funerals in Detroit were a sign that it was already too late for many. Detroit had sadly earned its "Murder City" moniker. Forced layoffs, population decline, and dramatic increases in unemployment, poverty, and crime was the reality for far too many.

Enter Father Alex

Unbeknownst to me, another Detroit priest, Fr. Alex Steinmiller, was also experiencing a sense of restlessness. A Passionist, Fr. Alex was in charge of group retreats in Detroit and was with Catholic high school students almost every day. As busloads of young people left him each day, he worried about their futures and those who had never, and probably would never, experience the comforting retreat atmosphere. Follow-up and ongoing connection with young people were equally troubling concerns.

In his journals at the time, Fr. Alex described his feelings: "Coming into this month, I was entering the third year in Detroit of working among young people in a retreat setting. In the spring of that year, I had already been teaching at Bishop Borgess High School and wanted to be immersed with the young. There was something going on within me that I named 'restlessness.' It focused on those whom I was not reaching—the young, the 'out there'—those *not* coming to the retreat house.

"I sensed many threads to the ministry, including the power of married couples' relationships, the young people not being reached, peace and justice and vocation. But these were not integrated. I had begun to challenge the perspective of the retreat house ministry, especially its slow opening to 'under-privileged' youth. But I did not know where the restlessness would take me."

The challenge of the retreat experience is to discover where one is in life and to decide what to keep and what to change. Once the retreat ended, the greater challenge was to keep the resolutions alive. How do we keep the spirit going, especially if we want to make a major shift in the way we live? If we look at the violence that surrounds us, do we see ourselves running away from it or bringing alternatives to it? How do we sustain the spirit and follow through on these discoveries after the retreat is over?

Even though we had not met, Alex and I shared a mutual restlessness about "those living in environments of poverty," those disconnected, who could not or would not come to any place of prayer or spiritual discovery. They therefore had no exposure to the positive energy such opportunities offer. This is how Fr. Alex describes it:

"I was assigned to St. Paul of the Cross Retreat House. I enjoyed working there but I got restless after listening to these horrific stories from families about their children who were runaways, kicked out, addicted or out-of-the-church."

Our restlessness with the Church and school institutions evolved from our feelings that we weren't in the place where we needed to be, doing what we felt we needed to do. Our feelings could be compared to a doctor who's dissatisfied with *just treating* cancer. We felt the urgency to get to the cause. It is not like we disagreed with treating patients. We just wanted to stop the need to have so many patients.

We wanted to take up that challenge—to find the cause of the spiritual cancer that surfaced in violence and to do so "before it is too late." We were impatient with expanding emergency rooms and funeral homes. We wanted to find the "ounce of prevention" and bring it to those most in need; those being "left behind" while so many were improving and moving out.

When we met, Alex was still in graduate school at the Catholic Theological Union (CTU), working on his thesis comparing the nonviolent philosophies of Dr. Martin Luther King, Jr.; Mahatma Gandhi; and poet, social activist, and scholar of comparative religions, Thomas Merton. I had studied various spiritual awakening experiences in and outside the Detroit area. It was during all this searching that I came across his name. He was in charge of the only retreat house serving youth in Detroit: St. Paul of the Cross Retreat Center. When we met, I listened to his restlessness.

He wanted to reach students who were going to Detroit's public schools, like Cody High School, that was on the northwest side of Detroit, near his retreat center. He wanted to connect with young people because of the violence that was prevalent there. Every spring, there were two major riot-like clashes between black and white students at the school. Alex, in his attempt to implement a serious program at the school, wore a specially designed t-shirt that read, "The Cody Alternative." It was a reminder that there was a nonviolent alternative to violence within the school.

The "Provider" and the "Nurturer": Both/And, Not Either/Or

In getting to the root cause of violence among young people and reversing the process, the first step, as far as I was concerned, was finding out what our youth were and were not getting from their homes, families, friends, and churches. What were they dealing with and what challenges did they face in their lives that led to deadly outcomes?

The best place to build relationships to understand young people at risk due to poverty, as I saw it, was in the public schools. I believed I should first go into the schools and see first-hand the effects of what marriage, family, culture, faith, and values had on young people.

Based on my own intuition and past experience, I felt the next step would be to go into the metro Detroit community and connect with married people older than twenty-five years of age and young adults eighteen to thirty-five years of age. Alex and I would use what we learned from the schools and the community to design and offer retreats and other follow-up programs for young adults— single, married, single again—with a priority on those confronting the challenges poverty was forcing them to face.

Every well-rounded child needs a provider and a nurturer. If that child has this within a harmonious parental mix, it is wonderful and rewarding. In general, the provider readies young people for secular life: schools, work place, and public service. The nurturer prepares them for sacred life: faith communities, churches, and community service. In brief, schools are for providing education to live and work in a pluralistic society. The nurturing of values and spirituality are seen as coming from the home and spiritually-centered gatherings.

What happens during a cultural revolution caused by economic shifts? What happens when the schools do not seem to be efficient and the churches do not seem to be effective? We can easily be caught between a rock (Church) and a hard place (State). "Separate-but-equal" begins to show its dark side, not just in education, but in positive values and mature spirituality.

They eventually work against each other, often unknowingly. The results are very well known and usually surface through violence. I began to ask the question, "How could a good idea of keeping Church and State separate-but-equal not work? Look at what is happening to the young people. By our fruits we will know."

It is considered illegal in public schools to explore values that are spiritual in nature. In failing schools where do we find common ground when the home and community are "at risk" of becoming violent and we cannot engage a solution? In disruptive neighborhoods where do we find common ground when families and neighbors are strangers to one another and cannot speak the same language?

We watch the secular response for young people: charter and magnet schools emerge, leaving the majority of young people behind. The administrators and educators are trained to manage and measure youth through the prism of academic standards and outcomes. They want young people to know what they need to know to work and be productive in society. This is the provider's way. It is good to do.

Paul Tough, author of *How Children Succeed,* says public education is not designed to measure or build soft skills. This line of reasoning makes me think of the qualitative outcomes that most seek to measure: integrity, character, grit, and unconditional love. There is no consistent public system-wide method to help youth identify or engage the culture of home and family. There is, as Tough acknowledges, no ongoing development of intercultural competence so students can gain knowledge and comfort with people of different backgrounds.

Exploring the development of such soft skills would open the door for people to gain awareness of equality and social justice issues across cultural, racial, ethnic and neighborhood boundaries. But this is more natural within a sacred system designed to nurture such awareness.

Early in our journey, we came to understand that reinforcing these skills is the key to engaging the violence that young people bring to other young people.

But how do we measure soft skill outcomes? Standard educational institutions do not even think that way. They may imagine in theory but cannot imagine that way in reality. Most people know that to provide for young people who lack positive nurturing is an exercise in frustration at best, and in failure at its worst.

How do nurturers see? They revere the mystery within each person as a gift to be discovered. Consider a mother who nurtures. She sees her child differently than the provider does. She would not analyze whether to keep or get rid of the child. The caring, healthy mother, or father, never sees a child as a problem. They may have problems but they are not problems themselves. For them, it is always unconditional love and constant nurturing, no matter whether the child meets certain measurements or not.

The nurturing of a child empowers spiritual values to give young people the foundation to discover their true gifts and their true selves. The nurturer can present healthy choices based on the growth of their wisdom as to why a child acts a certain way or where that child wants to go in life.

Without a consistent and unconditional love relationship in home and in family life, the schools and churches are not equipped to nurture. Many "challenges" become very serious, life-long problems for young people that seem unmanageable. Those young people may be left behind. They will be drawn to find relief from some addiction or self-destructive way of life.

Senator Walter Mondale of Minnesota was chairman of the Labor and Public Welfare Committee's Subcommittee on Children. In 1974 he sponsored the Child Abuse Prevention and Treatment Act (CAPTA), commonly known as the "Mondale Act." The Child Protective System (CPS) comes from this bill.

At the time there was a strong reaction stating that it was an attack on the American middle class family model. Others said it would set up groups in neighborhoods to evaluate how families raised their children. The lack of a proper home life would be a national health problem. Since 9/11 we have been hearing a similar debate on how far to go to enter into people's private lives. Now we say it may be justified. It is a matter of "homeland security."

I often wonder why we use the word "home," yet we cannot nurture the values that make a home. I wonder why we use the word "homework" when so many young people in poverty communities do not have one home in which they live. As I wondered then and do so now, I am aware of the fear of many and the lack of awareness of others. We are aware of the light needed to be given to both the families and young people with whom we relate and the people who support us to do so. But it is illegal to do anything.

I met with a group of people from the country of Jordan in early 1974. They were Chaldean and had come to work at the Ford Plant in Dearborn. One of them asked me about the public schools and what they were like. The father was concerned if his son would receive a good education. I was concerned for his daughter, since she looked Hispanic and could easily be taken for one. Their family roots were Islamic and the schools at that time were only just beginning to address the need for bilingual education. When I went to the school I did not know how to raise the religious issues with the Principal.

It was about much more than just language. It was the Chaldean's way of praying, their way of touching or not touching.

Along with this challenge was the decision to bus for interracial harmony. What would happen if the young people would be bussed from one side of town to the other? What would happen if there was a fight because of what someone did?

I remember Tim, first introduced as Hattim, whom I met at Southwestern High School. He asked me, "Why do we have to be bussed? What is racism all about?" Tim said he just wanted to go to school, get what he needed, and then go to college. Tim wanted to know "why do they talk about racism so much?"

How could I respond to his questions about education without expounding on the challenges to his family's way of life? How could I speak to the quality of education without explaining how "our differences" fuel the potential for violence?

The Middle Group

I remember back to that first day when I walked into Western High School in 1973 when the young person asked me, "Did somebody die?" I was not ready to respond. From the little I was hearing in the community, I wanted to share cultural and family values rooted in faith. I just did not know how.

I left that day determined to find a way to wake young people up that would be legal for me and empowering for them. In the beginning I wanted to listen. I went to the cafeteria and ate with young people. I went to the second school in our community, Southwestern High, where I met a young girl in the lunch line by the name of Kathy.

"Why are you here?" she asked.

"I am just here to listen to whatever you want to share," I answered.

"Why?" Kathy shot back.

I was put on the spot. It would not be the last time.

"I do not know," I honestly replied. "I just think young people know what needs to be done to get ready for their future. They just do not get a chance or 'time out' with a coach to figure it out."

After lunch, the Principal, who erroneously concluded that I might be pushing religion in his school, decided I should leave. What I considered a bit of divine intervention, the school's fire alarm went off as he walked me to the exit. The whole school had to leave the building. Outside, I met Frank Briglia, a counselor.

"Hello, how are you?" he asked, which led to an extended conversation outside where I explained what I wanted to do in public schools. "Wow, that would be great," Frank replied. "Come inside with me."

It turns out that Frank was the counselor of Kathy, the girl I had met in the cafeteria line. He told me she was about to be kicked out of school. Kathy was one of the young people he considered part of the "middle group": ordinary young people who were not getting much attention until they had a problem.

Academically-gifted students get adequate recognition, in terms of planning for their futures. At the other end of the spectrum, young people who are violent or disruptive tend to be punished or expelled. If young people have a talent for the arts or sports, it may give them a sense of importance.

Too many young people do not have a caring adult in their lives. They may not have someone who encourages them to find their "spark," and follow their "life direction." What do they do to be recognized? Will the recognition be what is best for them? Will it be unconditional, without any other agenda beyond love?

Frank wanted to know my thoughts about reaching this middle group. We felt that the middle group represented about eighty percent of the students at the school. They were not getting much attention. These young people usually were not good enough to get scholarships to college and not bad enough to get into trouble. That brief discussion led Frank and me to start a program at the school.

The principal still had his reservations about me being in his school, but a series of events, like a stabbing or a near riot where my presence was helpful, encouraged him to at least tolerate my working with Frank.

Rejection Led to the Cornerstone for the Mission

I was in three schools: Southwestern, (the school attended by the famous Dr. Ben Carson who separated conjoined twins), Western, and Holy Redeemer, (a Catholic high school, now closed). The majority of students who went to Southwestern, which is also now closed, were African American homeowners. Western was primarily Hispanic and becoming more and more international. Holy Redeemer was multicultural with a third of the students from the suburbs and the majority of their parents being alumni. With gentrification many of the people who lived in this community were gone: pushed out, moved out, or dead.

My original thought was to have some sort of relationship between Catholic and public schools. There were about 3,000 young people going to school in these three southwest Detroit high schools: 300 in the Catholic high school and 2,700 in the two public schools. I thought that if we can get the 300 to relate to the 2,700 then we could find a way to mutually help and strengthen one another: a method that would become known as "Peers Inspiring Peers."

The parents and guardians of the young people in the private high school did not want their children to be with "those kids" in public school. That led to my going into the public high school without them.

Not only was the resistance from the Catholic school side huge, there were serious suspicions from public high school officials who could not get past the fact that I was a priest, and therefore "my mission had to be to proselytize." Eventually, I thought it best to let go of the idea.

It is important to point out that the rejection of our early efforts to merge public and private school students was the "blessing through rejection." If we had not been discarded, we would not have found the clarity of focusing on faith and spiritual direction to begin among young adults out of high school and those eighteen to thirty-five years of age.

The obstacle to mixing the Catholic and the public schools led us to build our foundation outside of both Church and State institutions. In other words, rejection became the cornerstone of focus: LIFE, now known as Life Directions. We felt the separate-but-equal approach that was supported by the separation of Church and State was not working. We heard the strong resistance to the "Mondale Act." We knew that without the nurturing in the home the schools were at risk of not educating as they hoped and that they would eventually close.

But there was nothing we could do. Early in our journey, we knew we needed to build a self-structured way of nurturing values and spirituality apart from the school system and outside of the faith-based structures. There was a need for ongoing community involvement. At the time, I had developed a talent for contacting and building experiences to awaken values that would lead to a desire to follow up and deepen the values discovered. To effectively work with young people, I needed experiences designed for young people.

What happened next was an amazing grace that would continue to unfold.

Fr. Alex, who ran a retreat house with youth experiences, was trying to get embedded into the public schools. I was already in the public schools, focusing on finding a youth-oriented retreat house. In fact, I officially met Fr. Alex after calling him in search of a retreat house. For many reasons, his retreat house was "booked." He felt a kind of rejection like I did at Holy Redeemer High School.

I remember our believing the real reason for things not being possible was that the church did not want certain people who would cause problems. The second person I met at Western High School was a person who had been kicked out of Holy Redeemer because he was caught with drugs. It was then that we developed a way of reflecting on what we heard. We would later call it "logo-praxis."

When we would hear people's opinions, we would listen to their feelings—positive or negative. We would listen to their body language; this we learned from poor people who had to learn how to survive with no power to change the system. We would then yield to the authority against us and pray to discover any way to reach those at risk of self-destructive choices, before it would be too late. We had developed a "Tao" way to "yield" called "The Water Course Way." To yield is to submit. Do not resist, just adjust and wait for the Power Greater Than Human to do what only God can do.

Together, the two of us found a user-friendly retreat center in Canada, across the river, that was owned by fellow Redemptorists. We now had a retreat house where we could bring young adults out of high school and help them launch into something that would be a new way of life.

PARABLE OF GOING AGAINST THE STREAM

Two young men came to fish. As they were doing so, they saw people taking injured people out of the river and putting them into an ambulance. One of the young men asked, "Why are people coming down the river injured?" He was told not to ask. The hospital nearby was full. The nurses were doing a great job. The doctors were excellent. The system works well. "It has taken a long time to work out the bugs. Do not mess up the process with your questions." The two young men remained quiet. They waited for the ambulance and the workers to leave. They went to get a canoe and go upriver.

1. What does it take to be willing to go upriver and find the cause?

2. If they do not go upriver, who loses?

3. The people taking care of those who are hurt feel needed. What will be the risk of seeking to get to the cause of violence?

CHAPTER TWO

THE TEAM OF FIVE

The week after Fr. Alex and I met, I took six young people I had met in the community to a TEC (Teen Encounter Christ) retreat in Chicago. Two seniors came from Western, two from Southwestern, and two from Holy Redeemer High Schools. We traveled to be with a fellow Redemptorist who was in charge of the Chicago TEC program. I was looking for a common experience for the seven of us that would inspire us to come back to Detroit and "build something," as I wrote in our journal at the time.

While driving back, I purposely listened to the young people's conversations. I wanted to hear what they had gained from the experience. The word "superficial" kept coming up in my mind. The young people had fun together and they talked about a few things they did that were sort of spiritual.

It seemed to me that what they had just experienced was more of a social weekend with spiritual overtones. It was not a transforming experience. It was not going to bring them to a choice-point: violence or forgiveness. The retreat format did not deal with the challenges inside of their life experiences. It was not designed to gently and humbly show a way for young adults to let go of their past so they would be free to claim their futures.

Also from my experience, most retreat directors presume that young people have a family life to which to return. The spiritual director, if asked, would say the young are probably connected to an adult community—a private school or a faith-based community—that sent them.

Four of the young people in the car with me did not have that set of dynamics. I thought about Lynda, a senior that I had met while doing a home visit. Her younger sister had a baby she named "River Free." He was the love of her life. The two of them were living in a home with another teenager. "Teen Homes" were more common than most people wanted to know.

These were the people that I wanted to reach. Now that I was driving these teens back to where they call home, what would happen to them? They would be like fish out of water after the TEC retreat. They would not have any peers to sustain their inspiration. They would be headed for a spiritual downer after "the upper" of the weekend. It made me sad knowing they would be going back with nothing that would help them recognize and overcome the dysfunction in their lives and communities.

Values Conflict

I was scheduled to do an all-girls Catholic high school retreat two weeks after the TEC retreat. I had asked two of the young women to be with me, along with a young adult college student, Jeannie, who happened to be also an alumna of Holy Redeemer High School. I wanted to use some of the dynamics that would be needed to encourage looking at issues many of us want to often avoid, especially trust.

I was extremely hesitant about this retreat. I knew we lacked the important mix of cultural, social, and economic backgrounds from the city and suburbs. I was concerned that this trip, too, would be another "natural high" for the girls, with no real rootedness in "the power of love to overcome fear."

Sister Pat Glaab, a Sister of the Immaculate Heart of Mary Congregation (IHM), whom I knew from Holy Redeemer, helped put the retreat together. The way I remember our first evening was like oil and water in the same pot. There was no way for it to mix together. It was one of my first experiences in managing a "values conflict" that was non-resolvable. This is not to be confused with "needs conflicts," which can be resolved.

I had two groups of people the same age coming from two completely different life experiences. The majority of girls came from one high school, so there was a sort of solidarity of mind. They did not have to deal with economic, social, or racial differences like those who were going to the public school.

Being rejected by the majority of the girls who wanted to do "their thing"— not mine—caused me to go deeper and reflect on the kinds of retreats we needed. The concept of "life reborn through rejection" was becoming clearer to me.

I lowered my expectations for the rest of the retreat. We had a good time together, and we all left as friends. It would be the last time I would do such a retreat, but it gave me the impetus to contact and recruit with a way to follow up and do community organizing in a different way.

I left the retreat feeling very sad for the young women. They were the result of their lack of experience. I knew the young people in public schools. I knew the richness they had to offer would be as empowering as the values of those in the Catholic School would have been for the other girls. I had found this truth by stepping out of my comfort zone. I was grateful for knowing both groups.

This lost opportunity turned my sadness into resolve. I wanted to find ways to go beyond the separation of Church and State. I wanted young people in faith-based schools and their peers in public schools to inspire each other. By separating faith from knowledge, both were lacking. The private schools could deselect and avoid engaging a pluralistic society. The public schools could develop the elimination of the importance of values to guide knowledge.

I remember when my parents moved to an all-white community in 1952 in St. Louis County. I was leaving our integrated grade school in the city that was established by the Archbishop in 1947, when I was five years old. I remember the changing neighborhood and the "white flight." Now I was facing a similar kind of discriminating issue. What was I to do with what I was finding?

I knew it would not be easy; nobody ever said it would be. But I believe that bringing strangers together is a way to find the truth that has the potential to set both sides free. They can know the joy of discovering that "a stranger is a friend I haven't met yet."

This cultural, social, and economic mix was also very important to Fr. Alex, who had gone beyond his community's commitment to diversity:

"Some Passionists, not all, dedicate themselves to working with totally different cultures. Way back, I made a choice that the only way I could address my racism was to immerse myself into another culture."

After leaving the seminary in the summer of 1968, Fr. Alex decided to move in with a black family on Madison Street in Chicago. The experience, he says, began what he calls his "recovery from racism."

"I do not think a person can be their personal best without being in relationship with diversity," Alex said while reflecting on his journey. "We weren't created by the Creator to be solely with people just like ourselves. So, if I can prove that you can grow from being in a personal relationship with a white guy—that is what I did. From being streetwise in the '70s, I learned that many black kids are raised *not* to trust "whitey." My desire was to go into an African American school, for example, and help a child realize 'Hey, I can trust this dude. This dude likes me. This really works!'"

Looking to a Way to Awaken the Spirit

I had started the peer-to-peer groups in two public schools by December 1973. By the following March, Fr. Alex, a married couple—Judith and Alexander MacDonald—and I had designed our own retreat. We called it "Life Search." With Jeannie, the college student from the all-girls' retreat, and Agatha, an English teacher from Holy Redeemer High School, we built a team to ensure peers would be inspiring peers. Lynda from Southwestern and Ann from Holy Redeemer were on the team as well.

One of the four young men invited to the retreat was Jim, who was graduating from University of Detroit High School. The advisor who invited the young men saw this retreat as a way to give them space to sort out what transitioning from high school to college would be like. Jim stayed to himself in the beginning. He was part of one of the five groups of six young adults; none of the participants knew each other before the weekend.

We invited them to create a skit. Jim was really shy. Lynda, the group's team captain, invited him to take on the role of a husband. I could see him freeze. Watching how Lynda casually shared that she would be his mother-in-law changed what was happening. By the end of the weekend, Jim was comfortable with the whole retreat. He started to build up his confidence to lead. He became part of the team during the second weekend.

Three other young adults joined with three adults for the inaugural weekend. Now they would be giving the same opportunity for twenty-four other young adults to experience. We wanted to find a way to start so that the young people we wanted to reach would feel connected to the team leading the retreat.

As we drove back to Detroit after that second retreat, we reflected on the experience. We were getting closer to our passion, but most of these young adults came from a school, faith community, or family that would receive them. We wanted our retreats to be much more inclusive of the people who lacked such "accepting conditions."

The retreat we had just left was a spiritually-supported group spending quality time together. It was great to build a team. Now we wanted to invite those who did not have a strong family or faith base. We wanted the process to be structured so that young adults who were strangers would discover together a truth that would encourage them to forgive and be free.

This would best happen if the boundaries were clear and a maturity level was present to deal with conflicts that would be discovered. Just being together as young adults was not enough. We wanted to ensure that all could see the excellent power and strength of values that can give positive direction to one's life direction.

What this retreat gave us was a foundation of "achieving young adults from many cultures." They would be ready to wake up their peers who did not have the experience of family and community life centered on spiritual values.

An example of discovering a hard truth about forgiving and forgetting is found in the story of Pascuala Herrera, a college graduate living on the west side of Chicago. Pascuala was physically-challenged. She wanted to make a life; she wanted to marry. And she did. She was in a leadership role in focus: LIFE, growing in her awareness of her talents, using her talking skills to advocate for others. She is the Professor/Coordinator of Learning Services at Harper College in Palatine, Illinois. Pascuala married and very much wanted to have a child.

She struggled with the loss of one child, but she did not give up, hoping against hope for another. She joined our retreat team to encourage others to believe in themselves. She shared how she turned obstacles into opportunities. She and her husband, Isidro, decided to adopt a child. They did not know that Pascuala was pregnant as they were completing the adoption process. Eight months later, they had a biological child. Pascuala was so happy that her adopted daughter would have a sister! She just knew all would be all right.

Pascuala told her story on one of our focus: LIFE weekends. Someone in the group shared thoughts of what her story meant: "So, once you relaxed with the adoption, you could get pregnant." A long pause followed. Pascuala explained, "What I did not tell you was that we had two miscarriages and were told that because of my wheelchair way of life, I could not carry a child to birth. What I also did not say was that we had changed hospitals and had a different doctor.

"I was so angry and hurt at the hospital and the doctors. I got in touch with how I felt. We were disrespected. It took us a while but we did something I would never have thought. We forgave the doctors and sued the hospital and the doctors to stop the injustice that could be done to others."

A group discussion broke out on the floor. "How can you sue and forgive? If you forgive, you're supposed to forget, right?" I could hear people talking over each other. I called for quiet to catch our breath and shift the mood into learning what we do not know.

Forgiving a wound does not remove the wound. Healed, we remember the healing that happens when forgiving invites the other to receive forgiveness. If it happens, then reconciling can happen. For some, to confront them for the wrong they have done is a way to invite forgiving to heal them.

The shift in mood brought on many questions from the group.

"Is that why I forgive and am at peace, though we are not reconciled in my family?" "Is that the reason I had to get out of my abusive marriage, when he would not stop?" "Is that what it means to have tough love?"

The reflections kept coming. Then I said, "To stop injustice is important for the sake of all people including ourselves. Does that make sense? I remember Marguerite, a paraplegic, telling me she was fighting for my future rights. She was going to court to fight for barrier-free buses and someday I would need them. She said, "You are a TAB." I thought she was referring to a soft drink. "No," Marguerite corrected me. "You are 'Temporarily Abled-Bodied.' That is an example of what a forgiving person is doing to people who do not know the 'why.'"

What we discovered is amazing. As with Pascuala, the young adults themselves, as they met, would bring to life the healing and the encouraging values that open each other to being transformed by the Power Greater Than Human.

Developing the Hunger

In making connections with students in the high schools I visited, I quickly saw the need for a network of intergenerational peer partnerships. In order to encourage a community-wide response to eliminate violence and self-defeating attitudes which keep students from successful graduations, we needed to engage school administrators, teachers, students, families, and adult mentors. So I began to look around for young adults, being especially conscious of the need for married couples and spiritually-centered men and women.

I also wanted to face the real, painful conflict among "Blacks, Browns, and Whites," as so many named it. So I kept my eyes open for partnerships within all three groups. It was important to me to have an association of culturally-sensitive, racially-diverse leaders from the business and neighborhood communities. This would be essential in order to follow up on the inspiration and direction we would provide young people in the schools and young adults on the retreats.

Looking back, we were putting into place two separate-but-co-equal ways of developing a hunger for life—a justice-building way to resolve conflicts in secular life and a peace-building way to manage conflict in sacred life. "Justice" centers on all people being treated and respected equally. In public schools we designed inter-generational dramas. "Peace" empowers forgiving to be the spiritual energy to sustain the struggle. On the retreats we used a set of dramas to create disrespect of values and re-create forgiving to heal the hurt. When working together, there is a joy in building justice and peace that never ends.

We gradually discovered two interdependent ways to grow in knowledge and wisdom. First, the knowledge we seek to awaken— in young people especially—is the building of peers to inspire their peers to take responsibility for their lives and not blame others or any situation. This value would become the centerpiece of all our work and activities for those under the age of eighteen. Second, the wisdom we lifted up from the elders for those older than eighteen is the embracing of diversity among all people of good will. This empowers forgiving to be a universal way to manage conflicts into a community of gentleness and humility.

There was a young man whose parents were born in Syria. They only spoke Arabic and were not involved in his activities and the people he was getting to know. He became interested in a particular girl, and thought she was also interested in him. He started to want to "get more serious," as he put it.

I am not sure what happened, but she broke off the relationship. He was furious; he had lost his honor. She happened to be a Mexican

American. He felt ridiculed. He told me what he was thinking of doing. It would be really ugly.

I brought him to a meeting with a married couple in their home. In the course of the evening, he told what happened and what he planned to do to the girl. The father said, "If you do, we'll have to turn you in, and it will hurt your future. Can I give you another way of looking at it?"

His "yes" was weak, but it gave the father the chance to share that the girl might have felt he was coming on too strong. Maybe it had nothing to do with him. Perhaps it was more about the girl herself. If she really cared about him, the father said, she may come back when she felt more secure.

What a gift to have this father do what the boy's own father did not know was needed.

But we also learned that there is quite a difference between fifteen-to-seventeen-year-olds who are fairly dependent and so strongly influenced by their peer groups, and those eighteen years of age and older who are independent and may have an anti-authority attitude. It was an amazing awareness but a painful ordeal for us. It led to keeping these age groups apart during spiritual-centered experiences to awaken a hunger for the Power Greater Than Human.

To those in middle and high schools we sought a way to encourage positive values that would give direction to a young person's life. To those beyond high school, we hoped to awaken a hunger for the spiritual life, and for each person and group to find one's Life Direction.

We had concerns about our retreats and the young people participating in them. As Fr. Alex noted in the journal about our efforts at the time, "It was the beginning of an idea which would germinate slowly—contacting the young, coming to have shared community experiences, and a follow-up process."

The "germinating idea" needed committed "gardeners" to help it take root, sprout and grow into something that could drastically change how young people perceived, reacted to and participated in violence. It was a process that, of course, required money. But, more importantly, it required a cadre of individuals committed to "the walk," no matter what obstacles, false starts, wrong turns or jagged curves were on our path.

Meeting the Team, Connecting the Threads

We had started building connecting points, and we made a major discovery, which continues to be a defining insight. The work in the schools and on the retreat was not sequential. It was not like we did the work in the schools and those young people went on retreats with us. It was illegal to do so.

We were in two different worlds, two separate arenas—the world of reflecting in a sacred context and the world of reflecting in the secular field. The challenge was finding a way to relate to both—apart from each other to begin. Then we would be free to invite each world to meet the other.

Each situation would have what we came to name "anorexics." The first group is anorexic to values: wanting to control the truth rather than discover a relationship with the common good. The second group is anorexic to inclusive spirituality: wanting to control the Power Greater Than Human, rather than the other way around.

How to build a hunger for values and inclusive spirituality among young people and young adults was—and continues to be—the challenge. In reflection, I realize that seeking the answer to that question really moved us to the real insights that eventually led us to the indispensable value of forgiveness. We first came to this insight by discovering the trends of marriage in the twentieth Century.

As a society, we avoided extreme violence within married life in the early generations of twentieth-Century society. Most people married, had children, and stayed together until death.

Fr. "Jo Jo" Dustin, a fellow Redemptorist and a famous banjo priest who was on the *Johnny Carson* show, explained to me what happened to his ministry after World War II and the Korean War:

"Everyone use to come to Church to find the person to marry. Then entertainment picked up with television. After World War II and even more after the Korean Conflict, marriages began to separate, and more people got used to raising children alone."

I told him that I noticed that, after the Vietnam War, the phenomenon really exploded. We started seeing the dropout rate in public schools and the "drop-off" rate from parishes after high school. In other words, after grade school, young people in public schools in poverty areas started dropping out in greater and greater numbers. In the private school, young people started dropping out from their faith community after high school.

I had read about Robert McNamara, one of Henry Ford II's "Whiz Kids," the group charged with reinvigorating Ford Motor Company after World War II. Although, McNamara ended his career as head of the World Bank, he is probably best remembered as U.S. Secretary of Defense under the Kennedy administration and the man who was part of leading the country during the height of the Vietnam War.

I remember thinking that married life probably would not be a value high on McNamara's priority list. Mobility and speed would be. The pressures against marriage are enormous, especially when resources are so fragile due to the lack of jobs and money and all that is possible to support families.

We believe in the "law of gradualness." Put simply, moral laws are ideals. But when we face choices that make it seem impossible to keep all the values, we need to determine where we are on the road toward the ideal. I need to follow my conscience and do what is best for everyone, including me.

I remember a prostitute I met when I was a twenty-three-year-old seminarian in Milwaukee, who said to me, "You say I am sinning by turning tricks? I had my baby with a professional baseball player. She's four pounds. The hospital released me. I have no insurance. What choice do I have?"

Who was I to judge her? I remember her challenge. I asked myself the question, "If we do not get to the cause of such a sad situation, is it enough for us to just take care of people? What happens to the child?"

When I went into the public schools, I knew I was not free to speak. I was in an environment where the issues this young woman was managing could not be explored. In sports I played defense, so I trusted my instincts and kept it in my heart, though it was and continues to be painful to do so.

A chemistry teacher at Southwestern High School once addressed this topic with me. He said he believed the public schools were trying to do whatever the other half of a marriage was not there to do. The "half" there was the single parent. So whatever was not provided, the public school would seek to fill in. This would not work for most young people.

The sad truth is even if they have two parents and both work full time, you can still have a half-parent situation. It is not about the physical connections. It is about the quality of the provider/nurturer relationship. When it is done together with the same two parents, it is easier to show how a permanent unconditional love relationship can work.

This is by no means an indictment of education or church systems. It is the simple fact that neither institution was built for young people—the customers, so to speak—that come from single parents. Both the Church and the School are meant to compliment two parents. If there are a few coming from single homes due to death or some other reason, their peers, the Church, and school systems can work well together. But not when it makes up the majority.

Our challenge when bringing young people in high schools into motivation groups and young adults on the retreats together was further complicated by the task of including those with families and those without such in a home. The conflicts would surface between those with one set of values and spirituality and those with a different, if not completely opposite, set.

Let me share a story that happened many years after we began our work in public schools. I was working in a high school where there were a lot of dropouts. I learned that a form of prostitution was going on at the school. A young girl in a group session asked me about the baby in her belly. She wanted to know if it would go to heaven. I remained quiet as the other young people in the group responded. My only comment was, "It is sad."

What I did not know was that she had a pimp in the school who found out she had spoken to me. As I was going from one floor to another a few hours after that session, I felt hands on my back and I was thrown down a flight of stairs. After checking to make sure I was all right physically, I looked up at the young man. "It is sad what you just did to yourself."

He laughed and walked away. When some young people heard what happened and what I had said, they asked me, "Why did you say that? Why do not you get back at him?"

"Yes," I agreed. "He was wrong. I do not think I can change him. But I shared with him and now I share with you, that he did not change me. I was in control of my becoming violent. I want to find a way to free him from being violent to himself. That is what he showed me. What he did to me, he has done and continues to do to himself."

To manage tensions is the intuitive way to want to turn divisions into diversity. When it is wanted, the knowledge needed with the skill to do so can develop and be acquired. In these learning and transformative settings lies the pearl of great price: forgiving the hurts due to rejection and the reconciling that goes beyond any deception or seduction by either one.

The memory of the faces of hope strengthens my desire to live the journey to turn violence into peace-building for the young people who have never met anyone who would choose to forgive rather than to be violent. The joy this gives me is what I want to encourage others to have by wanting the next generation to live life and to live it to the fullest.

Cold and Floundering

Our first December, in 1973, was bitterly cold and floundering. It was a month of a solidifying relationship between Fr. Alex and me, defining moments and the significant meeting of the right people.

After those retreats in 1973, we began the task of grouping people together. We had three couples: one European American, one African American, and one Mexican American couple. We also had four young adults out of high school and six seniors still in high school that joined our effort to move forward.

December 1973 was a month of real wandering and grasping. I was the only one of the five eventual co-founders who was devoted to the work on a full-time basis. Fr. Alex was finishing his Master's thesis as he was petitioning his Passionist Provincial Fr. Paul Boyle to join me full-time.

Our team of volunteers poured over everything, reviewing the results and our experiences in schools to date. We had accepted what we could not change. Only a few chose to stay with us after our initial exploratory meetings. We knew we needed a strong follow-up process after the weekend experiences. The question was: how do we find people to be a stable foundation upon which to build?

We preached from pulpits and turned to Marriage Encounter adults to join us. We did home visits with people who showed interest. We continued inviting adults who were concerned with the quality of life—or the lack thereof—for young people in financially-challenged communities.

At the same time, I was working in two high schools. Since I wanted to change the image of my priesthood from being identified only with death, I called myself a "Life Worker." I knew why I was in the schools: to wake up young people before it was too late. But I would not be free to express the faith that would drive me to want to be with them. In the early centuries after Christ, when many feared the world was falling apart and governments were collapsing, the hermits created ways to hold on to what they valued while at the same time managing to stay apart from the world. They called themselves Life Workers.

I saw myself as a hermit with a similar role. I wanted to hold on to life by creating a hunger for positive values and inclusive spirituality in environments where traditional "systems" were inadequate and violence was blatantly real. Remember, this was the era of Watergate, Vietnam, anti-war, and civil rights demonstrations and scars from human rights conflicts. The riots in Detroit may have been history by 1973, but the killings continued, especially among young people who were dropping out of school.

Enter Alexander and Judith

When I was preaching at the Redemptorist parish in southwest Detroit, Alexander MacDonald came up to me after the service. He looked at me with intensity: "I liked what you said. If you have time, come by our home. Here is our address."

That very afternoon I rang the MacDonald's doorbell. Alexander answered. I met his wife Judith and their six pre-teen children. I did not know it at the time, but they would become co-founders of our life work.

They shared with me that they had gone to Holy Redeemer High School. Alexander worked at a Chrysler plant; Judith was a stay-at-home mom. They were going to send their children to public schools. She asked me very bluntly, "What are you doing about children in the public schools: not just *our* children, but all children?"

Judith later elaborated on the concerns she shared with her husband in a reflection about our first meeting.

"When we first met Fr. John, we were concerned about the safety of our children and the decision we had made to stay in the city of Detroit. The city had gone through the race riots, where businesses had decided not to rebuild and had moved out, leaving the streets in a blitz. There was redlining with middle class families making a great exodus to the suburbs.

"We heard horror stories about the public school system, which is where—if we stayed in the city—our children would be going. We could no longer afford to send them to private schools. Family members encouraged us to vacate the city, if we had the means to move. This was the 'responsible thing' for us to do as parents, they insisted.

"As parents, this put us in turmoil. In the midst of all this, God gave us the answer; it came to mind, in reflection. If things were as bad in the city as we thought, we'd be running away; we'd be selfish, only thinking about our own family. We had to want for *all* children what we wanted for our own. We began to see those being left behind in declining neighborhoods and schools as part of our family. We made the decision to stay in the city, and we never looked back.

"We decided to work with Fr. John in order to create support systems in schools and neighborhoods that would help our children and other children hold on to positive values and virtues, by being with fellow peers. Being supported, we would inspire them to make positive choices in their lives. One of the fruits of young people making positive choices usually leads them to do what is necessary to have successful careers. 'Success' for us, as parents, is our children growing up to be kind, loving, compassionate young adults who use their talents in the service of others."

The MacDonald's faith challenged them *not* to flee and to do what was best for their children and ignore the needs of others. They also wanted their children to be enriched and empowered by multi-cultural and socio-economic diversity.

In early 1974, I asked Alexander and Judith to go on a Marriage Encounter retreat. My intent was for us to gain insights into how married life grows, is strengthened and brings life to others. They came back on fire, with a discipline that moved us into a pattern of a weekly sharing of our spiritual life to empower each other to live our values and encourage us to find a way for the children to live. On those occasions, we would reflect on what happened to us as we pondered questions that came to us. Actually, the practice became a well-defined three-year tool that we co-created called "The Word of Life."

While I focused on the Life Worker aspect of our mission in the public schools, Alexander and Judith concentrated on the follow-up side of our Life Search retreats, as we first called them. Our common goal was to model married life and single life as two unconditional, loving commitments. We wanted to demonstrate what happens when a lifetime commitment to each other for the sake of our children includes all God's children.

Enter Sister Rosalie

In early January 1974, I was seeking to encourage Holy Redeemer students to assist me in reaching their friends who were struggling at the two high schools where I was working. I was leading a prayer service and could not get them excited. A young woman announced a song that got them going. When we were near the end, I asked, "Do you have another one?" She answered "Yes!"

This young woman had no idea that her "yes" would lead to her being the fifth pivotal young adult joining Fr. Alex the MacDonalds and me. Her name is Sister Rosalie Esquerra, an Adrian Dominican. With her, Fr. Alex, and the MacDonalds, we were to become the co-founders of our life work.

The five of us began to share our stories with one another. The MacDonalds wanted their children to be ready for the world made up of many different cultures and faith communities. They also wanted their children to make a positive difference in life. Sister Rosalie (her Religious Name at the time was Sister Maria Antonia) wanted to reach young people in public schools who were dropping out and dropping into violence. Fr. Alex's passion for public schools and my determination to be part of the solution to violence became the magnets that have held us together for these forty years.

Three of us met every Friday morning for prayer. We prayed as people sent on a mission. We prayed to bring peace out of violence and that we would not leave anyone behind who could be reached. In the evenings, I reflected with Alexander and Judith, whom I had come to know through Holy Redeemer Parish. Fr. Alex was part of St. Theresa's faith community. He met Will and Tina O'Sullivan who were very close to the young adults. Sister Rosalie prayed with St. Gabriel's faith community. She met Ruben and Bertha Godinez. Their children and Alexander and Judith's children were a natural fit.

The day we met together was sort of formal. We talked about our common interest in young people at risk. By the second time we met we were beginning to trust each other. It did not take long for us to be aware that we were not the typical group of adults. We called ourselves "The Incredible Team for Mission Impossible!" We were three cultures, three married couples, and three single young adults—all of us dedicated to working with people outside our denominations.

Alexander MacDonald always said "we must do this in a loving way." Judith's passion was making sure that whatever we did, it was done with integrity. Young people are always dealing with issues that compromise their values, so Judith always approached our decisions like a mother would treat her child: lovingly challenging the young person to face issues right on.

The three couples became very clear on their partnership with Fr. Alex, Sister Rosalie, and me. They appreciated our spiritual leadership, but, as married couples, they were positioned to challenge young adults to make choices and do so in an ongoing support community. They would be able to model a marriage. They would also be able to encourage all of the young adults to accept what they cannot change without judging and to have the courage to change what they can. This would be their way to deciding what to do with their life. The couples would share the wisdom that comes with life.

It made sense. We did not want to teach a class. We sought to challenge young adults to discover what they are going to do with the rest of their lives. Having three married couples who were raising their own children and willing to make time for young adults was the gift that launched our work to be based on a solid spiritual foundation.

Sputtering Start

In February 1974, Life Search was officially formed. Our fledgling group of 30 or so now had a name. We were intent on restructuring to ready ourselves to be a "gift for others."

We developed a three-part approach. First, contact through public and Catholic schools and through churches. Second, rely on the experience of Life Search team members who had been working with us. Third, build a Life Circle that focused on ongoing growth led by a married couple.

Our dream was to generate funds that would allow us to take on full-time young adults in their twenties and thirties to do what we were doing in the schools and in the communities. These young adults would become "Life Workers."

Alexander and Judith became increasingly involved with our efforts. Soon they became Life Search Directors, along with me. They were the facilitators; I was the co-leader. Together we would direct the work for those finishing high school along with adults who cared about them. Fr. Alex's team would take on the responsibility to select and train Life Workers. Sr. Rosalie, with her strong ties with the Hispanic community, would ensure we were doing what we were doing with quality—doing so in both Spanish and English.

As I mentioned, Fr. Alex and I had arranged to hold our retreats at the Redemptorist Center right across the Ambassador Bridge, about ten miles past the U.S. and Canadian border, near the city of Windsor. Because of our Marriage Encounter work, a promising relationship had been built between Detroit and Windsor among married couples. We just had to reinforce that relationship. In this way, finding married couples and adult single people to work with us spread into Canada.

We had not thought of it at first, but by having the retreats in Canada, we all had to go through Customs. It was a perfect way to ensure nothing illegal would be on the retreat: a non-verbal way of saying "all is safe."

Watering the Soil

By October 1974, our retreats were growing with healthy numbers of young people attending, but effective follow-up was still a major challenge. The city of Detroit was our major focus but we were making inroads in the suburbs. Father Bob Morand, the pastor of St. Teresa's Parish, who had experience in the African American community, joined our efforts. Working the weekend retreats were groups of young adults from the city, as well as from different parts of the suburbs and Windsor. The structure for community work was starting to develop, but salaries were needed if we expected to keep youth workers full-time and engaged.

I spent much of the first few months of 1975 working alone because Alex was finishing up his thesis on non-violence. Our proposal to the Archdiocese had been rejected without explanation. Fortunately, we found a way to resubmit and it was approved in May of that same year.

Life Search had a $63,000 budget. Amazing!

Restless: Till We Rest In Peace

A restless heart was the source of our zeal. Francis Xavier went to India from Portugal in 1541 because he wanted to respond to an unmet need. His zeal was centered on bringing spiritual food for the hungry and spiritual truth for the thirsty. We were restless, not for the hungry but for the anorexic. We knew people were fed up with answers that did not work. We also knew they were dying of spiritual malnutrition and did not know it.

What Francis found out by following his heart describes what we found within our mission within the communities where our walking created a path. As I read a letter he wrote, I thought of the many very intelligent people--far more educated than me--who would make excellent spiritually-centered people to do our mission.

We could not deny what we discovered. We did what Francis challenged those who see the need to do: "Forget our own desires, our human affairs and give ourselves over entirely to God's will and his choice."

The restlessness we felt then and continue to feel now is the inspiration that keeps us on mission, sustains our enthusiasm and encourages us to continue. We continue to draw encouragement from what Paul told the people of Philippi: "God, who began this good work in you, will carry it on until it is finished…" (Philippians 1:6).

What They Can Do for Others. . .

I am fast-forwarding about ten years just to emphasize the importance of our retreats in the lives of young people. Here's a reflection from one of our young adults, Karen Kerrigan, who in late 1984 made a focus: LIFE retreat (called "Life Search" at the time). Karen met a number of young adults and found a spirit of belonging and friendship that continued her interest in the "circle meetings" which explored values, spirituality, and life choices. Each person was seen as having unique talents and gifts. They asked questions to invite insights into each other's lives. They reflected through the Word of Life which was like a beacon, shedding light on issues and concerns they were facing.

The people who attend an initial weekend are invited to go further on their growth in their spiritual journey. The purpose of the focus: LIFE Two weekend is to encourage young adults in their late teens through their thirties to explore how they want to live their lives as being gifts for others—having their talents make a difference in the lives of people different from them.

Karen moved on with her career continuing to encourage her peers and those younger to look at how God is calling them. She has stayed in touch with us and recently wrote to recall meeting and networking with "many people from many different cultures and different areas" of Metropolitan Detroit. "Life Directions, as it is called now, was a place of transition for me," she wrote. She was grateful to have this way to move from her college years to her young adult career as a teacher.

"It also was a place for me to begin again, just after losing my father, when I was twenty-two," Karen continued. "Near the end of my young adult journey with Life Directions, I was co-directing focus: LIFE weekends and exploring my life journey and a deeper way in spiritual direction. I am grateful for the many opportunities for growth and community, teamwork, and leadership that Life Directions provided me with when I was a young adult."

We have served many Karens. It is both rewarding and humbling to have been welcomed by young adults to meet as peers and awaken a desire to find their "life directions." Moving past high school has a set of challenges which family and friendships may support, but to have a place to sort out choices with peers who want to be open to growth is worthy of all the work we continue to encourage others to make possible.

But it is more than what it does for young adults; it is what they can do for others, especially to promote ways to stop violence in relationships, in communities and in our cities. This is what makes the "circle" important and complete.

Focus: LIFE Incorporated

Back to our story: it was July 1975. My community at Holy Redeemer sensed it was important for us to have our own offices. There was a "walk-up" to an abandoned furniture store owned by St. Gabriel Parish, just west of Holy Redeemer. Fr. Alex had completed his degree, and his Provincial had released him from his work at their retreat house. The walk-up had a divider between our living quarters and offices. We used a room for a makeshift Reflective Chapel, and the rest of the rooms became office space. We named the facility "focus: LIFE" in the spirit of an organization born out of the 1967 riots called "Focus HOPE."

The building was located near a party store owned by Arabs. Down the street from us was a very large mosque. On any given day, we heard Spanish and Arabic mixed with English. The neighborhood sounded like the United Nations with rich and diverse dialogue right outside our door.

We had found funds from faith-based communities to hire "Life Workers", six young adults from three cultures, to work in six community high schools and their surrounding neighborhoods. We had continued to contact and recruit through our network of relationships, which continued to expand. By the end of 1975 we had held fifteen Life Search retreats in Windsor.

Agatha was the first of the six Life Workers. She came with a great deal of experience with high school students. Though she did not know Spanish, she was very much at home with people of many cultures. Pat was the son of a couple who knew Fr. Alex. He was a hard-working young adult, who was willing to give two years of his life to initiate our project. Agatha, Pat, and four other young adults made up the team of six Life Workers.

By January 1976, we had developed our very own twelve-step process for "the anorexic to values and the anorexic to inclusive spirituality." We had two methodologies written up and printed in manuals to use with our staff and volunteers. We aimed to put in place a paradigm shift with our identified disciplines attached. The method of our madness involved engaging the cause of violence and showing how forgiving is the transformative energy coming from the Power Greater Than Human.

For our work among those under eighteen years of age, the central shift was to engage the young people to discover through reflecting with their peers that they are victims because they want to be, more than because they have to be. This continues to be the core of the challenge: to have peers who are rooted and taking charge of their lives and inspire their less-achieving peers to embrace the positive values that work for them.

We also made another painful discovery. Agatha was our only adult Life Worker. Within that first year, four of the other five young adults moved on for various reasons. Later on we learned that to do our work demands a way of life that has an internalized vision before we can lead others. The learning was tough, but the lesson has led us to develop volunteers and staff with a way to integrate values and spirituality that is balanced and life-sustaining.

What was more challenging was to take on the issue of the "anorexics to inclusive spirituality"—those who want to control their relationship with a Higher Power. This group wants to define, not *discover*, that relationship. We worked to refine what we now call our "three-phase way" of developing a hunger for spirituality that challenges the anorexic to inclusive spirituality.

The first phase centers on challenging young adults (eighteen years of age and older) to move from an "entitlement" way of life to a point where they see life as a gift freely given, not earned. This would lead them to being thankful *for* each other and *to* each other. To want what others have and resolve conflicts with violence disrespects the gift that we all are from the Giver: the Power Greater Than Human, however we define this Higher Power.

The second phase is all about inviting peers from the first phase to go out and build networks of justice and *right* relationships based on healing with unconditional love. This has been the work of encouraging every young adult and mature adult to discover his or her "spark"—passion—and to choose a Life Direction for the sake of those who need what they have. They are "a gift for others." We all can be self-giving or self-serving; it is our choice.

Phase Three is about turning division into diversity and hostility into harmony. It begins with reflections on people's lives: trying to glean the needed spiritual and personal resources, "address the mess," and empower peers and those who care for the next generation. This phase brings the message of "the gift of forgiving our enemy." My enemy is my friend whom I am choosing to forgive. Not to do so is to continue the mess: the killing of the young in more ways than just physical.

Bill Kilburg, a seventeen-year-old high school basketball player who had just won the state championship, thought he was "the king of the hill," until he joined us for one of our retreats. In an exercise, we blindfolded him and sent him on a "trust walk."

Donna, a female paraplegic, led him blindfolded along the way. The young man discovered that every talent he had for playing sports was a gift to which he was not entitled. Why? Donna did not have any of them; yet, she had more joy than he did. She took him over to touch but not see a flower. She helped him "see" life through her eyes. He became aware. He became grateful for his talents. But more than that, he became aware that his life is a gift so he should enjoy it! How does that happen? He gives his gifts and talents to others, for their sake.

The purpose of this kind of exercise is to awaken the spirit of trust—a child's trust. When we can trust someone in that way, we can be vulnerable. So many youth have been hurt because they once trusted and had been betrayed. They learned to hide from it. If we do not trust, how in the world are we ever going to entrust our gifts to anybody?

This young basketball player thought he was important because of his athletic abilities. Donna showed him that he was important because of himself. The experience changed his life and what he did with it, and Donna had no idea what she had done for him by trusting him and being trustworthy to him.

We had ways of awakening forgiveness as the most healthy and life-giving response to violence. We sensed we were ready to become a not-for-profit corporation with our very own 501(c)(3) tax exempt number. Seeking a grant, we brought together nine of the young adults and adults with whom we worked. We started our own board with bylaws. Judith MacDonald was the first Chairperson with three African, European, and Hispanic American board members. Six of the ten were young adults. Four were adults in focus: LIFE leadership. We were now poised to ask for donations on our own and not as part of the religious communities that supported our beginnings.

Walking by faith and not by sight, we had no way of knowing that the institutional religious support we had relied on for so long would altogether disappear.

THE PARABLE OF THE ROCK IN THE WAY

A little boy wanted to play football in the lot next to his house. He asked his dad for permission. His dad said "yes," as long as the little boy used all his strength to clean the field.

"Dad, there is this big boulder in the middle of the field. What am I to do?"

"Use all your strength," the father replied.

The little boy got a big stick. He tried to pry up the boulder. But the more he tried, the less it budged. "What am I to do?" he asked.

"Use all your strength," his dad repeated.

"I am," the boy complained.

"No, you're not. Use all your strength."

The little boy used a rope around a tree; it did not move. He pushed his shoulder against it. It moved a little but not much. Finally he sat down and wanted to give up.

"Son, you did not use all your strength," his father said.

"I sure did. What did not I use?"

"You never asked me for help," the dad said.

As you look at doing something important in life, reflect upon this parable.

1. What does it say to us about what you need before you start? If you think of your strengths that are needed, you may not think of the strengths you need to be a servant and not a savior.

2. What is the reason the father let his son do what he did? Would you be willing to do the same, to wait to be asked the question? To be patient is to let God do what only God can do, let each person be free to ask.

3. What do you think was the discovery of the son at the end? Will he remember the lesson learned in a way that frees him to be patient with others? Spiritual anorexia is challenged by the person with the addiction asking questions before receiving answers.

4. What does this story say about knowing your strengths and limits and ensuring you have the synergy you need to complete the job? Burnout and being on fire look the same from the outside. Within your heart you will know the difference. When you see what is not working, you rejoice to have eyes to see. You look for those who need you to share their spirit which has given them the power to live before you met them.

CHAPTER THREE
THE ROSE BETWEEN

In January of 1976, Sister Rosalie A. Esquerra moved from being a volunteer to becoming full-time co-director of focus: LIFE. Having a woman, a "Mexicana" (as she calls herself), and an Adrian Dominican was a wonderful gift to our mission.

Sister Rosalie brought her talents as an educator and her way of looking at life to complement the direction we were seeking to discover. She expanded focus: LIFE to engage the Spanish-speaking community. Her gentle touch encouraged people who tend to stay distant from faith-centered people to want to meet and usually end with a hug of compassion and solidarity.

Slowly, Fr. Alex and I came to know the roots of Rosalie's journey which she began to share indirectly. It was confusing for us at first, until she explained how she learned to be cautious:

"You need to understand that I do not want to impose myself on anyone. It was part of how I was raised. And it is part of people who are positioned to be in the minority, with little or no power. It is sort of a survival. I am not sure, but it may be one of the effects of being conquered, being oppressed as Mexican people.

"We wait for your response to the situation or to the question. If you can hear what is not said, and you respect me for wanting to know what I know, then I begin to slowly trust you. If you do not want to control me and you do not want me to meet your needs while giving me a sense of being used, then we begin to build the bridge of being trustworthy. You seem to be worthy of my trust.

"Also I want to let you know that I will not organize people to do something that they do not understand and agree to demonstrate. Once I was asked to have a hundred people in a march for justice for immigrants. I asked to know the strategy to ensure everyone knows the issues. 'Why do we need to do that? We want strength in numbers,' the organizers told me. Because I did not do what they asked, it almost cost me my job. It is that important to me *not* to use people."

Being white and male and a priest, I was grateful that Rosalie was willing to trust us as a fellow team person. I continue to be even more grateful for her teaching us, for lack of a better word, to do what we need to do to be worthy of trust. And once we are trustworthy, it is even more important to remember to be loyal.

1986 Nobel Prize winner and author Elie Wiesel said that the Jewish people were the ones who put their fellow Jews on the trains to their deaths. I knew the meaning of the word "Oreo." I remember thinking Al Jolson's minstrel show was funny, until someone told me what it meant to African Americans. It was *not* complimentary.

Also because of her sensitivity to "the little people" walking *with* us and not *behind* us, we are very cautious to take a stand on an issue of justice as Life Directions. Our bylaws state that we will not take stands on controversial issues. We want to wake up people to the issues at hand. We encourage all to first be informed. Then each person's authority as a person will do what conscience challenges each of us to do.

Affection is Effective

I will never forget how Rosalie shared her affectionate way of being with "Santo Niño." She has a tender relationship with Jesus, fashioning as she remembers it by her grandmother, "Grandma Moses of Arizona." All the saints were her companions, especially the Little Flower. It was nothing to hear Rosalie say, "Little Flower, at this hour, show thy power." Her little way was the way to hear God's will and to encourage others to develop their own little way to relate to the Power Greater Than Human.

Rosalie grew up helping her mother raise the "boys," as the seven were called by her mom and dad. She remembers how she so wanted her dad to be there for her. She believes that a father's love for his children is so important. She makes this remark often when she sees "dads loving their children."

The color of her skin was something she was made aware of when her mother prepared her to be a Sister. As she remembers it, Rosalie was packing her things and her mom was putting lemons in her bag. Rosalie asked her why she was packing lemons for her. Her mom said she may want to use it on her skin to be lighter. She remembers feeling sad because her mom had taught her that the last four letters of Mexican is "I Can." However, she just took the lemons and to this day she loves eating them!

Her love for children wants her to bring them all to smile. She sees any child who looks sad as her challenge to cheer them up. Her sixteen years of teaching first-graders gave her lots of opportunities to bring them joy. When she was a principal in Las Vegas, she encouraged her staff to "bring smiles" so the children would know how much God loves them. It never fails that she wants everything to look so happy and neat, with candies for everyone.

Fr. Alex and I saw ourselves as pioneers, like Lewis and Clark, looking for the "passage." As I look back, I am profoundly grateful for Sister Rosalie's dedication to the young people on the margin. Fr. Alex and I are strong-willed, and neither of us is shy about expressing our passions. Like the "odd couple" analogy indicated, we differ on issues and circumstances and debate them with almost obstinate enthusiasm.

At the time we did not know that we were going to bring to surface the results of injustice, as we worked within two separate-but-equal worlds: the spiritual life of the faith-based communities with our private schools and the secular life of corporate America and our public schools. It would be our commitment to young people falling through the cracks and young people living in broken relationships and neighborhoods that sustained us, as we searched for life out of death, joy out of sorrow. Both worlds did not need to be separate. We were seeking to find the common ground to raise the next generation of compassionate people to "rediscover the values and the spirituality" that make life grow for all people of good will.

The "rose between" came to symbolize young people falling through the cracks caused by separate-but-equal Church and State when family life is not working. The relationship between a husband and wife is the supernatural way that brings both to excellence. As forgiving leaves this relationship, the climate for violence begins to grow.

We wanted to face the challenge to go past the analysis. We did not come looking for those who had it all together. We reminded each other of the privilege to be in the middle of the mess of life as it is. We also encouraged each other to remember that God can make a way out of no way. He built creation; He can fix it, if we let Him.

Peers Mentoring Peers – It Works

The idea that young people are part of the solution shows itself when they mentor their peers who are just two or three years younger. After waking up to values that give direction to their lives, they want to do the same for others. With a little coaching from adults, they can do in everyday life what they do on the basketball court. All it takes is team spirit and the knowledge that we can lean on each other as we are growing up!

Pat Trainor, our full-time partner who you will meet later, found such a diamond in the rough, almost literally. One day, one of our young people, Rory, was away from everyone sitting alone under the stairway at Martin Luther King, Jr. High School, minding his own business. Pat sensed he was by himself for a reason. He asked Rory's name and if he would not mind joining him and a group of ninth graders.

"For what?" Rory shot back. "To hear how they are making it or not at King?"

Rory eventually accepted Pat's invitation and his "yes" led to a great year for the group and for Rory. Pat gave him so much on-the-spot training that, by the second session, Rory really came "out of the box." He was ready and willing to lead. Pat recalled how Rory addressed a group of his peers in need of inspiration:

"You guys are messing around and got an attitude that reminds me of myself last year. I was so smart; I flunked almost all my classes. Then I came to Life Directions. I started to listen to things that spoke to me. Now look what I just got."

What Rory "got" in his first semester as a sophomore was a report card with all 'A's. He passed it around the group. They shut up and started to listen up.

Rory graduated from high school in the early 1980s. By that time he was already working as a volunteer young adult leader on the east side of Detroit. It kept him focused, he said. Rory went to culinary school, graduated, and now owns his own catering service specializing in ribs. He caters some of our events and is always ready to share his story from thirty years back with his wife and kids enjoying it every time they hear it. Rory learned a lot from the training sessions and it is great for him to be a role model for peer mentors now thirty years his junior.

For many young people, "belonging" is a tough value to make work positively. It is especially true when another value, change, is looking an eighth-grader in the face. We know that most young people drop out between eighth to tenth grades. It is one thing to say that it is because they chose the wrong crowd, when they went from middle school to high school. It is another thing to offer an alternative.

The peer mentors that were in our Peer Motivation groups and had become Certified Peer Achievers, "made it." They found out what worked and learned how to make school work for them. They also got involved in activities going on in the community. They learned how to be safe and secure by building the right friendships. Peer mentors are an alternative that works!

Peer mentors, like Rory, are stronger and more effective when they can be mentored by married couples. We found this relationship gives the wisdom needed to guide and encourage. It worked for us as adults and we sensed it would do the same with the younger adults. Married couples were—and continue to be—extremely important, as Sister Rosalie details:

"Father John, Father Alex, and I each had a married couple with whom we prayed with every week. We each had partners. The idea was that the richness that comes from committed relationships is the value we hold up as married life. In visual terms, the married couple is the depth needed to sustain community. Single people, including religious people, represent the breadth of community. We gather people to reconnect with the roots. Sometimes a married couple is so focused on 'family,' that they may be closed to other relationships.

"We seek to bring married couples together to be with other married couples. It becomes peers inspiring peers. It is the way couples encourage couples. At the same time, single people can look to expand, yet be unaware of losing our balance in relationship. When the two ways of loving live and work together, the results can be amazing."

Many young people face the challenge of being sexually active. It is for some a rite of passage, for others it is recreation, and for still others it is "practicing for the real one."

A group of high school seniors had been meeting with a spiritually-centered married couple for a few months. They had talked about all kinds of things, but when the topic of sex came up; they could not help but share their shock: "Are you serious? You have been married to each other for ten years? Isn't it boring?"

"We love each other," the husband responded. "We want to be together and we do not have to be true to each other. We want to be."

As he shared this value, the young men in the group were quiet, not sure what to say. Then his wife spoke to the young women: "Would you girls want the father of your child to have been sexually active before you married? Or better still, would you want to marry before you have a child?"

Cecilia, one of the young women in the group, could not stop herself. Before she knew it, she was talking: "People your age thought marriage was better before having a kid. People my age think having sex is better before getting married. If a kid comes, we deal with it."

"What are you going to teach your child?" asked the husband.

"To be married, have sex, and then have a child," Cecilia answered.

"Why teach what you do not do?" the wife came back at her.

"Because our way does not work," said Sharice, another young person in the group. When she made that comment, everyone became quiet. They were all amazed at the conversation. They knew they could not talk with their parents. They knew they would not want peers in their school to know what they said. At that point, they all agreed to explore why it was that they could not be honest in school and at parties.

Waking up to values works when adults are comfortable to be themselves, and remember doing "good" has a way of making things better. In preparing couples and young adults to mentor teens, we are up front with this value. To say "no" to any negative behavior does not work as well as saying "yes" to positive choices.

Vale La Pena

As I look back, I realize that our married couples were positioned to listen to the source of tension caused by broken relationships within marriage and family. The powerful energy of unconditional love listens to young people differently. Especially, if like Alexander and Judith, they feel the challenge of living in a faith community with their children attending public schools, and living in communities with the issues of addictions of all forms, as well as racism and class separatism.

Judith and Alexander, from the beginning, were part of the central team. They were the first married couple to encourage young adults to be part of the solution. They never worked with us in the schools; they were the reflective, prayerful support people for young adults in their homes. A married couple or two mature adults were the key to young adults staying centered and reaching out, speaking and living the value to serve their peers who weren't rooted in their families.

This is how we found God's way of making a way out of no way. We began to feel the power of forgiving for our journey to find the cause of violence. In Spanish, it is referred to as "Vale La Pena" which means "it is worth the pain." In English, it is "worthwhile."

The fidelity of those who are *not* in positions of power over young people is essential to ensure young people see a role model that cares. Alexander and Judith, with eight kids, weren't rich as the world sees richness. They had no authoritative roles in either the schools or the churches. They were an ordinary, hard-working couple doing extraordinary work.

They did not need money to hold their position as a married couple who could inspire, challenge, and motivate other married couples to join the mission. Ruben and Bertha were hospitable and very accommodating with their home. They were so supportive of our building community that it encouraged others to want to join the work. Will and Tina were so outgoing and vivacious. They kept us balanced and able to not take our challenges too seriously. Being a biracial couple, their awareness of issues of discrimination gave us an insight into prejudice that was freeing for us and encouraging for the young adults that looked up to them as role models.

Judith always insisted that the "sacred" would guide the secular side of our mission. Her husband, Alexander, adamantly reminded us of how we "professionals" did not give him or his friends the wisdom we have. So we were to walk softly and not pre-judge people to be "wrong," as we would say. He made us very sensitive to the broken and to the ordinary person. He helped us avoid idealistic, "full-of-ourselves," philosophical conversations.

"The fidelity of those not in positions of power" was a real insight the couples helped develop. They were very clear that we never consider anyone who worked with us as "volunteers." There are self-supported people and people who are financially-supported. The self-supported, by definition, tend to be more committed than the financially-supported. As Judith would remind us, "The world may say we are a volunteer organization but we pay to do our work. We do not have to do this mission. We want to do our mission. We are just as committed, if not more so, than the financially-supported people."

Consider this: when the government decides it is going to address a problem, such as violence among young people, it throws money into salaries and staffing. But when those salaries and money dry up and go away, those financially-supported people, who were so dedicated to the young, go away with them.

I remember being told by a politician, who will remain anonymous, that the government funds us to fail. That is why, most times, funding is set for five years. It is designed that way so that it ends after the first year of the next term. As we sought support, this insight, joined with Alexander and Judith's, gave us pause if we were to be awarded a large sum of money. Staff loyalty would need to be tested to see if they would be dedicated to what we value or to the money.

With their insight, we learned early that we should never base what we are doing on the financially-supported staff. We should respect the difference between the shepherd and the hirelings. The shepherd stays with the sheep when the wolf comes. The hireling runs because he is paid. This insight from chapter 10 of the *Gospel of John* has many implications to bringing values and inclusive spirituality back to life. As the years progressed, we would return to this insight often to encourage each other to stay the course.

Once at a reunion of some of the young adults who used to meet with Alexander and Judith, a man, who had become a grandfather, shared that he was thinking of taking his own life. He had made a mistake and could not forgive himself. Alexander's gentle way of listening had given the man the power to see himself as Alexander did. Alexander had no idea the grandfather was contemplating suicide until he confessed. "Thanks for saving my life," the grandfather said tearfully, "when you did not know it was almost lost."

Strength in Our Differences

The "rose between" is the ideal that draws us past competition to complement, past jealousy to joy, past fear to love that hopes against hope.

As Sister Rosalie took her place within the mission, she moved us to see the children at risk as our source of inspiration. She helped us discover that our differences would be the diversity needed to find the way to a truth that would set us free. Our friendship and our common vision became our impenetrable bond.

Sister Rosalie wrote with deep conviction and rich emotion on how she saw one challenging aspect of her working with Fr. Alex and me: "To be between two strong, independent men of God is a tearful, painful experience. It was three of us hammering out how we see life."

Rosalie walked with conviction, talked with compassion, and stood with character for "her kids," as she named them. She had returned from a long stretch in Central America where she experienced rebirth and renewed rootedness in her values and culture. While journaling, Sister Rosalie described how she, too, had a strong-willed personality to reckon with:

"I was beginning to learn how to speak again. My strong, deductive way of speaking would not let go. I could not leave. I believe in the principles so strongly, I could not but stay."

When violence broke out at Western High School and a young person was stabbed, Sister Rosalie and I happened to be on the scene. I pressed down on the wound. She called 9-1-1. When the young man was taken to the hospital, we had a heart-to-heart conversation, sharing our visions and our mutual desire to help young people at-risk. It was a life-changing moment for both of us, although we did not know it at the time.

She told me of her desire to help young people stay in school, especially people of color, as some described them. She was directing a federal program called Emergency School Assistance Action (ESAA). She had fought for bilingual education to challenge the system *not* to see Spanish-speaking people as needing Special Education. She told me how she organized to keep bilingual programming together at Webster School in southwest Detroit, when busing for integration passed.

As she finished sharing, I asked, "Why do you want them to stay in school? Is this all you want for them?"

That question led her to network her program with our developing work. She brought an amazing set of skills to our retreats and our working among married couples in the community. Gradually she wanted to do more than engage the educational system. She wanted to do what we were doing: waking up young people to values to give direction to their action. She knew this was her deep passion. She did what she had to do in order to transition from being Director of ESAA to joining Alex and me.

Rosalie came on board at a time of extreme challenges and profound breakthroughs. We were rejected by the Archdiocese in regards to funding. Inter-Parish Sharing (IPS) was the only means of financial existence that we knew of at the time. We heard second-hand that school administrators had considered removing us from public high schools because we lacked a professional way of doing business. We definitely felt the tension and experienced the antagonistic, dismissive attitudes of school administrators. But, since no one articulated their concerns directly, we were battling phantoms. Sister Rosalie's experience of being a school principal gave us the guidance and direction for our work within the schools to move onto solid ground.

Our numbers were growing on the retreats and in the schools. Detroit was beginning to recognize focus: LIFE. But making headway into racially-polarized communities was still a major challenge. There was also much uncertainty and internal debate about what we were really all about. Were we building something beyond ourselves? Were we truly a gift to others?

Father Alex and I were having a "come-to-Jesus moment" over the slow growth of Life Workers. Fr. Alex was frustrated with those who joined and quickly quit when the going got rough. It was a painful process. I was mostly concerned about the rootedness of the effort. Was the turnover a sign that this plan of action with youth workers was not the way to go?

It was the input, patience, and steady resolve of a religious woman named Sister Dora Lezovich, an Immaculate Heart of Mary Sister, who had come aboard as an Associate Director which helped lead us through a transition from youth workers to a professionally-trained team. She was there to keep our balance as we weathered our unsteady vessel through uncertain and choppy waters.

Settled Structure

Our funding proposal to the National Campaign for Human Development was denied. Focused on those falling through the cracks was not seen as spiritual enough for some and too secular for others. The lack of stable funds was a huge issue. We needed to expand, but we were running out of operating capital. Our financial reality said "cut back" but the urgency of our mission screamed "move forward!" Fr. Alex and I met before all the pastors of the local parishes to plead our case. After we spoke, Monsignor Clem Kern, a powerful person dedicated to "those living in an environment of poverty," was the first to make a $100 donation—"a C-note," as he put it. Msgr. Kern also spoke on our behalf before the pastors:

"The letter telling us about the kids you serve is good. But we do not need it. I work with broken people and keep beggars alive. We all know what you're doing. You want to wake up kids before they come to my front door. I want you men to know I believe in them. I hope you do. Why else are they doing this thankless job?"

We raised almost $10,000.00 in ten days.

Then an amazing thing happened. All Saints Parish near Southwestern High School needed a Pastor. Fr. Alex and I were approached. The people involved in making the decision knew that our full-time work was with people who do not come to church and that we had no agenda to recruit them to join. The parish had some essential needs that would be part-time, at best. If we would meet the needs they identified, we would have a home and a small stipend to compensate for the ministry we would do for them.

We took the position and moved in. But what came with it was even more amazing. Almost overnight we had just expanded our meeting space. We began to run our ongoing growth programs out of the basement of the church rent-free.

We now put even more attention on challenging ourselves to our vision. We worked to shore up our self-supported structure by building young adult groups to sustain the spirit of the Life Search Retreat, now known as focus: LIFE. We also invited adults to join our Advisory Board to help support our continued financial needs. We redoubled our community work by visiting homes, talking to families, and building stronger networks outside church circles.

For three years, we had been "listening to life." Although there was much uncertainty, we felt that we were part of a major movement of spirituality. Being in a place with visibility gave us credibility among ministers of all faith communities. More people heard about us. We actually had a meeting of major world religions to explore what we have in common and how it would relate to those who go nowhere to worship. From the Muslim tradition we heard the power of prayer and fasting, from the Buddhist tradition we heard the call to contemplation, from the Jewish tradition we heard the dream of a better world, from the Christian tradition we heard the power of forgiving. Encouraged by this conversation, we found young adults who wanted to come on our focus: LIFE weekends to discover how they might be part of the solution to violence.

We were not able to maintain our reflective gathering. But for that brief moment we grew in confidence that we were bringing hope to those falling through the cracks created by young people leaving high schools and young adults leaving faith communities. We were able to hear what was missing from their lives. It put in place a challenge to wake up a hunger for values that would come to life through the search for a way to find out what we have in common.

The "Three-Culture" Concern

Part of our mission was to get "Blacks, Browns and Whites" involved and engaged with focus: LIFE. If the "community" component of our effort was not strong, there would be no way to contact, recruit, or offer experiences and work with those who had "anorexia to values and inclusive spirituality."

Fr. Alex, who was deeply embedded in "race work," reflects on his and our collective roles in bridging ethnic, economic, and social gaps:

"We were two white guys and a Mexican engaging primarily with the African American community and later with Hispanics and Native Americans. But in our heyday, we had a great impact in the suburbs, too. White young people bought into the fact that they could actually build bridges with the city. I think that was our 'forte'—we were the only legitimate program that bridged young adults over nineteen years of age with their peers in the city."

"Culture" is a word we prefer over "race." The latter can be divisive. It can bring us to focus on historical wounds and long-embedded differences. Culture, on the other hand, speaks to our shared experiences. Culture was "stolen" from African Americans when they were brought to America as slaves. The vestiges of this "theft of their roots" were festering in black communities, as Fr. Alex recalls:

"I had to learn not to ask too many questions. Sometimes white folk, in an effort to control the situation, ask people everything about themselves. I learned to be very careful and respectful when I engage in order to stay on common ground.

"My experiences with African Americans have enhanced my life and understanding of our differences. For example, I never realized there was a worse slavery after the original slavery until I moved into an African American community in the Ensley section of Birmingham, Alabama. Black folk, after they were freed, found themselves involved in a form of slavery that was less genocidal but more lethal. They were put in jails for minor infractions such as staring at a white woman or spitting in the street. In jail, they were used as free labor, and this went on for at least twenty years after slavery.

"After reading *Slavery by Another Name* by Douglas A. Blackmon, I realized the vestiges in Ensley. You would not believe how many single men I met between the ages of thirty and fifty living in my 'hood' that have absolutely nothing: no driver's license, no jobs, no savings, and no value."

For many European Americans we tend to want to let go of our roots for a better life; we want to be "American" and speak English, and we often disconnect ourselves from any culture based in our past. For some Hispanic Americans, Europeans fashioned the Native Americans in what we call Mexico into a whole new culture.

For us in Life Directions, cultural diversity is the common ground upon which we want our mission to stand. We would hold up its value. We found African Americans surprised and Hispanic Americans grateful for our wanting to encourage their values and ways of life. Without cultural rootedness in this sense, we are all victims. To *not* truly know ourselves and our culture makes it harder to enrich one another, support each other, or bring our inherited gifts to what we could refer to as the "concert of cultures." Our approach is that a culture is what receives the faith. When it does receive faith, it supports and encourages justice for all, especially "those living in an environment of poverty." Once we know, from then on we are responsible for being victims. It is our decision to dare to be different for all, not just for ourselves.

Sister Rosalie was more aware of her culture and history; she could clearly see the connections between Detroit's Hispanic community and her Mexican and Central American cultures. She had a voice rooted in that historical familiarity and a way to speak to our shared "disconnect" from an authentic place.

The organizing of the young adult groups to sustain the spirit of the Life Search retreat was done in three areas: the city of Detroit, its suburbs, and the greater Windsor community. In Detroit, we had young adult groups who were primarily African or Hispanic or multicultural. In the suburbs, the groups were primarily "Americans," whom we called "European Americans." In Windsor they were simply called "The Canadians."

The groups, called circles, gave "space" to reflect upon their lives and discover direction. They came together seasonally to celebrate their diversity, to surface an issue of justice: education and jobs were the two more popular topics that would encourage community service.

In the suburban communities and in Windsor we found structures in place to encourage young adults to come on retreats. In the city, it was different. We had built the structure of youth workers to build the bridges. It would be a long process. I distinctly remember the first interchange meeting Fr. Alex and I had with African Americans at St. Bernard Church's Cultural Center. They spent the first two hours of the meeting just checking us out. I was grateful for Rosalie's advice: "Do what you need to do to win their trust. Once it happens, do not break it."

We believed that inclusion of culture was essential to building bonds within diverse communities. It was from this "three-culture" approach that we would look to ensure our Life Workers were represented. Our married couples of many cultures convened the young adult circles. In this way our reflections would make valuable connections with the young starving for inclusive spiritual values.

Lowered Expectations

By the end of 1976, the country was in a different mood. Among the people with whom we lived, the era of scandal and GOP backlash had come to an official end. President Richard Nixon's successor,

President Gerald Ford, was defeated by Jimmy Carter. To quote people I heard on the streets, Ford was beaten by a "peanut farm-owner" from Georgia who was seen by many as a religious man.

Focus: LIFE was also in a different place. The value of youth workers trained by us and sent into the high schools as role models was not sustainable. It was not working. There was a need for a more professional team. Agatha, who knew me, and Pat, whose parents knew Fr. Alex, were completing their commitment as Life Workers. When we moved from the young adults in schools to professional people, Agatha and Pat were perfect to lead that transition.

Facing the Struggle

With professional people in the schools, the quality of our work improved. We demonstrated results that teachers and administrators appreciated. At the end of that year we received a standing ovation after making a presentation about focus: LIFE before the school board. We considered the meeting a breakthrough and were encouraged to expand our programs to other public schools in the city.

There were a few unsettling incidents that happened within and outside our core team. Within focus: LIFE we needed closer accountability among salaried staff. Once, a staff person resigned in the middle of the year, only to have the young people with whom she was working leave as well. The support from the parishes was waning. Fr. Alex met with one of the key leaders for young adults within the Archdiocese. "We wanted to be part of an area-wide gathering of all youth programs. After listening to my request, this 'leader' said that what we had asked was 'outside his job description.'"

His response moved Father Alex to write, "This really aggravates me! The one man who has the recognition by all as having the 'authority' to draw all youth ministries together refuses to do so."

By March of 1977, we knew our struggle to secure sustaining funds from within the parishes to support our Life Workers was to end by June. It was one of the most painful times we had experienced. We were left sad and empty but more determined than ever to find "a way out of no way," to do what we felt the Lord had sent us to do.

The decision made us more determined to build our support community. The suburbs and Windsor young adult circles were growing. We decided to focus on the young adults in the city and for us to work in the schools directly. For me, it meant that I had to commit to the slow methodical "three-culture" process of engaging and meeting with families of different cultures in their homes, businesses and schools. We would build relationships rather than hiring staff from within the culture.

Oddly enough, being resisted by church and school institutions gave us a spurt of renewal and direction. We were reminded that to be a Christian, we must glory in rejection, strife, and powerlessness, to love with no conditions. This is what we do because this is what He did. It took a great deal of support from the young adult groups from the retreats to want to continue to be faithful to the mission.

Readied for the Alienated

I wrote in May 1977, "I sense it is happening! We are bringing the whole process into clearer perspective...beginning to hear the rhythm and making balanced decisions."

Reflecting on this writing brought back memories of our strained but steady growth in leadership and focus. Our dream was coming to fruition despite continued setbacks and challenges. Sister Phyllis Paquette from Canada, a Sister of the Congregation of the Holy Names of Jesus and Mary, had joined us as a part-time associate director. Sister Rosalie, in particular, was ecstatic. With Sister Phyllis on board, she wrote, "The possibilities for expansion and getting the ship in order to move have promise."

The parishes made us a generous offer of $25,000 but there was a caveat: we had three days to raise matching funds or we'd lose all the money. We contacted the Redemptorist, Passionist, Adrian Dominican, and the Capuchin Provincials, as well Bishop Gumbleton, the auxiliary bishop of Detroit. Our hope was to give it our all and accept the rewards or rejections as blessings. We did it! We met the challenge.

We had trained enough people to co-direct the Life Search Retreats. Focus: LIFE staff had representatives from three different cultures working in full gear together. The neighborhood visits were starting to pay off with more and more married couples and young adults serving as peer leaders. We strengthened our community outreach with the "focus: Family" program that was developing "slowly but not speedily," I wrote at the time.

Even though I felt things were coming together, I must admit that I had my doubts. Besides the institutional opposition, it was no cakewalk making neighborhood connections. Making something happen among families in neighborhoods with an imprint of oppression can be hard and dispiriting work. It is unbelievable how fearful people are to share their lives and families with the family-less. As an example, Fr. Alex was visiting homes near Northwestern High School, which was a west-side high school. He was having a good time with one of the families, until one of the children told him that there might be a contract out on his life. Fr. Alex asked what he meant, and the young man explained in detail:

"The Cascade Street gang sees you as a threat to their turf. You've been hanging around their corner and they do not like it."

Fr. Alex knew of the gang called Young Boys Incorporated (YBI). They were mostly ninth-graders. He did not remember ever meeting any of them face-to-face. That made it even clearer that he needed to stay out of that area of the city.

The real struggle, at the time, was entering into the lives of people in a non-threatening, non-manipulative way. Violence closes many hearts and doors. I wrote about this, asking, "How does one gather a desperate group of people who seem to be running, running…but to 'where' is ambivalent at best."

During a solicitation meeting with an executive at Chrysler, he asked an intriguing question about our organizational structure and the future of focus: LIFE. How do we intend to continue a process beyond ourselves, he asked, when the organization was "relational"—meaning people were involved because of their relationships with Fr. Alex, Sister Rosalie, Alexander and Judith or me? "How would you continue your work and pass it on to others?" the executive wondered.

It is a question I struggled to answer. But the question laid the foundation to ask, "Is this the work of God?" To explore this question, we needed a way to evaluate our vision, mission, and values.

Needed Evaluation

Richly diverse attendance at our Life Search weekends was growing exponentially. The school situation started to shift in a positive direction. Under our leadership and with help from the likes of counselor Frank Briglia, relationships and patterns with school administrators and teachers were developing, and the wheels of healthy engagement clicked along nicely.

In October of 1977, I met with Bob Newsome in Chicago so we could begin the process of developing evaluation tools for our organization. I was introduced to Bob two years earlier by my mother. He has since passed away, but, at the time, he was an expert organizational psychologist who specialized in putting together systematic ways of evaluating what companies do.

We valued truth in relationships, and Bob had a paradigm that broke down the five essential ways to influence people. One way was to set up a stable system to give people a sense of order and security. Another was a system of clear direction, rules, boundaries, and regulations. Still another way of influencing people was to receive them: be a listener, a healer, someone who cares for people with a non-judgmental response. The fourth way was to be a charismatic leader for whom people are willing to die, though they often cannot explain why. The last way he described to influence people was to be wise and compassionate: be someone who can deal with all the implications and consequences of any situation and find the jewel of wisdom that builds cohesion.

We needed a system where all five variables worked together. I turned to Bob because we wanted to look at the five years of our work to honestly access if what we were doing was really for God's people or just a nice do-gooder program that was all about us. Were we meeting our own needs or doing something that would make a difference because God sent us to do it?

Bob gave us the analytical tools we needed. I brought him modules and tables to review. He did go through them all and give me advice. Finally, he helped create the six-month evaluation process we needed.

A New Chapter in Our Saga

In Detroit Fr. Alex, Sister Rosalie, and I, along with a few others—people on our Board of Directors and people actively involved as volunteers—began using the tools Bob Newsome had put together to create evaluation forms. We sent them to hundreds of people so they could give us their input and feedback about our work.

Father Alex and I found the initial responses to the mailers encouraging, as Rosalie documented in her journal writing:

"John and Alex were like two little boys in a place where sports equipment can be bought and each boy can buy a whole basket full of what they wanted…seeing their eyes light up; their voices get excited was a real treasure."

We were ecstatic with the conclusive results indicating that we were doing good work that needed to continue. But our in-house analysis would not be enough to convince the Archdiocese or other institutional sources to expand their funding of our work. So six focus groups, led by our organizational psychologist Bob Newsome, included administrators from the public school system and faith-based communities. They went over the evaluations.

Collectively, they came up with nineteen major recommendations. First, we were told that we needed to create a real fundraising board that would sustain the vision and mission of our work. Secondly, we needed to build up our self-supported people to become the ones who would be integral to our succession plan. As John Sanford, an African American neighborhood lawyer and one of our board members put it: "focus: LIFE, now called Life Directions, is a vision that affects how you look at every aspect of your life. If you do not have the vision, the work is impossible."

Our evaluation was thorough but not thorough enough to open the floodgates of funding. In fact, shortly after completing the process, the Archdiocese informed us that it had no funds for our work. Worse yet, Bishop Gumbleton expressed concerns about the continuation of our work.

"Physically, all of us are tired," Alex wrote in the journal. "It is been a long haul and it seems to be an uphill battle. It is very difficult to continue with hope, when the support does not come from the leadership of the church. We do not want to become embittered; we want to remain faithful."

And faithful, we remained. The founders accepted the challenge of developing a whole new way of looking at our operations. Even with funding unsecured, the work of a handful of adventurous wanderers had been validated by a broad spectrum of analysts. We were indeed doing God's work. Only now we were doing it with renewed focus, as Fr. Alex so aptly described in our journal:

"We are beginning a new chapter in our saga. Our process has been carefully evaluated and we move accordingly to the Lord's will."

THE PARABLE FOR THE KID ALMOST LEFT BEHIND!

There is an essential intuition that needs to be valued in order to stay true to the challenge of getting to the cause of inequality.

A boy of five could not play baseball. His seven-year-old older brother was very good. Their father started a team in which the kids who knew how played the first half.

The team was winning, 20-2. Everyone was cheering for them. The father put the second team in the game. The team lost 40-20.

The five-year-old was in right field. He sat down and would not come in. The father brought the whole team out to right field.

"Johnny, why won't you come in?" he asked.

"I am scared. My brother will kill me!"

"Why?"

"'Cause, I lost the game for us."

The father lifted Johnny's chin and said to the others, "Sons, when Johnny learns how to play, we will all win ... someday. But unless Johnny learns, we'll all lose. See, in life we cannot leave anyone behind. If we let people be losers, we'll all lose."

1. Reflect on the story from the viewpoint of the players. What value did the father teach? When young people see

each other being educated, what are they learning from those who have more talent and opportunities than what they have?

2. Reflect on the story from the viewpoint of the father. What did the father remember in order to make sure all the children came out to be with Johnny?

3. Reflect on the story from the viewpoint of the schools and churches where we live. What does the parable call us to explore as possibilities for the sake of all God's children?

CHAPTER FOUR
FINDING BARNABAS

"You want to get to the cause of violence? You want to motivate people to be self-responsible and able to manage their own lives? Do I understand you?"

These were the questions that Fr. Lloyd Thiel, the Capuchin Provincial, asked me when I went to him for counsel. After I explained the purpose of focus: LIFE, which we changed to Life Directions, I remember his long pause before responding:

"This will be much more difficult than what we are doing. We are dealing with those who need direct intervention: food, clothes, shelter. These needs are immediate and essential for survival. In a sense it is easier for people to understand these needs and to show ways to respond. What you want to do is get to the cause of people being in this condition. Know it will be harder for people to put their arms around what you are setting out to do. But I really want to encourage you. I'll help you with a small fundraising idea to get started."

I am forever thankful for Fr. Lloyd's mentoring me into "friend-raising" and the importance of knowing the core message of our mission: get to the cause and let others meet the needs of the effects of the cycle of poverty, which is violence.

We had studied the work of Fr. Bruce Ritter of Covenant House in New York. We knew a number of priests who do great work to comfort the hurting and confront the hurtful. "If you want peace, work for justice" is a great sermon, but where do you find people who want to support this value? I remember thinking that we were in Detroit, the city of inventors. I began to pray for people to support our inventing a way to get to the cause of violence.

"Cause" is the operative word. Many individuals and agencies are adept and amazing at treating the effects or after-effects of violence—when it is already too late. Our work is to slow down the shooting and the killing. We see many who are not going in that direction. But how do we tell their stories?

Recently I read the work of Fr. Greg Boyle, a Jesuit in South Central LA. He has powerful stories of "street kids, gangs, and tattoos" and has done a phenomenal job helping them come out of chaos.

We have a different mission. We set out to wake up young people and young adults *before* they are caught up in such violence. We want to get to the cause and break the cycle. We center on prevention. We tell the stories of young people and young adults who are on the solution side of violence, who want to grow into being peace builders.

We want to tell the "good news" of young adults like Sandy (not her real name), a girl who *was not* killed. Our challenge was to tell her story and find a donor who wants to believe peers can inspire peers through self-responsible choices to live. It is a challenge I am grateful we continue to want to face.

A reporter from the Detroit Free Press once came to the campus of Western High School, seeking to interview Sandy. It was on a Monday. The previous Saturday evening, Sandy's girlfriends from school had attended a party. Their parents weren't home when they called each other and agreed to go out. Things got out of hand. A fight broke out. All three girls were shot and killed.

Somehow, the reporter found out that a fourth girl, a close friend of the others, had turned down their invitation to accompany them to the party. The newspaper reporter was intent on finding this young woman to ask why.

When the reporter found her, she shared how her friends had come over dressed for fun. They wanted her to join them. Sandy's parents weren't home either; no one would know. But Sandy did not feel right about it. She said she was not sure it would be safe. She did not want to say anything to them. She just said she was not feeling well. As I read the story, I realized she said something really powerful. She had declined to go because she had joined this group at her school called Life Directions.

"We have been encouraged to think about the consequences of our actions before we do things," she explained. "So I thought about the consequences of going over to these people's home and I chose not to do it."

Three dead young women was the real "story." One young person living: how would this story make news? This is an example of the many "untold stories" that we remember. Who wants to support what we call "logo-praxis," which translates into Sandy's way of processing before acting?

"When something happens, will I be able to reflect before acting? I'll keep it to myself to hide from being bullied. I know what it is that I want to do. I am the only one who needs to know. I have 'named' it. I found the meaning, the value that will guide my decision. I am free to decide what to do. I am in control of what I will do." Being in control of ourselves can lead to what one of our staff tells young people, "I want you to have an 'M.D.' after your name, not a number under your picture."

When the young ladies rang our student's doorbell and invited her to the party, she was able to get in touch with her feelings and decide the invitation did not feel right. It was against what she valued, and she was able to connect what she did value. She had been equipped to see peer pressure for what it is. She said "yes" to her life direction and "no" to her friends.

I know the prison system is like a "gang education" system. From city to county, from state to federal prison, the "management and leadership" training for violence is there. The recidivism rate and the dropout rate are statistics most people hear but never "feel" and "embrace" or "understand."

The gangbangers I know have the loyalty that I as a teenager had to a labor union. When I see their tattoos, I see that they often see it as a sign of their religious affiliation. Seeing as we do gives us a way of understanding that encourages us to know the cause is not family and belonging as much as it is making money and survival.

Dealing with the cause can be as simple or as complex as we make it. If someone I trust challenges me to change and if someone loves me just the way I am, then it is up to me to take charge of my life direction. It is simple to say, but it is very difficult to do, depending on how long I have built a pattern or, to be more accurate, dug myself into a rut. "If only it would never have gone this way": this is the dream of Life Directions.

I honor the thousands of young people and young adults who are alive and whose stories center on their dream, their life direction. I am grateful for those who believe the value of getting to the cause. I am grateful for those people who support peers being the solution to the problems their peers face every day.

What We Knew and Did not Know: Following Our "G.P.S."

It is one thing to develop an evaluation plan of our young and developing organization. It is quite another to implement the recommendations. Our funding, for the most part, was program-centered, coming from faith-based communities. They believed in the mission. They were encouraging of our first Board of Directors, all of whom were young adults and adults in the focus: LIFE process.

The importance of forgiving was core to getting to the cause of violence. Those of us who were doing the work in the public schools were accountable to the board selected and trained by those of us who founded the work. We developed the board to know that the word "accountable" means this is where we count on you, and you can count on us. "Lean On Me" was the song that captured the spirit of the board.

Those who were full-time in the mission would work with parishes and seek support from the religious communities that sent Alex, Rosalie, and me to do what we were doing. We would do fee-for-service type agreements marketing our experience with youth in public schools and young adults in the community. Faith-based groups that wanted to learn from us would give us a stipend for our teaching, preaching, and organizing.

In the fall of 1978 we knew what we knew, and we knew what we did not know. What we did not know would set us on a search to find our way. As I look back, I remember turning to the Word of Life. We had come this far with the Bible as our "glasses to correct our vision," We call the Bible our "G.P.S."--God's Providential Signs. It constantly recalculates, depending on the destination you enter.

The place to which I turned was the Acts of the Apostles. How did they face their financial challenge? Alex and I were giving to focus: LIFE the stipends we received. We were following the example of Francis of Assisi. We had "sold," so to speak, all we owned. Sister Rosalie, Fr. Alex, and I were all "consecrated religious" with congregations supporting us and sending us forth. We know this works.

What we did not know was how to secure funding for those who have the talents, knowledge, and skills to do what we do. Patrick

Trainor, an educator and psychologist, was the caliber of person who would need a compensation package that would respect his needs.

Joseph, a Levite born in Cyprus and whom the apostles called Barnabas, which means *one who encourages*, sold a field he owned, brought the money, and handed it over to the apostles. (Acts 4:36-37)

Finding Barnabas became our quest. Frank Briglia represented our work in the schools. I asked him if he knew anyone who would believe in our mission to get to the cause of violence through forgiving and simultaneously be positioned to give or get the funds needed for qualified staff. Frank had partnered with our Life Workers and with Agatha. He knew the difference. He knew we could produce quality people. He agreed to join me.

We had built quite a track record inspiring potential dropouts to make school work for them and their peers. Frank could speak to the results. He suggested I meet Judge James A. Hathaway, who had just served as Chair of the Detroit Public School Board. He was responsible for hiring, among other decisions, Arthur Jefferson as Superintendent.

Walking into the DAC (Detroit Athletic Club) would become the opening day of my learning a life-changing lesson. I was about to find our Joseph, surnamed Barnabas, whose common sense and talent to inspire his peers would be the partnership that would take a "small operation on 8300 W. Vernor" to the campus of Marygrove College. We would expand our work to Chicago, San Antonio, Tucson, New Orleans, and Marion County, Oregon, using what Judge Hathaway would teach us.

"Find Barnabas, if you want to sustain the work," is the principle that we embrace. Paul does the mission; Barnabas sustains the mission. Their partnership carried them to the founding apostles in Jerusalem. Once that relationship was in place, Paul was sent to build with another "Barnabas." When I would get discouraged and doubtful, "the Judge"—as I affectionately referred to him—would do for me what Barnabas did for Paul. He would come get me and keep me focused (see Acts 11:25-26). He would work with me to secure support to do the work, always remembering "those living in an environment of poverty" as our first priority (see Acts 13:2).

I came back to the team to share my conversation with the Judge: "Make sure we have a 'firewall' between what we do for those eighteen years of age and older and what we do in the public schools. Money raises money. The funds we have will get us started. We need to think of people we know who would want to hear our message and have the means to invest in continuing the mission. They will want to hear from the young people themselves. We also need to get the message out to the public. We need to become known."

Sister Rosalie, writing in our journals, reminded us how we turned to our young adult circles at zero hour to build our first Board of Directors:

"It was three o'clock in the morning when we finished writing, and that morning we were calling people to sit on the board because we had to have 'the thing in' by eight a.m. the next morning. We called people that were walking with us. I still remember just asking if they would be on the board."

Two challenges immediately were before us. First, keep the spirit of the young adults. We wanted to encourage them to orientate those who would join to build ways to have sustainable funding. Second, attract people positioned to give or get what we needed to be financially sustainable.

Fr. Alex did the entry to our journal years later. His reflections still captures that tension: "We were pretty strong on maintaining our values. The difficult thing was finding funding for programs aimed at people over eighteen years old. The mentality is, 'If they do not have their lives together by eighteen or nineteen, forget it! It is throwing good money after bad for at-risk young adults.' That perception was the big challenge.

"That was painful. We had people who either wanted to change the formula, water it down or take it in another direction. You see, Life Directions is not Catholic. It is inspired by Christian theology. Our fear was that it would lose its identity as a nonprofit organization with spiritual values at its core that worked in the secular world."

Frank Briglia joined our discussions. I asked him to share our conversation with the Judge. Frank said the Judge made it clear to put the priority on our impact in the public schools on dropout prevention. The results of our work among young people in public high schools would be the outcome to promote. It is going to be like starting a business.

"As I see it, the Judge said what I have been saying to Fr. John," Frank explained, paraphrasing the Judge: "'You do what you do to prepare yourself to be in the schools.' I mean, you're a priest but you do not broadcast your training or the studies you did to get here. I just want the young people to get what you give them. That way they stay in school and have a life with the tools they need to survive."

Frank had been on our focus: LIFE weekend with his wife Nancy. He knew the power of forgiving as transforming all kinds of people from all walks of life and religious traditions from Catholic to Christian to Muslim to Jew to Anonymous. He saw the respect that all received. He wanted to promote it for his parents but not for the young people in the public schools. It seemed to be too risky due to the separation of Church and State.

As we sought to build a board that would focus on fund-development, I asked each of us who started this work the same question: "How have you been prepared to relate to the challenge of generating funds?"

I reflected on the fact that I had been groomed to meet this challenge at an early age. My family opened a small confectionary when I was nine years old. We built our customer base with "penny candy." When I turned twelve, my dad had me take care of the vendors. I learned how to keep books—money in and money out.

Also, my dad had each of his children to open our own bank account. His principle was simple: "Spend the money you take out of the bank, always leaving money in your account and you will not run out of it!" What an amazing training I received.

Fr. Alex remembers that his father was a salesman. "My father was on the road all the time, selling." Alex looked at his natural talent to be the front guy a lot of times in the media. He could put together "sound bites" to catch people's attention. He realized one of his many talents was to give "the elevator speech."

Fr. Alex's talent to direct individual and group ways of reflecting on justice and peace gave him the reputation among religious leaders, especially those who related to his retreat center. His knowledge of the challenges we needed to face to move from dealing directly with the results of injustice to keeping our focus on its cause would position him to speak clearly to the issue of "an ounce of prevention is worth more than a pound of cure."

Sister Rosalie was a first-grade teacher. She also had been a school principal. Her educational and administrative experience would be invaluable to ensure we would be accountable to those in authority. This would give us the credibility we wanted to be positioned to work with the system. On one hand, we would be supportive of the school's outcomes for attendance and academic improvement. On the other hand, we would be able to organize the achieving peers to inspire their less achieving peers.

The Religious Sisters had given quality education to so many in the South when the schools were segregated. The fact that she was a "Sister" gave us the credibility of not proselytizing but caring for each person as a person no matter what their culture or creed. Sister Rosalie had worked with the Detroit School Board on implementing and maintaining bilingual education. She had organized parents and community leaders. Her talents and her experience would guide us through the issues we had to face.

Judith was a triage nurse and a mother of eight. Her ability to assess people in pain and to stay focused on the cure positioned her to lead us to put in place sustainable ways to ensure people can be on their own. She has the natural instinct for three things: first, people who met her would immediately become relaxed and willing to talk; second, she had a way of telling people things they may not want to hear, but needed to face; third, she knew how to talk to professionals about what needed to be done.

Her children would become the first group of young people to receive our inter-generational programs. We had a lot of fun testing the idea of "kid search," a retreat for those twelve and under. We did it once, and that was enough to know our work would start at thirteen years of age!

Alexander rounded out our team in a way that we grew to appreciate. He is an extremely friendly person. Everyone just likes to meet Alex! But what many would not know at first was his ability to know what he does not know and identify why he does not know it.

After he graduated from Holy Redeemer High School, Alexander worked his way up at Chrysler into quality assurance. His quiet approach to what was happening would give us insights after meeting people and finding programs that we would have missed without him. His major caution in the challenge to generate funds was simple: "Do not let money determine the direction of the mission. It is the other way around. Also let's make sure the ordinary parent can understand what we are doing." The phrase I came to use to describe Alexander was KISS--"Keep It Simple Sir."

The First Question to Answer: What Do You Do?

As our journals indicate, we were "all over the place" as far as raising funds to attract and keep professional and reliable personnel. We knew our foundation was the spiritual formation of young adults from eighteen to thirty-five years of age. They are the parents and leaders for the next generation. We knew their experience among diversity of culture, class and creed would be the seeding of a powerful energy base to lift up forgiving as the alternative to violence.

Life Directions can be understood by using the analogy of a three-story building. The first floor is focus: LIFE which begins with a retreat and continues as a Life Circle involving single and married young adults. We had circles in the city, suburbs, and Windsor. Married couples were leading the ongoing growth after the focus: LIFE weekends.

The second floor is the high school young people to motivate each other. We were in a number of high schools from the southwest to the northwest side of Detroit, and just recently to the east side. We were truly a city-wide organization working in the schools.

The third floor would be for the high school young people to mentor eighth-graders to make high school work for them. We wanted to pilot two ways to approach young people and families—in a mentoring way for those coming into the high school and in a community way for families to build ongoing communication, with a view to bridging the gap for families who never went to school in the United States or who may never have graduated from high school.

The Second Question to Answer: Do You Have Any Staff Beyond the Founders?

We could find engaging and committed volunteers such as Will and Tina, Rueben and Bertha, Floyd and Renee, Chuck and Lee, John and Carol, Gayle and Angela, Rosemary with Ken and Darlene, and others. Judith saw all of them like her and her husband as "self-supported staff." She was clear that without the self-supported people we would never continue to do the work. We would not have our foundation in the community and in our spirituality.

Bob Newsome and I met again in November of 1979 for "future planning." We had worked out a kind of bartering system. For $300 a day, I worked as a consultant for systemic change for his project and he would continue to provide systematic evaluation services for focus: LIFE.

Patrick Trainor, who worked for Bob, was temporarily assigned to work with us pro bono. Given our financial resources, both Bob and Pat were truly a gift for a great deal of young people. Their professionalism and dedication was a powerful combination.

Pat had an interesting set of talents with a big heart for the oppressed. A holdout from the liberal '60s, he had long hair and a thick beard. Pat was once a high school counselor and a teacher and had worked for the Illinois State Office of Education. When we first met, he was not fond of management and was not exactly tolerant of rich people. Pat also had some experience working with religious orders for systematic change. When he came to focus: LIFE, he felt, based on his experience, that he had a fairly good idea how to solve many of the problems of "those living in an environment of poverty" and address violence among youth.

"Great," I responded. "Get in the car." We drove to the east side of Detroit. "Okay," I said. "Get out of the car. I'll pick you up in four hours." Then I drove off.

When I returned at five o'clock, Pat was visibly shaken: "Man, I did not know what to do," he said. In my head, I was thinking, "but, you were the one with all the answers, remember?" Pat trusted me enough to stick with our work. He gave us an invaluable talent that would match our team of five. He became the point person to train and manage staff beyond those of us who began the work.

Sometimes people with all the solutions can be part of the problem. They see themselves as the gift and fail to understand that everyone has gifts. It is our challenge to encourage everyone to discover their gifts and want to be part of the solution. Many people believe they have answers. So often they do not think they need to learn the right questions. If you ask the wrong questions, you'll never get the right answers.

Pat was lost on the east side of Detroit that day. He was happy to see my car come around the corner to pick him up. I wanted him to share that "wandering into the unknown" feeling before joining our efforts. I remember saying, "Pat, if you want to find the lost, sometimes it is good to get lost."

When we go through what Pat experienced—and I do not care what talent you may possess—it is humbling. Humility is the flexibility of growth. If we have not been humiliated, we do not have any way to learn humility. When we have been shamed, when our worth is doubted by many, then we are ready to be sent to serve— not be served. We can "take it" because now we have been stripped of pride and a false sense of self-worth. When we can go to the extremes of "nothingness" we are free! The only way to understand us and what we do is to get lost. If not, we'll never understand what it is like to lose. Then, when we find "the lost", we may not know how to be with them.

The Third Question to Answer: Do the Schools Trust You?

"We are still not certain as to what we can expect," Rosalie wrote in late 1979. Our work in communities and schools were starting to pay off. We had asked the young people we served to bring their friends, and did they ever! Things were going so good at Southwestern High School that one thought there were free tickets to a popular rock concert in the library where we met on Thursdays. The groups were getting too big to serve, and we were forced to cut down the numbers.

When asked about this period of growth, Sister Rosalie recalled the school administrators who quietly checked us out for a long period:

"After a while the public school administrators started to view us less as intruders and more as partners in helping young people. It helped that Frank Briglia, who walked with us, was also on our team."

Sister Rosalie was a huge asset in our moving forward. She was embedded in Detroit's Hispanic community in southwest Detroit. Rosalie had all the educational experience needed to respond to academic concerns and criteria. We were all conscious, respectful, and very sensitive to protocol. We let administrators know that we understood the schools were in charge and that we were there through their invitation.

In 1981, after the evaluation process, the co-founders started making deliberate choices to build sustainable funding, based on our being very public with our programs. As we felt freer to work in the schools and the surrounding communities and to seek public funding, Ruben Godinez and Alexander MacDonald, two of our Life Circle leaders, asked us to make sure we stayed steeped in our spiritual values. We were grateful for the counsel. We wanted to do our best and let God do the rest. It is easy to wander off the path when seeking funding. But in the long run, it is very important to stay true to the mission.

The board wanted to ensure that we had a real firewall between the work we were doing with young people under eighteen years of age in the schools and their surrounding communities and our work with young adults and adults through the retreats and ongoing growth.

Our spiritual programs and activities built our reputation among faith-based communities. They turned to us for training and mentoring. We did so on a "fee-for-service" basis, signing contracts to train people in parishes for mission work. This did not fund our work in the schools, but it helped us financially to support and offer retreats to those who lacked the funds to attend. We were struggling, but full of joy, knowing we were doing our best and it would all work out.

The Fourth Question to Answer: You Know What You Know. Are You Ready to Go Public?

"Something is happening! It appears to be subtle. Maybe it is that we have been doing this for such a long time we are seeing ourselves differently," Father Alex wrote with a mixture of optimism and fatigue. "We are tired of working with inept ministers. We continue to get requests from schools for high school retreats but we won't get money unless lay people come forward to help us raise it."

Father Alex also noted how we were "planting seeds to grow in the suburbs and youth ministry teams to be established." At the same time, Pat Trainor and I began visiting suburban parishes seeking support. The affirmative responses were few and far between.

Our board was doing their best to find creative ways to raise money from outside our network of church support. I remember our young people designing, stuffing and mailing Christmas cards for a stipend. For a brief time, we sold Amway products with the hope of creating an independent revenue stream. It was a yeoman's effort, headed by volunteer Angela Thomas, but it never worked out. We even offered staff training services to agencies like United Cerebral Palsy, Inc.

We were sailing our struggling ship through uncertain waters. The "fatigued crew," to quote Fr. Alex, was anxious for powerful winds to boost our tattered sails. This moment of "hitting bottom" was the moment when we would let go and never be the same. It was the moment when the value of "Barnabas" joined our team of five.

That day I mentioned earlier, when Frank took me to the DAC, the Judge was coming off the elevator. Frank said, "Judge, I'd like you to meet a priest who works with me at Southwestern."

The Judge was in a hurry to get back to court: "Hello, Father.

Frank, I do not have time now. Call and make an appointment."

Frank understood and made the appointment. We met. I shared how a group of us started a not-for-profit named "focus: LIFE." I told stories of how young people's lives were changing through positive peer pressure.

The Judge listened very carefully. I'll never forget the attention he gave to us. Then he spoke, "Frank, you've seen this program work?"

"Yes, I have. I work with Fr. John."

"All right! I'll check him out and get back to you."

"When?" Frank was persistent.

"Next week. Hope you enjoyed the lunch, Father John. Thank you for all you're doing for young people."

At that point he agreed to continue to explore how he might help us.

Little did we know that a few Barnabases were on their way!

I remember taking Judge Hathaway's comment at the time as a sign that he could not help us due to restrictions from the bench. It was not until I talked with his son, Attorney Thomas M. J. Hathaway, that I realized his father had indeed taken an interest in focus: LIFE.

"Dad was big on supporting people but he had one rule; they must never embarrass him," Tom recalled. "Dad used to say, 'I will support you unless you do something illegal, dishonest or you embarrass me…and then I will go after you!'"

Turns out, the Hathaway Family knew Father Alex Steinmiller intimately. Tom said the family had been attending the St. Paul's Retreat House since the end of World War II. It was there the family came to know Father Alex:

"Father Alex was a young priest, who gave great talks and was always talking about the work he was doing with young people," Tom recalled. When his dad realized that Father John was "hanging out with *their* Father Steinmiller," it was an "ah-ha moment," Tom remembered.

I did not give up on Judge Hathaway. In early 1981, we eventually connected. During our brief meeting, he asked a series of probing questions: "What do you do and how do you do it? Is there separation of Church and State…you know I am a judge…" on and on he went.

According to Tom, his dad had investigated us thoroughly and was ready to commit, mainly because he felt we were a results-oriented organization.

"Dad said, 'Tom, there are a lot of programs out there but this one actually presents results.' He said he was going to look into it and he did. What he discovered was a group of good, dedicated people doing good work."

Beyond the Questions – Let's Get Started!

Judge Hathaway paid us a visit with a well-known Detroit TV and radio host. These two very sharp people, with business-savvy, razor-like brains, immediately summarized our need: we did not have any money.

"I'd like you to meet a friend of mine, Fr. John Phelps," Judge Hathaway said, introducing me to his friend. "He has a unique program that works to stop dropouts and the violence that comes with young people being on the streets. Would you interview him?"

The celebrity agreed.

I look back on this moment and remember it as the beginning of focus: LIFE going public! And we never have looked back.

I was interviewed on Hathaway's friend's radio program. Later, he told famed sports broadcaster, Ernie Harwell, the official "Voice of the Detroit Tigers," about focus: LIFE. Ernie became our first high-profile spokesperson. Once, he was broadcasting and between pitches yelled: "And HEERREE'S Father John!"

To stay within the boundaries imposed by the bench, Judge Hathaway recruited his son, Tom.

"I was just coming in and out, doing things my father asked of me," Tom remembers. "I was already on different boards and commissions and had my own agenda. But then, I visited the Vernor Street location and saw what was going on and I said to myself, 'Wow! These are real people.' I was amazed at how competent the staff was and the fact that they were all there working for low salaries when they could get better elsewhere. They really believed in what they were doing. It was an amazing group.

"I started to believe all the stories about the program I had heard anecdotally from my father. It took a while, but it slowly sank in that this was an organization that is really changing and saving young lives. The way I framed it in my head at the time was like this: 'This is the Lord's work and I have the opportunity to do what I was called to do.'"

Tom became a very close decision-maker. With his father's quiet guidance they started tapping into their sphere of influence on behalf of focus: LIFE. Tom was happy to share more details:

"We'd hold luncheon meetings and ask people who came to write a check. I was helping my father, who'd call and tell me what was needed. Little by little, we did more fundraisers. My mother got involved and we recruited our friends and before you knew it, we were raising public money for Life Directions."

A real Detroit legend and philanthropist who gave a lot of money to social justice causes was part of the Hathaway's circle of friends. The philanthropist jumped on board with a serious intent to bring in more individual donors. During one of our first high-profile luncheons a successful auto dealer said he had to go but, before leaving, he gave us a $1,000 check. To this day, Sam Lafata claims it was the most expensive check he did ever written for a social cause. Maybe he was joshing, maybe not. All I know is that he set the tone for giving that day and he has not stopped.

With the help of our growing sphere of influential backers, we held more fundraisers. In 1981 we threw a fancy affair at the Gourmet House in St. Clair Shores. All sorts of influential people were in attendance. The next year, we honored Walker Cisler, who was introduced to me as being one of the five architects of the Marshall Plan. Naming the famous Mr. Cisler as our honoree attracted the attention and support of the CEO of Detroit Edison and the head person of Michigan National Bank.

We have had many financial supporters but I consider Judge Hathaway and his son, Tom, as our first and second Barnabas. The judge knew the challenges in the public schools. As Chair of the Detroit Public School Board, he dealt with wayward young people. His son, an attorney, was also concerned about the numbers of youth living their lives in fear of violence or behind bars. I have my definition of a Barnabas but Tom's differs slightly:

"John looked at me as being his Barnabas, but anyone with funds and resources can be one. It is a partner, a collaborator," Tom says, adding his own personal motivation: "Most do it as their vocation; I am doing it as my avocation. As the Barnabas, I am trying to enlighten people to the fact that they can help. Even if it is just money, they can help. But more importantly, I can recruit more people to join us as they understand what Life Directions is, what we do and why what we do is in everybody's best interest."

Fr. Alex made a major connection with a friend of the Passionists. This man owned a recycling operation. When I met him, Fr. Alex had arranged for us to talk. I began by sharing how we are sort of in the recycling business. He was very kind to me; he probably knew that I was just getting used to "selling" our program.

"Father, let me tell you that I believe in what you're doing because I used to be a tough young person myself. If it was not for a priest I would still be the agnostic I was in college. I grew up with many of the experiences of the young people where you and Fr. Alex work. I changed because I said to myself, if this man Jesus could not get any of his followers to die for him and the president can have bodyguards and he started a religion that is built by cowards, it must be right."

What I learned from him was a powerful insight. Many of those who want to contribute to us have grown up with some of the challenges the young people we reach are managing today.

Every worthwhile organization needs a Barnabas, someone to support the vision financially. If that someone does not believe in your vision, he or she may give but they are not your Barnabas. If they believe in your vision, they are unconditional partners. If the money is running low, they will do all in their power to keep walking with you.

If an organization does not have at least one unconditional Barnabas, chances are it won't make it. When I look back over our forty-year history, it is amazing how many people have been a Barnabas to us or a friend of Barnabas. We know that money makes a mission grow. It does a great deal to build sustainability. We would never have impacted the lives of so many without the resources we received.

But keeping Judith's insight in mind, we want to remember the self-supported adult circle leaders and mentors and the young adults who offer the retreats and work with our teens. We wanted the mission not to be controlled by money. Not everyone who gives funds believes in the mission. What has become important is to ensure the peers who have the spirit of Barnabas test those who give. We need to discover if the vision and the mission is their reason for giving. Only peers who give are positioned to test the spirit of others.

How do you find your Barnabas? Well, to quote the Judge, "you have to kiss a lot of frogs." If you're working with young people, your Barnabas will probably have had a history that understands the youth you're trying to serve, or they have had a long history of working with young people.

Though our definitions may differ slightly, we celebrate the tremendous results of their unconditional love. We entered the 1980s with a new kind of direction, backed by funding that was not tied to or dependent on our religious communities. We were bringing in enough money for quality staffing, beginning with Pat Trainor with promises to expand. In mid-1981, I wrote:

"All the cogs are being oiled; the parts are being replaced or updated. The machine is about ready to thrust ahead."

Indeed, focus: LIFE was growing up. But, just like a young person entering puberty, our growing pains were just beginning.

THE PARABLE OF THE PITCHER WHO NEEDS NO ONE TO WIN!

The team my father began when I was five started to do better and better. As the season went on, the kids who knew how taught the ones who did not know how what they themselves knew. It took time, but eventually it worked. And they began to win.

One day the pitcher thought he was the best. My dad asked him, "Are you the reason we are winning?"

"Sure am!"

"Okay, you pitch," my dad ordered. "When you get three outs, you win the game." The pitcher went to the mound, and only the catcher was on the field to play on his side.

The coach had everyone bunt. The pitcher could not get anyone out because he had no players but himself.

"Son, you're good. But remember, we need each other to win."

1. Reflect on the story. What value did my dad want to teach our team? What value did he want to teach the pitcher?

2. Reflect on what happens when some people forget they need others to be their best? It is not so much about winning and losing. It is more about those who have someone to show them and others to make resources an investment in those who have less.

3. What difference would such an attitude toward life—that we need each other—have on the struggle of those who are being "left behind"? Do you have any insights that come to you about "separate-but-equal" opportunity?

CHAPTER FIVE

QUALITY ASSURANCE AS BLESSED ASSURANCE

I went away for the month of November 1980 to organize our programs and activities into manuals and workbooks for the staff and volunteers who would want to learn from us. While I was away at a Redemptorist house in southeast Wisconsin, a *Milwaukee Sentinel* reporter came to interview me. He matter-of-factly asked if I really thought our program was going to work. I held up the Hebrew and Christian Scriptures and said, "If this book works, the program will. If it does not, then it probably won't work."

We are constantly amazed at how our walking creates our path. From the beginning we have lived the principle, "you cannot lose your way when there is no road." For me, Life Directions has always been about walking beyond what I know. This is also the inspiration of the mission. The mission is to do what we do for the next generation. I do not know who's going to follow after me, Fr. Alex, Sister Rosalie, the MacDonalds, or anyone involved with our mission. I do not know, and I do not need to know. We walk by faith on an ever-expanding pathway.

During the 1980s we really became more focused on our

organization's sustainability. We wanted a not-for-profit corporation with a sustaining business support system for our spiritually-rooted and values-centered programs. Most nonprofits are one or the other; very few are both. Like a train traveling two rails simultaneously, we rode separate tracks: one of spirituality, the other of values. To stay with the analogy, we sometimes felt like two unirail trains moving side-by-side.

It is difficult for a not-for-profit seeking public funding to uncompromisingly maintain its spiritual values while meeting the requests of the funding source. We remained true to our values. No matter our adjustments and new ways to do what we do, "forgiving" as *the* way to manage conflicts was our core message. We came to call it our "brand." It is essential in both worlds to remove the cause of violence.

In a promotional taping, I was asked why we started focus: LIFE. I explained that violence committed by young people begins at earlier and earlier ages with each passing generation: "In 1973 it was fifteen-year-olds killing other fifteen-year-olds. In 1993, it will be eleven-year-olds killing eleven–year-olds. By 2013 it will be seven-year-olds. We need to find the way to see forgiving as the response to violence one person at a time."

During the decade of the '80s, certain people who identified with our principles came forth and added essential dimensions to our work. I have already mentioned Pat Trainor, Judge Hathaway, and his son, Tom, in the previous chapter. But there were others, such as Fr. Bob Morand, who was the Pastor of an African American faith community, St. Theresa's Church. We shared their desire to create an orderly manner in which to empower African American young adults to mature in their faith-life. Sister Phyllis Paquette, based in Windsor, was attracted to our work in public schools and among young adults. She sought an international partnership that would allow us to further develop ways to connect young people with values, who were cut-off from mainstream churches.

Focus: LIFE was in six high schools in Detroit: two in the northwest, two on the east side and two in southwest Detroit. The anorexia to values among students of younger and younger ages accelerated our programming in Detroit's educational system. Tom Hathaway describes this period as the "second leg" of Life Directions:

"It is when they were really getting into the schools. Most people think they are dealing with young people within communities, but Life Directions found that most young people spend their formative years in schools. So we are dealing with what made Detroit the 'Murder Capitol of America' at that time.

"Kids impacted and involved with violence were getting younger and younger. Middle school students were already developing tendencies that were destructive and would destroy their chances of getting through high school. Life Directions knew these numbers because they were in the schools and saw the kids that never showed up. Violence was one of the reasons. Many did not come because they were frightened."

"Culture" Vs. "Race"

"How do we have the cultures share in a way that keeps us enriching?"

This question, posed by Sister Rosalie in our journals, underscores our multi-cultural approach to serving youth in public schools. The east side of Detroit is almost exclusively African American. The southwest side was multi-cultural and multi-lingual. This is where Sister Rosalie sought to design an area-wide, multi-cultural team. Northwest was much more racially mixed with an equal number of "Blacks and Whites," as they described themselves at the time.

It is interesting how we evolved from that restrictive definition.

As I mentioned before, we found ourselves using the word "culture" instead of "race." When some people think "culture," they think theater or the arts. We think of three interrelated elements: first, the hierarchy of values a culture holds; second, the way we express ourselves as a culture; and third, how we organize our thoughts, relationships, families, and communities. This is the real genius of individual cultures. Unfortunately, it is not always seen as "genius." It is seen as a problem, something that is perceived to be in direct contrast to our pluralistic way of leading.

Sister Rosalie compliments me in her writings, describing my "amazing mind for picking up the unique traits of ethnicities" and tapping into the "puzzle pieces" of different cultures. She's very kind, but what Rosalie described was a result of my "walk" within the schools. What I discovered was a complementary worldview of different cultures and how valuing "culture" could be an enriching alternative to fear-based violence.

One day I received a crisis call from the principal of Western International High School. A parent was threatening to shoot the department head of bilingual education for flunking his daughter. The principal hoped I could help. When I arrived, I asked the nationality of the teacher and the parent. One was Chaldean, the other Jewish. Because of my Arabic, bilingual friends, I was able to intervene. I could speak to the value of "woman" in the Arabic culture. What happened in school was not a violation of the value. I invited the father to explain to the Jewish teacher his concern.

Once I found the value that was being challenged and found a way to express it, both the father and the teacher were free to manage what happened, breathing forgiveness. We found ourselves engaged in an enjoyable conversation about the way in which we navigate living in a pluralistic society. We were able to have a respectful talk about how each complemented the other's values of marriage and family, love and truth. Violence was deescalated through shared cultural values.

Remember, focus: LIFE came into existence six years *after* the race riots in Detroit and across the country. There was still so much misunderstanding about culture and how it relates to violence. There was not a lot of reflection in many homes, so the young people we met in schools were unaware of the depth of their culture.

For instance, they do not reflect on the fact that we did not arrive in this country for the same reasons. Some cultures came against their will—slavery. Others are here because they want to be here to build a better life—European migrants. Others came to America with an attitude of ownership of the country— what we call the "Entitlement Attitude." And then there are those who were born here, misnamed as "Indians," and forced to live on land reserved for them—Native Americans. We are not invited to see one another as immigrants to a nation where people lived and had formed many tribes before we "discovered America."

Many do not value the understanding that we have all been victims at one point or another. We found that truly understanding culture could lead us away from violence and toward a path of building bridges and creating harmony among one another. We are searching to go beyond separate-but-equal to stand together on the "common ground" we call the United States.

The issue of ethnicity is also impacted by factors such as owning or renting a home. Where you live can determine the types of opportunities you have or do not have. Your zip code can pretty much determine what kind of educational or health support systems you may have or what transportation challenges or opportunities are within your neighborhood. For many African Americans, who are integral to our mission, there were two different kinds of challenges: race and economics. The economy had shifted in the city, and sometimes issues which had been perceived as discriminatory were really the result of this economic shift and the loss of resources.

The key for us was respecting and honoring the strength and tradition of African American culture. We learned about Kwanzaa, which originated in 1965. To see seven integral values building up the African-American culture is a wonderful awakening to life. The seven days before the New Year dedicates a day to each value: *Umoja (Unity), Kujichagulia (Self-Determination), Ujima (Collective Work and Responsibility), Ujamaa (Cooperative Economics), Nia (Purpose), Kuumba (Creativity), and Imani (Faith).*

We brought these values into our programs. This path proved to be a way to bring positive energy to the culture of a people who were still besieged by the vestiges of slavery, racial oppression, and the modern-day dilemma of disproportionate unemployment.

Much later, in the 1990s, when we started our work in Tucson, we met Native Americans who were like a hidden group in the city. They lived in their own little ghettos, so to speak, a little tribe in the middle of the city. They faced real racial discrimination that impacted their ability to gain a strong education which would have allowed their aspirations and desires to grow. Yet, this small tribe of ghetto-dwellers was solidly rooted in tradition, family, dignity and self-worth. We had to truly understand that dynamic before attempting to get into the schools and awaken the spiritual values and hunger amongst the Native-American young people we sought to serve.

Misunderstanding culture creates unnecessary tension among people with shared values. Many Vietnamese Americans struggle to understand why African Americans—a people who have been in this country since it became a country—are not seen as legitimate, strong, and equal players at the table. Many Vietnamese have little understanding of what it was like to be a people who had been brought over here against their will and stripped of their African culture, values and traditions. The Middle-Eastern people share a similar sentiment, but many of them were invited to this country for employment. They came to America with expectations that they were going to create work and jobs. Many were brought to the table almost as equals.

I remember walking into a school and a classroom with about twenty African American ninth-graders who eyed me suspiciously. This was the day after the Rodney King incident. I had to remember that Rodney King did not ask to get beat up and that it was people of my color and my culture and my gender who did it. Why *would not* those young people look at me and remember what happened the day before? Why *would not* they react suspiciously or angrily to me?

When I approached them, the ones who had elders who provided roots told the others to shut up and listen. The ones without those roots just stared at me. "I was trained to be afraid to be with you," I said. "You may think that I have nothing to say to you. What happens if we both decide to come to know each other? If you kill me, who wins and who loses? If we learn how to live together we all will win some day."

As I spoke, I remembered the firewall – separation between Church and State. I knew I could not say what I was thinking. I was working to accept my fear as my friend. What was the fear? It was death. Why in the world should I be afraid of dying when, as I always say, "my 'Boss' rose from the dead." Was it just a nice sermon? I preach, "What is there to fear? The Master's last breath was forgiving the ones who took it." But emotionally I needed to be in touch with what was happening within me and continue to let my spiritual way of seeing influence what I would say and do.

When I know my dark side and can partner with people of other cultures who are completely different from me, I begin to see them as a gift. When I partner with people of other cultures, they have a gift for my culture and I have a gift for theirs. Also a faith tradition that is different from another faith tradition should be seen as a compliment, not as a conflict.

In the 1980s, we created the "Parish Enrichment Mission" series with a priority on challenging church-going people to engage others who had become distant from their faiths. We were looking for adults over twenty-one who wanted to make a difference in the world. We sought to awaken, among faith-filled people, a call to reach out to those who were not aware of a Power Greater Than Human. We put special emphasis on reaching the African and Hispanic American communities throughout Detroit.

Through our community work, we were challenging the concept of Christian-based communities. A faith-based community is meant to express its way of relating to the Power Greater Than Human. The values and principles upon which the community is built are to influence how they hear what is needed and how they choose to respond to the challenges young people face.

When the community is Christian, the Christian Scriptures and the traditions that have been part of their journey offer a great deal to our moving forward. The Golden Rule—"Do unto others as you would have them do unto you"—is integral to the Christian community, but it is not exclusively a Christian mandate. Other faiths—Hindu, Muslim and Mormonism—have similar tenets.

Embracing culture, not race, lets us see life as including everyone, not excluding anyone. Exclusivity leads to tragedy. Take an exclusive golf course as an example. Who are they excluding and why? If we live life excluding others, we may put up boundaries. Faith communities may believe they are superior to other faiths. Nations may believe they are better than other nations. We create competition as nation states. Pretty soon people who become threatened by others' existence may want to take the others out.

Cultures are as diverse as creeds. If we have been born African American or Asian American, let's be the best! If we believe we are chosen to be Catholic or Protestant, let's be the best! If we have to be against one another in order to be for ourselves, it may be that we really do not know who we are. I feel bad for those who have to find something wrong with others, because they do not know what is right to say about them. They are out of control of their relationship with a Power Greater Than Human. That is what anorexia is: when we think we are in control. So we are in control of our Creator--really?

I remember challenging a group of Catholic Christians on their thinking that people of other faiths needed to change. I said, "What would you think if I told you that Jesus does not agree with you? Open to Matthew 25:31-46 and read how people who do not know Jesus at all are going to enter heaven. Check out the Last Judgment. It is in 'The Good Book.'

"I stand on solid ground. People of all faiths or no faith are able to go to heaven. When we are with others and they are with us, let's see the way the Master did. It is not our decision to determine anyone's culture. We know the 'melting pot' idea does not work in life. In focus: LIFE we approach every person's creed with the same level of respect. Let's all be our best and let the Man Upstairs do the rest.

"What would you think if I called all of us non-Muslim or non-Baptist? When I use a negative word before a name, the 'non' part says, 'I think you are not as good as I am.' It may even suggest we are in competition, which will never encourage common ground."

To use a comparison, culture is to creed what a wife is to a husband. Any culture can join with any creed. Any creed can embrace any culture. It is the bond of unconditional forgiving that brings the relationship to fullness.

Ten Years Strong

"The staff continues to work well together; spirits are good. Work has begun in the schools. Life Search (focus: LIFE) is generating some really excellent programs and activities and we are in four new parishes for the coming year. Thank you, Lord, for keeping us in the palm of your hand."

Sister Rosalie's reflections captured the spirit of our growth in the mid-1980s. We were able to bring on more professional staffing.

The board established committees (youth programs, executive, financial, public relations, fundraising) that focused on specific tasks and decisions.

We were at a choice point in our journey. Essentially, we wanted to do more than our resources allowed. We were certain of the quality of our work. Young adults were on fire with building a better world. Teachers were encouraging more and more students to "give them a chance." Creativity came about through a team that was formed as a result of the two programs: focus: LIFE weekend for those eighteen to thirty-five years of age and older, and the Peer Motivation program in the public high schools.

But how could we do more?

We hired our first Asian staff person, David Fukuzawa, who encouraged us to write our first multicultural manuals and workbooks for training others. These manuals were based on what had come to us within the first ten years of focus: LIFE. David encouraged us to write down what we had learned in such a way that others could read it and use it in what they were doing.

We worked on an unpublished book – *From Reflection to Action in a Multicultural Environment.* It had a five-chapter reflective section that captured the core of "our walk." We wrote about how all we do begins with the question: who am *I*? From there, we look at the culture, asking "who are *we*?"

This led us to a chapter on our work for justice in the face of inequality. Continuing "the walk," we called for peace-building through forgiving. In the last section, we were training others to do what we advocated because we are all called to be self-responsible for the sake of the next generation.

By the end of the year of 1984, we found ourselves talking to our board about another evaluation; this one would be "third-party" enough that it would give us needed public credibility. At the time, we had no idea the University of Detroit would step up and fund an evaluation study with outcomes that even caught us by surprise.

A Disguised Blessing

In late 1984, I made this disturbing citation in our journal:

"I heard today of the drastic cuts in parish (fee-for-service) support come July 1985. Alex and I are in deep thought. We do not know what to do; a forty-eight percent cut for all intents and purposes. What will happen remains to be seen."

What happened was a blessing. Frank Stella and Tom Angott, wonderful philanthropists and very involved with the Community Foundation for Southeastern Michigan, heard of our plight. Frank paid us a visit and, like Judge Hathaway years earlier, immediately zoomed in on our dilemma. The cuts indicated that focus: LIFE was not a part of the Catholic Church. We could awaken the values that any faith community shares, but we were not close enough or intertwined enough with the Catholic parishes for them to fully fund our needs.

Frank and Tom talked with Mel Larsen who had worked with high schools. Mel saw the value of what we were doing. He knew our challenges and potential. Mel suggested we get an evaluation from a noted institution that could lift our work in the schools and lead to new sources of funding. Frank and Tom thought it sounded a bit risky. Who knew what the study would reveal? They promised to stand behind us no matter the outcomes of the study.

The movers and shakers somehow arranged for the University of Detroit to do an in-depth and thorough evaluation. I recall the verbal battles I had with the evaluators and our fights about performance outcomes. They were instituting a "needs-assessment" way of looking at life when I insisted that a "values-opportunity" way was what we did.

From our experience, we knew that seeing young people as

problems to be solved does not work. Seeing young people as mysteries to be discovered is the better way to go. So I strenuously argued that in helping young people find their strengths and talents, they would look for problems and come to solve them independently.

The obstacle, as we saw it, was that the people doing the evaluation seemed to see those helping young people as "the solution" given to the problems. They simply could not wrap their heads around the concept that the solution is the same age, culture and gender as the problem. Most academically-trained people look for a certain type of academic matrix; they have a hard time seeing young people as the solution.

It made sense. We were seeking to raise public money. People who might give want to know what problems we "professionals" are solving, not what talents we are going to awaken in young people. I have often thought that if baseball scouts approached their jobs the way academics and social workers do, we might never see a baseball game. Scouts have to look for talent in the person they are evaluating. We knew the talents needed were the peers who could influence their peers to take charge of their lives.

It turns out, in spite of our differences on what outcomes to evaluate and measure, the researchers found that the young people involved with Life Directions stayed in school at a significantly higher percentage than their peers who came from the same social and economic environment. They got along better in class and participated more actively. Our programs worked. Young people were making school work for them!

I was struck by the language of the evaluator. There needed to be two groups: the controlled group and the contaminated group. The young people we impacted and woke up to their talents as a gift for others were called the contaminated group. We would have called the groups by positive names: one is "in the mess," and the other is becoming the "messengers." This was our first "professional" discovery that prevention may be talked about a lot, but the evaluating world into which we were invited thinks intervention. Seeking funding requires verification, ways of evaluating outcomes.

Fifteen years later a similar third-party evaluation indicated that young people impacted by Life Directions had higher reading and math scores. This was conducted in Chicago by the "10,000 Tutors" organization that evaluated all types of programs that impacted young people at risk of dropping out of school and into crime.

We were not aware that the evaluation was going on by the Chicago Public School System. I am not sure if my conversation with Mayor Daley the month before he, as Mayor, took over the Chicago Public Schools, had led to such an evaluation. What I had asked of the Mayor was the need to have a common evaluation of all community-based programs that seek to make a positive difference in the lives of young people. This could have been what inspired such an evaluation.

Whatever the reason, the evaluation presented us with hard evidence that our young people were in the eighty-two percentile in math and sixty-six percentile of reading. In other words, our program was among the best of all area programs in positively impacting math and reading scores.

What was the cause of our positive results? One evaluator said "the internal locus of control" kept young people we influenced to stay on course. The other evaluator said "their ability to stay on task made the difference." We reflected heavily on how we approached young people within their arena of academic achievement.

The answer, we found, was "focus"; our program helped students challenge each other to focus better. Think about a basketball player, for instance. He can be great on the court, but if he does not focus, learn discipline or how *not* to get distracted by being pushed around or being disrespected and violated, he'll never reach his full potential. To achieve that, he usually needs someone he trusts to encourage him.

Once young people learn the discipline of mental focus, they eventually do not need anyone else to keep them focused. When they can self-support and self-manage their own focus, they can do anything their talents empower them to do. When they hear the difference they make for others to excel, the "outcome" is amazing.

Even though we weren't designed to increase academic scores, upon reflection, we were able to articulate in a higher way the interrelatedness of intellectual and emotional maturity. When a young person walks into a classroom and the teacher creates a negative reaction in him or her for whatever reason, the feeling that comes with it—left to itself—will lead to something negative.

But if people are aware of the reaction and the feelings flowing from it, they can decide to be positive; the result will be different. That is what made the difference. When we put the insight in a spiritual context, it becomes all about vision. The quality of our vision lets us know our spiritual maturity. With spiritual insight into our seeing someone or some situation as what we control, we humbly accept that "my way to respond is in my control. What you do to me is under your control, but how I respond is my decision, not yours."

Once we become aware of this, then we understand why some of our choices have led to negative results. It is because we haven't learned to manage our dark side, which we all have. We want to awaken in young people their ability to know themselves well enough to make balanced choices for life to be their best and to be so for the sake of others. We want young people to take responsibility for whatever decisions they make in life.

The Detroit and Chicago evaluations and their outcomes showed us the power of such a way of approaching young people. The results made a difference in ways beyond what we ever could expect. It once again reinforced our steadfast belief in the mysteries to be discovered in the journey.

New Name, New Vistas, and New Directions

After the first third-party evaluation in 1985, we were in a great position to expand our work based on verified outcomes. We explained our three interconnected programs in language that was much more user-friendly and readily understood. These titles and the description of each program still exist today: the Neighborhood Enrichment, the Peer Motivation and the Peer Mentor Programs. Each has specific purposes and goals:

- **The Neighborhood Enrichment Program** approaches young adults from eighteen to thirty-five years of age and older. It deals with their discoveries of being given talents and shows them how to respond to opportunities. They can choose to be role models for those younger than themselves. They can inspire their peers to do the same – single, married or single again.

- **The Peer Motivation Program** brings young people who are on a positive path together with young people who are not doing well. They inspire the less-achievers to take charge of their lives and make a difference.

- **The Peer Mentor Program** brings young adults who are on a positive path together with selected young people. The goal is for Peer Mentors from high school to engage with young people from the feeder middle schools, along with adults who are the Adult Mentors.

We knew we had to rename ourselves. We needed our "brand." We were getting too big and were constantly confused with groups that had the word "focus" in their titles, especially "Focus: Hope," created after the Detroit riots to teach people transitional job skills after the auto industry started to decline. To be frank, donors were confused about the different "Focus" groups and it was not helpful to secure funding to wake up more young people to the fact that they are integral to the solution for their peers and for themselves.

Frank Stella and Tom Angott asked us to consider either merging with another group or changing our name. We started the brainstorming around the community and among ourselves. Nothing seemed to fit.

In 1987 we brought on a corporate firm, Plante Moran Accounting, who made sure our managing of our resources was above board and beyond scrutiny. We also had a professional, influential board that was very serious about our way of planning, governing, and maintaining continuity in everything. The board created three objectives:

1. Find available funding;

2. Get our name known;

3. Develop quality programming.

The first two goals were top priority because the board saw our programs as excellent; we just lacked exposure. With the third-party validation from the University of Detroit, entrée into schools was much, much easier. It made it even easier when Judge Hathaway, who had been chair of the Detroit Public School Board, mentioned us to the city's public school superintendent, Arthur Jefferson. The Judge knew what Mr. Jefferson was dealing with as far as the chronic dropout rate was concerned. The judge put Mr. Jefferson in contact with me. We were looking for an endorsement letter that would encourage corporations to "fund a school." Based on Judge Hathaway's recommendation, Mr. Jefferson was convinced of our credibility enough to write a letter asking people to invest in Life Directions.

Imagine the excitement of having Michigan National Bank come to see our program in action at Western International High School.

Their check of $35,000 helped us start our "Foster-A-School" campaign. To go from raising funds through labor-intensive events to doing more work with the young people and their families because of corporate support was a true miracle in the making.

As the '80s came to a close, we had discovered and mastered effective ways to reach young adults, especially "those living in an environment of poverty." We had built a strong Board of Trustees with a growing commitment to improving the quality of values among young adults within poverty areas. Our values were intact and corporate largesse had not altered our mission. We had stayed the course—our way.

Most significant, was that we had readied a new generation to lead. The young adults, who were in their teens in the 1970s when we began, were ready to pay it forward. By the beginning of 1990, it had become clear that our journey was about to expand beyond the boundaries of Detroit.

THE PARABLE OF HOW MANY TIMES HAVE I TOLD YOU?

There once was a young boy who was playing ball in his backyard with his friends. One of them hit a ball through the kitchen window. "Go get the ball. You live there!" they said to the boy.

The young boy went to get the ball. He looked around. He saw all the glass on the floor. But he did not see the ball anywhere. Then he looked up. His mother was holding the ball.

"How many times have I told you not to play baseball in the backyard?" He thought for a while: "Thirty-eight?"

With that his mother picked up a broom to hit him on the behind. But he ran out of the house. He was not sure why she was so angry. He knew how many times he was told.

1. Reflect on the story from the point of view of the relationship between knowing the truth and doing it. What does it say about the way we "tell" people what they need to do to make it in life?

2. What expectation did the mother have? Many are shocked when others do not do what they told them to do. Why do you think that is?

3. The son knew what he was told. What did the son lack? To be inspired to do what we know is right, we may need a peer who is actually doing it and wants us to follow. The question to ask ourselves is: now that we know what we know is needed to be involved in getting to the cause of violence, will we do so?

4. What awareness do you have of the reason people do wrong, break the commandments they have heard? Are you willing to walk with such people to encourage them to do what they say and to say what they mean?

Multi-city training week in Detroit.

Sr. Rosalie with children at a
Posada (1979).

Mural as service project by Peer
Motivation.

Field trip to Tucson for a healing community through "animal as healing"

Young adults celebrating life (justice event for the poor).

July 4th Parade in Detroit

Patrick Brennan, one for the original Life Workers (Staff in the schools) dance for joy.

Maria Bueno and Lourdes Chin (Chicago young adult & elder).

Fr. Alex in San Antonio with Fr. John visiting from the North (1994).

The Cookout is Community Service.

Honoree, Mayor Richard M. Daley with African Music Group (Chicago Salute Dinner 1996).

Fr. John, Merri Dee, Nelson Carlo – Chicago (1998).

Michael Wright mentored by Kevin Garnett at Farragut High School in 1994 promoted Sister Rosalie at Sunnyside High School in Tucson when he was playing the University of Arizona

Gleaners in Detroit Peer Mentors with Mentees and adult mentors in 2013.

"El Jardin" at Community Links

Restoring the Greenhouse in
Tucson.

8th Grade Mentees.

Parent Volunteers Pouring
Cement.

An Icebreaker with Mideast
Guests.

Peer Mentors at the Brookfield Zoo.

focus: LIFE Discernment Weekend.

Peaceable Gardens Board

Bench Painters at the Food Pantry.

Moving to the new Chicken Coop.

Garden at Amor De Dios Church in Chicago near Farragut High School.

With Cardinal George.

Let's Make Our City Beautiful!

Folkloric Dancers.

Making the focus: LIFE Candle.　　The Garden of Forgiveness.

New Friends.　　At Blue Man Group!

Northern Trust Bank's Vice President Darrell Jackson with students from
Marshall High School Peaceable Garden Board as he received Fr. John Phelps
2014 Humanitarian Award in Chicago

Partners for Peace Builders.

The Generations Together.

Welcome and World Peace Banner.

Planting a River Birch.

CHAPTER SIX
BEYOND THE HORIZON – EXPANDING BORDERS

I'll never forget the day of June 13, 1990. I was called by my Provincial leader, Fr. Jim Shea, who asked "John, how would you like to take Life Directions to Chicago?"

After almost two decades of wandering the labyrinth of the "Impossible Dream," we were celebrating the results of our board's work to expand into seven high schools and their surrounding neighborhoods. We had just finished redesigning our focus: LIFE Discernment Retreat to challenge young adults to take seriously where they were being sent to make a difference in the lives of their peers.

The central energy of the weekend in Detroit was to focus on a principle of faith: be ready to go when called without hesitating even if we do not feel prepared. We were hearing the outcomes of our first Peer Mentor Program at Earhart Middle School. The Peer Mentors from our first high school, Western, had done a magnificent job of ensuring the incoming ninth-graders made high school work for them.

"John, how would you like to take ..." There was a pause before I answered. Life Directions was not *mine* to take anywhere. What do I say to the person who has the authority to ask me to leave the work? He wants me to expand it. What do I say?

"Jim, I need to talk with our team. This is more than my decision. How much time do I have to let you know?" I replied.

"Three days," was all Fr. Shea said. Of course, I had made the co-founders and our board members aware of this possibility a few months before. I was asked to consider such an opportunity by Fr. Bill Nugent, who was on the Redemptorist leadership team. He had recently returned from Brazil, working among the very poor. He saw Life Directions as a gift for "those living in an environment of poverty" in this country. He encouraged me to consider testing the work to see if what we had created would be sustainable beyond our lifetime.

I gave a weak "okay" and hung up the phone. The next seventy-two hours was quite a marathon of conversations. Two complimentary challenges with this decision had to be faced immediately: how to begin our programs and how to get the resources to sustain the work.

The program side would be a challenge, but we were being given two locations out of which to work. A retreat center in Rolling Meadows, in the northwest suburb of Chicago, was available for our use. This would make it easier to launch our focus: LIFE retreat. That, along with a long history of the Redemptorists working in Chicago, made the decision fairly simple. Also I was told I would have two Redemptorists with whom to work with at the Retreat Center as I pioneered our mission within the poverty communities of Chicago.

The resource development side was a very different challenge. I would have the support of my Redemptorists in the beginning stages, as I was supported in 1973. The issue was not my support, but the support needed for the mission in Chicago. All funds in Detroit were for Detroit. My response was that I would ask some of our donors in Detroit if they knew anyone in Chicago where I could explore the possibility of "start-up" funds.

We were seeking to discern if the gift of Life Directions was rooted enough to expand. On June 16, 1990 I called my leader: "Jim, the team believes we are ready. It is a walk in faith but it has always been." With that, I began to work with our staff and board to make the move. I reflected on a journal entry I had made in May, just a month before the call:

"I believe 1990 has been a time when seeds having been planted generously are determined to break through hard soil, cement, weed patches, and dry lands. I see a sparkle of zeal in people's eyes, and we are beginning to have the time to refine some of our work. I sense we have turned the corner."

Through the gift of the unknown, we had faced many challenges in establishing Life Directions in Detroit. We were indeed ready for expansion. The lessons learned would help us make more prudent decisions. Our staffing had been refined in Detroit. It was strong, professional, efficient, and up to par. We had our evaluation outcomes from the Community Foundation for Southeast Michigan and were in the process of implementing our long-term strategic plan. Our program manuals had been written. This meant our lessons, philosophies, and programs were available for others. In 1987, we had relocated to Marygrove College. Grants and corporate donations were steadily coming in and our presence and activities in the public schools as well as our retreats were running and humming at their height.

In his reflections on this time period, Father Alex also believed it was time to put our core procedures to the test:

"We had this formula that worked: at-risk people are best served by engaging with their higher-achieving peers. This formula was flying in the face of institutional thinking. At the heart of the penal and public school systems, or any system that works with youth, is the thought that 'bad apples' need to be separated from others. We had a different formula that worked. So why not exploit it?"

The Second Site: Fr. John in Chicago, Illinois

Less than three weeks after Fr. Shea's call, I was on my way to Chicago with the Life Directions Board of Directors' blessings. Their only major concern was of liability: "What would happen to our operations in Detroit if Father John somehow needed our help?" It was a legitimate worry.

As in the beginning, we moved forward as a team. This time we had the right talent and expertise with which to work. The Board of Directors was in place with very capable people to lead the move. Ed McNamara, Wayne County Executive, was a member. Judge Adam Shakoor represented the judicial branch of government with Gerry Simon, an attorney who had many insights to give us as we set up our operations in the "Second City," as it is fondly called.

Sister Rosalie would assume my role as Executive Director in Detroit. Fr. Alex and Pat Trainor would partner with her. Fr. Alex was to manage the focus: LIFE side with a major fee-for-service with faith-based communities, who wanted training for some of its members to focus on young adults from ages eighteen to thirty-five. Pat Trainor would be asked to manage the programs and staff in the schools and their surrounding communities. The staff was ready to step up to the challenge with Rev. John Williams as a strong trilingual (English, Spanish, Mandarin) Project Director. Alexander and Judith, along with other couples, were in leadership of the circles. I alone would be setting up operations in Chicago.

The Redemptorist Community at St. Michael's Parish in Chicago gave me office space from which to begin my work. This way, Life Directions would have a city location from which to work. The two Redemptorists who came with me would focus their attention on the retreat center in the suburbs; I would be free to network into Chicago. The plan was to operate out of two locations. For our spiritually-based effort, we would use our retreat center in Rolling Meadows, in the northwest suburbs of Chicago. For our values-based work, we would use our office in Chicago.

There were also spiritual energy and sound reasons to start a Life Directions site in the Windy City. The Redemptorists are rooted in the Chicago land area with a 150-year track record in poverty and violence intervention in the city. Chicago's homicide rate among minorities in poverty was as disproportionately and alarmingly high as Detroit's. Lastly, we had a solid network of Redemptorist friends in Chicago on whom we could rely.

Before leaving for Chicago, I contacted a friend and a Life Directions supporter, Bob Mylod, the CEO of Michigan National Bank at the time. I asked if he knew a peer of his whom I could contact in Chicago. He did. Bob said he would give Barry Sullivan, the CEO of First Chicago Bank, a call and ask him to meet me. Then it would be up to me.

I arrived late for my appointment with Mr. Sullivan. After stepping off the elevator, I knew I was in the environment of a very important person. The whole floor belonged to Barry Sullivan.

"You're fifteen minutes late," he said with a smile, as I was escorted into his expansive office. I do not know what got into me but I quickly responded, "Well, you need to fix your parking system."

"Okay, you lost fifteen minutes," Mr. Sullivan retorted. "So tell me what is this all about. What is Life Directions?"

I answered with a question: "Do you have a mother?" After he answered "Yes," I continued. "Well, what would have been some of the choices you may have made if you had lost your mother at the age of fourteen?"

Mr. Sullivan listed a few things. He may not have handled the hiccups in his life during high school without his Mom's help. He may not have taken his college education as seriously as he did basketball and things like that.

When he finished, I told him about the young people we worked with in Detroit who have no one like he did in their lives--no mother, no father, nobody! I explained how these youth are going to make all the predictable mistakes, and by the time they wake up, they will be in their mid-twenties, without a school or education to back them up. They may be working but they will be frustrated. They'll probably have a couple of kids, and one out of three will be engaged, in some form, with the criminal justice system.

"We want to wake up these kids before it is too late," I concluded.

Mr. Sullivan was open to checking us out. "Okay," he said. "Tell you what. I want you to meet David Paulus and his partner Diane Smith. These two are working in the name of our bank in two areas of Chicago--Brownsville on the south side and Little Village on the west side."

Mr. Sullivan asked if I had a budget. The figure "$190,000" was my response. We figured it would cost $50,000 per school with $40,000 to manage the staff and volunteers for the programs in three schools. I knew this from our work in Detroit. Still, without really knowing Chicago, picking out a figure was risky.

I left Mr. Sullivan's office with contact phone numbers, and within three days I had created a $190,000 budget for three Chicago communities. That is when God kicked in.

I arranged a meeting with Steve Newton, principal of Farragut High School. It had been a primarily African American student population but an influx of Hispanic students had come a few years previously when their school, Harrison High, closed. This brought two cultures together with a history that was not necessarily in harmony. The potential for violence was palpable.

The LSC (Local School Council) had monthly board meetings. Mr. Newton offered to bring me to the next one. "If they agree, I will let you into Farragut, Reverend," Newton told me. I needed the approval of the LSC in order to receive the seed funding from First Chicago Bank.

The day of the school board meeting was total chaos. A young African American had been charged with killing a Mexican American classmate. There was a huge confrontation in the auditorium that night, and news cameras circulated everywhere. My instinct has always kept me alive, and I knew it was time to just absorb what I did not know, so I sat in the back.

Emotions were all over the place. The board chair was trying to start the meeting by getting other members to simply agree to the agenda items that night, which they could not seem to do. An elderly woman got up and started speaking in Spanish.

"Ma'am, you're in the United States. Speak English," a school board member interrupted in the midst of people who were very angry. People got quiet.

I knew enough Spanish to understand that the woman was crying about her murdered grandson. I feared the board member had unknowingly told this woman that she could not cry for a grandson who was just killed. I stood up and started speaking in Spanish and the whole place got quiet. "Who is this bald-headed, white priest speaking Spanish?" they must have wondered.

In the grandmother's language, I said *"Es muy triste. Yo voy a orar para su familia,"* which means, "I am very sorry. I will pray for your family."

I cannot say there was a cause and effect from my standing up for the grandmother but I can say that, at the very least, I had made an impression. There are moments when the breakthrough happens. When we are able to respond to violence in a way that does not accelerate it, like the stabbing at Western High School, it captures people's attention. It becomes one of those "How did you do that?" situations. "The whole place was ready to blow up and you are able to bring calm. How did you pull that rabbit out of your hat?"

Toward the end of the meeting, I had the opportunity to make a brief plea for support. I told them who I was and a bit about Life

Directions' dropout and violence prevention work in Detroit. I ended by telling them about our performance outcome evaluations and what we wanted to do at Farragut.

A youth minister from a nearby Catholic Church stood up and made a presentation and was immediately shut down because of the Church and State issue. It is interesting; that very person, Tom Howard, would join me six months later as our second staff person for Chicago. Tom just had to find out how I was received and he was not. He not only learned how but he has continued to be with Life Directions since that night. He is now a volunteer board member, after having completed sixteen years of being on staff, from Associate to Executive Director.

Since I had a thorough understanding of what we could and could not do in public schools, the school board agreed to add my request to the agenda. If the agenda itself were approved, they promised to get to it that night. I remember asking that they wait till the next month. I knew I needed to talk with some of the board members. I needed to learn how the LSC works. I needed to know what we were getting into by working with Chicago's schools. They agreed.

From that meeting to the next, three weeks later, I was able to meet with all board members but one. No one brought up the incident with the Spanish grandmother, but they were very gracious and welcoming. Again, I just chalked it up as another "God moment" that worked to my advantage.

The next board meeting was a bit calmer—no TV cameras this time—but it was still challenging. They were struggling to approve the agenda. About forty-five minutes into the meeting, Mr. Newton intervened on my behalf.

"You know, Father John was here last month and we never made a decision about Life Directions. He's here this month, and it seems to me we ought to make some sort of decision about his Peer Motivation Program and Life Directions."

They asked a couple of programming questions and said they would make a decision. In the interim, they would send a member of the community to Detroit to see our program before starting it in Chicago. If she saw what I described, we would be approved to enter the schools.

The chairperson made the recommendation, the motion was seconded, and it was unanimously approved by the board. A vigorous round of applause erupted. I thought they were clapping for me and our program. Wrong! Someone told me it was the first time the board had ever made a unanimous decision. They were dealing with all sorts of complicated issues, and here was a guy proposing a way to end violence in the schools. Who could vote against improving the drastically high school dropout rate in Chicago? Apparently, they were ecstatic to finally agree on something.

The representative from Farragut visited Detroit and reviewed our operations. She met with Sister Rosalie at Western International High School, which was similar to Farragut. I had no doubt that Rosalie would leave a lasting impression on her, not necessarily because of their shared Latino culture but because of Sister Rosalie's passion and practice with our programming. At any rate, upon her return, the Chicago School Board granted Life Directions access to its public high schools.

By January 1991 we had received funding, mostly from the bank, and we were able to operate in Farragut, Wendell Phillips, and later Lakeview and Clemente High Schools. We were also fully into our focus: LIFE weekend retreats at the center in Rolling Meadows in Chicago's northwest suburbs. Over a three-month period, we had four Life Circles representing four different cultures: African American, Hispanic American, Asian American, and European American. There was a special retreat for each culture. Later we would have a multicultural "Common Retreat."

The "Young Adult Circles" were on the north, west, and south sides of Chicago, along with the northwest suburbs. Married couples and self-supported volunteers were guiding the circles. The foundation of our spirituality was established in the community by the summer of 1991. The staff basically included a fellow Redemptorist priest, Tom Howard, a part-time administrative assistant, who also managed the retreat house, and me.

Mr. Sullivan's contact, David Paulus, who promised to help us build a board, threw a classic Chicago-style wine and cheese fundraiser on the lake. There, I met Nelson Carlo, one tough businessman. He was a *Puerto Rican* who joined the military in his late teens after growing up around the Farragut High School area. Nelson worked in steel construction and was well respected by the Mayor and other business and civic leaders. He was a member of Chicago United, an organization sparked into existence by the riots in the 1960s. He was known as the "Principal". All Principals would have a "Deacon," a role crafted by the Rev. Jesse Jackson, who would get the work done.

Nelson immediately got the gist of our program after I explained what we do. He agreed to start the board and what a board he put together! He was to be the Judge Hathaway of Chicago, our next Barnabas.

"You just explain the program and I'll close the deal," Nelson would say in his straight-to-the-point manner.

Meanwhile, back in Detroit, Judge Adam Shakoor, Wayne County Executive Ed McNamara, and Attorney Gerry Simon used their skills and expertise to build the protocols to start another board in another city. The whole process was not complete until 1993 but we were legally able to raise money under our Michigan 501(c)(3) status.

A Third Site – in San Antonio, Texas

Life Directions in Detroit was moving along like a well-oiled machine. Father Alex, who had just completed a fee-for-service contract with the Archdiocese of Detroit, was open to moving on from Detroit. The next Life Directions site happened similar to my going to Chicago, as Father Alex explains.

"My Passionist Provincial did not send me to San Antonio to work. I went to continue my education in Spanish. John and I started learning Spanish with Sister Rosalie but later we went away to language school in 1983 and '84 to learn Spanish. John retained it better. So I had planned to study Spanish at a language school in San Antonio for about twelve weeks. While there, to keep practice, I'd go over to a safe house, a building where a couple took in 'illegal' immigrants. At night, I'd sit and talk with them. That is how I kept my Spanish.

"John and I have always been sort of on the outside looking in; we are unconventional because we chose to do something different. That is our particular insight. So, when I arrived in San Antonio, I found out there were 385 drive-by shootings in one year. I thought 'Holy Cow!' I called John. 'Hey, Phelps, I think I have site number three. I am living in it.'

"We had never really thought about going into a city with a population lower than Detroit's or Chicago's, so this would be a new experience for us, but it was a challenge I felt ready to accept. Also, our approach would be completely different from Chicago and Detroit. Because I could not believe the stories I'd heard about the violence among younger kids in San Antonio's schools, I decided to start with young people in the thirteen-to-seventeen age bracket.

"I remember telling John, 'I have good news and bad news. We are starting, but we are starting with eighth-graders.'

"I told him it was part of the deal I made to get into San Antonio's public schools. In Detroit, Tom Hathaway's father opened doors that got us into the public schools. In San Antonio, I befriended a couple of high school administrators who wanted me in their program, but one of the administrator's said 'I'll make you a deal. I'll get you into our high schools if you start in the middle school where I used to work because it is a hurting zoo—nothing works.'

"The youth were challenging. Poverty has a way of hardening young people at a way too early age. In one of my first programs in a public school, this one kid came in and looked me in the eye and said:

"'Who are you and what the h.... are you doing here?'

"I returned his eye-to-eye glare and answered, 'I am a bald white man.'

"My reply totally disarmed him and the entire group looked up as if to say 'What?' What was so funny was after that brief exchange, all the kids stood up and started introducing themselves by description or what they looked like.

"There would be no retreat house in San Antonio. We found an abandoned, empty ice cream store on the south side to hold retreats. The guy who owned the store gave it to us for a song and dance. It became our first Life Directions office in San Antonio.

"My partner found me. I was sitting in this little house I rented in the barrio when someone knocked on my door: 'Hello, I am Sister Bette Bluhm and I heard you were thinking about doing some youth work here.'

"It was spring of 1992. Sister Bette, an Incarnate Word Sister, had heard rumors about a priest who had moved to the city looking to get involved in youth work. Bette shared my passion for youth.

"By 1993, Sister Bette and I were indeed soul mates. She stayed in a convent, and I lived in the rental house. At one time I shared the place with two teachers and a missionary. There were four of us and three dogs living in the rental home, and we had a great ole time.

"It took about five years to get San Antonio in good working order. By then, we were really rolling with five public schools, the training of young adult ministry teams in at least three parishes, and a whole lot of young adults working with us. Sister Bette and I were great together. We had developed a great team and had financial backing and credibility in the city as well. We fit together like hand-in-glove, but that is how God works. If you're on the right track with the right mission, He will send you soul mates."

The Fourth Site: Sister Rosalie in Tucson, Arizona

By 1993, we had started to merge into a National Board and were in the process of officially forming Life Directions National. While Fr. Alex and I were in San Antonio and Chicago, Pat Trainor was manning the ship as Executive Director of Life Directions in Detroit. We were strong in maintaining our values and core spiritual beliefs as we made this spread across the country.

At that same time I asked Sister Rosalie to join me in Chicago. Our work was expanding, and I needed her talent of selecting and training staff. Rosalie was already traveling to the southwest to see if there was a need and fit for Life Directions. In reflection, she writes how the exploration work led to our fourth site in Tucson, Arizona:

"We started to think about where in the West we'd like to go and I remembered Arizona, the state where I was born, had little resources. During a neighborhood community meeting in Chicago, I mentioned that I was thinking about starting a ministry in Arizona, and someone spoke up and said, 'Hey, I have an uncle that is a priest down there.'

"So I went to visit his uncle in Arizona City and told him I wanted to focus on the Native people. He suggested I go to Tucson and meet with the Pascua Yaqui and Tohono O'odham Tribes. So I went and met with whom the Native tribes called 'chairpersons.' The first thing I was asked by a chairperson was, 'Are you one of those people who's going to be here today and gone tomorrow?'

"I spent six months just meeting with the Yaqui and Tohono

O'odham (also known as the Papago) tribes, just exploring where we'd like to go with Life Directions. I had become so familiar with the tribes that a Tohono O'odham chairperson offered to give me living space on the reservation to start our program. Unfortunately, he passed away before it was time to make a decision about Life Directions working in Tucson. There was a change in leadership, so I refocused on the Yaqui people. They were very receptive and actually gave us a grant to start our work with them."

Sister invited Father Alex to work with her for a while in Tucson. In his reflections on that time period, he describes "a whole different world."

"Our focal point was Native Americans. It was a whole different breed of cat and a whole different culture. In some ways, I felt like I did back in the '60s when I lived with a black family. I was told that, way back in time, the Yaqui tribe had been driven out of Mexico by the Mexican Army and eventually landed in Tucson. So they had this stigma of having 'no country' and a determination to proudly claim and hold onto what they had in Tucson.

"We did our focus: LIFE weekends in the middle of nowhere, out in the desert. I remember one time, Sister Rosalie and I walked into this one little retreat house and inside were about twenty-five illegal immigrants sitting in the dark. They had just come across the river and were waiting for their ride."

Noting Father Alex's memories, Sister Rosalie added:

"I have always felt blessed to be able to walk into places and be received very graciously. One thing I always share with administrators is that I have been a principal of a school and I have taught in many schools. That lets them know that I am very sensitive to the challenges and the obstacles and responsibilities they have as educators and as a school system.

"Tucson is smaller than Detroit and Chicago. For me, that does not matter. My focus is the people with whom I have been sent to work. If it is 10 or 200, it does not make a difference to me. It is all about building relationships.

"As our CEO of Life Directions, I thought it appropriate to invite Father John down when I made my presentation to the Yaqui People. By then I had introduced myself and had talked to many people. They knew me fairly well. But I had to make the presentation to the board in order to get official approval to work with their people, and I asked Father John to walk with me on this. It was appropriate protocol.

"It was interesting. The reception was; 'We know Sister Rosalie. She's been around here. So why does this man have to talk?' After I told them he was the President and CEO of Life Directions and was there at my invitation, they let him say a few words.

"For me, it was an interesting diversion from the norm. There is always that issue of a woman and a woman of color; people are always surprised with what I bring to the table. It is like they are surprised that I have contributions. It is that whole labeling thing: 'you look a certain way, so you must be dumb, stupid, unqualified,' whatever.

"Culturally, I am so used to white people taking prominence, so I was surprised when Father John was kind of put aside. 'How could this happen?' I thought. But, being who I am, I was not going to let them throw him out. We came out of it okay, but it was just a different reality than what I had grown accustomed to seeing."

Apparently, Father Alex was more attuned to negative attitudes towards Sister than she was at the time, as he explains in his recollections:

"Rosalie had a real uphill climb in Tucson. The whole program was marginal. I never thought we were in the mainstream where corporations and major nonprofits would embrace us and, to be quite honest, it was the fact that Rosalie was not only Mexican but a Mexican woman. Unfortunately, racism was alive and well."

Sister Rosalie recalled how the Yaqui people had a reservation out of town, but they also had a settlement in town. "It was about a ten-block, poverty-ridden area that they have occupied for many, many years. When I came to Tucson, the casinos were just starting, and the Native People were using what they gained to develop their own neighborhoods. They were moving from living in cardboard houses to building cement homes for their people.

"The neighborhood on which I focused really blossomed while I was there. I was working with the school children who had become my entrée into the communities. I became very close to the adults. I took a course on Yaqui culture, and some of the adults and young adults from the course joined us on our retreats.

"The Yaquis funded us for about five years, but after it ended, I moved down to the Sunnyside area. It was a more of a multicultural setting with a strong Hispanic presence in the area. In the Mexican culture, like others, children are a joy for us--to be protected and loved.

"Getting established in Tucson was no big deal to me. I never had the feeling of failure; I just walked the walk: went into the schools, talked to the teachers. They sent me the students and, through the students, I was able to accomplish our community work. We had the involvement with young adults and at least three retreats a year.

"What happened in Tucson was a reflection of 'who I am.' What comes out of me is looking for ways for people getting to know one another in a way that they will value the differences.

"I remember when I first began in Sunnyside High. A Sister brought a family to visit us with a baby in their arms. I asked if I could take the child and show it off to the other Sisters at the convent. They let me take the baby, but when the Sister brought the baby back to the family, the parents told her that they had to take it home and bathe it in Clorox. When she asked why, they said, 'Well, that Sister touched our baby!' The other part of the story is that by the end of the year, the family was glued to me.

"It is that whole thing of being 'who I am' and people coming to the conclusion that I am okay, I guess. I thank the Lord for the gift of being in the midst of the negative, staying positive, and people being drawn to me."

The Fifth Site: Fr. Binh Ta in New Orleans

Sister Rosalie's success in Tucson was replicated elsewhere. In 1996, Father Binh Ta, who started as an intern in Detroit when he was a Redemptorist seminarian in training, wanted to start Life Directions in New Orleans. The Redemptorists had great contacts there and Sister Rosalie had already visited and assessed the site to determine if the schools would be receptive.

Fr. Binh wanted to engage the Vietnamese young people and young adults as the second generation was facing the challenge of enculturation: the assimilation of their traditional culture with western culture. He remembered how we had brought to surface the loss of cultural identity among other young adults within the African and Hispanic American people. He also recalled how we had identified the loss of core values as the educational system of the United States would ready young people to work within a pluralistic, capitalistic society.

Fr. Binh was a "boat person" who came to our country after the fall of Saigon. His family went to one of the transitional camps in Arkansas. They valued education for their children. Binh went to high school and then to college as a science major.

During his years of study, he became attracted to the mission and ministry of the Redemptorists, whom he came to know in Houston. During his formation as a Redemptorist, he interned with our team in Detroit. He was accountable to Pat Trainor who was to mentor Binh's role as Executive Director in New Orleans.

The entry point into New Orleans was through the Redemptorists.

We had a long history in the "Lower Garden District." Our reputation as Redemptorists was deep and well respected. As Binh began to build relationships within the city, he came upon Walter L. Cohen High School, which was near where he was living with the Redemptorists at 2030 Constance Street.

Sister Rosalie had gone to New Orleans and found Sara T. Reed High School, which had a large population of Vietnamese Americans. It was destroyed by Katrina in 2005. At the time Sister went there, there was a unique challenge in the school. The cultural divide between the African and Asian Americans was subtle but strong.

There was a dropout rate among Asians that was seen by many within their culture as "losing face." Sister was able to show how Life Directions would address this issue. When Fr. Binh showed up, he was immediately accepted by the administration and faculty.

In New Orleans, the school-side of our work was not the challenge. I saw a need to put in place the spiritual development of young adults from eighteen to thirty-five years of age that would be multicultural from the get-go.

We had not been in New Orleans three months, when we already had the beginnings of a Board of Advisors. Our Provincial leadership, who had invited us to come, joined our board. Fr. Monroe Perrier, affectionately known as "Fr. Monie," was the first member of the board. Through contacts made by the friends of the Redemptorists, we started building relationships in the business and corporate communities.

As we were building relationships in the schools and in the business communities, Fr. Binh and I saw the need for him to have a partner. This partner would be the first person to initiate Life Directions, directed by the co-founders and mentored by Pat Trainor into the role of Executive Director.

Fr. Binh and I saw the essential need for a strong partnership with whom to bring to the surface the work of Life Directions. Today we know that partnerships at the center of our work can determine the make-it-or-break-it factor.

It was Martin Luther King Jr. Holiday in January 1997. Fr. Binh and I went to a celebration in King's memory held at Xavier University in New Orleans. I asked one of the Sisters of the Blessed Sacrament (SBS), if she knew anyone who might be interested in connecting with our work in public high schools among African American young people. I knew her community of Sisters was dedicated to African, Native, and Haitian Americans. Sure enough, she pointed out a sister who had just finished her Master's Degree in Youth Ministry, Sr. Gilda Marie Bell, SBS, from New Iberia, Louisiana.

Fr. Binh and I met with Sister Gilda Marie and shared what we were about to launch in New Orleans. She was very interested but wanted to consider whether this would be consistent with their reason to exist as Sisters.

The joy we experienced when we heard from Sr. Gilda Marie that she was open to joining Fr. Binh was hard to describe. We just knew all would work out from that point on. I began to do an orientation for their partnership. Sister Rosalie led an in-service training of our programs. We were able to bring down the materials we had developed for our three programs and for the focus: LIFE process. We were up and running by March 1997.

Looking Back to How We Lost Control

What follows are some bittersweet discoveries that called us to step up to the challenge of replication. We needed to be much clearer on the issues that needed to be addressed with gentleness and humility.

In 1998, we were now in five sites. We needed to step up to review the condition of our work, the sustainability of our resources, and the central staff to live the vision and do the mission of Life Directions.

The two years from 1998 to 2000 helped the co-founders see the good, the bad, and the not-so-good. We thought back to 1987, our first strategic planning session with Plante Moran in Detroit. We used the same three major goals as our frame of reference: our funding, our marketing, and our programs. But we also remembered back to 1978 when our internal evaluation identified that the internalization of our vision and mission before taking on leadership by our staff was more critical, only to be followed by having a strong board to sustain them.

Without these previous moments of truth, I doubt if our lessons learned would have brought us to discern what to create and how to respond to the challenges we would face within each site, and collectively from the five together.

What came forward as the greatest lack was not what others were doing or not doing. We found that we, the co-founders, needed to be up front and clear with the boards, the staffs, and the volunteers. They needed to know that the heart and soul of Life Directions is our inclusive spirituality.

We knew that the results others saw came from being rooted spiritually in "forgiving." But we had not explained in detail what makes it possible to bring peace out of violence and to have achieving young people be the solution that would draw their less-achieving peers to self-responsible and balanced decisions.

What we discovered—and painfully so—was a three-fold truth. First, we had done a good job explaining our programs in the schools and in neighborhoods. Second, we had designed our manuals and workbooks to develop all three programs. Third, what we had *not* done well was explain to the boards and our donors the spiritual foundation upon which the programs rested. What became even more painful was when we hired staff who did not internalize the value of "forgiving" as the core of our mission.

Looking back, the insight from our 1978 evaluation is non-negotiable. A person is suited to lead the mission and values of Life Directions to the extent that the vision is embraced and reverenced through experience of doing what we do best: "forgiving to respond to violence." We did not attend to this need. We also did not realize that the original fundraising board of Detroit had begun with the young adults from our retreats. There we had no need to explain our spirituality.

We believe divine grace kept us moving forward as we expanded faster than we could manage. It gave birth to the gifts we have in place to bring our boards, our programs, and the staff to a level of excellence. It is good to keep this in mind as we share how we went about discovering what needed to be done. We built our board and staff, training and developing out of pain caused by not doing so in the first place. The forgiving we offered in our programs would sustain us through the conflicts that would arise among some of the board members and staff.

The level of the business side of Life Directions was maturing. The quality of programming in the schools was solid. We were having National Board meetings and overnight board retreats and staff with volunteers meeting to support and encourage our growth. Everything seemed to be coming together. We had momentum because of our winning reputation in five cities. In Chicago, our influential alliances helped us reach unprecedented heights in record time. Much of that was due to the connections with Mayor Richard M. Daley.

The month before he took over the schools in 1995, we were able to arrange a meeting with the Mayor. Nelson Carlo; Bill Farrow III, a Life Directions Chicago board member and First Chicago Bank Vice President; and Victor Dickson, the regional manager of Sprint, joined me. Mayor Daley said he was familiar enough with the program that he wanted to ask me a direct question. "If I gave you the school system of Chicago, what would you do with it?"

I paused before replying: "The reality is there are more than 400,000 young people of school age. Many of the undocumented are not registered, and those who do not sign up are not counted. Having said that, I'd first start with the school board; looking at the teacher as the producer and students, under sixteen, as customers. I'd operate like a major business, making sure the person in charge knew how to run a business. What we do at Life Directions is develop a hunger among young people that makes high school work for them and college a possibility, and then have them become peer mentors for eighth-graders.

"As you may know, statistics can lead us to think all eighth-graders make it to ninth grade—that there are no drop-outs. We know the reality; most dropouts occur between eighth and tenth grades. At best, we are one of a multiple set of resources needed. With families fragmented, we need to change how we do business. It is not working, and most of the issues are between the people in the community and the people in the schools."

Daley listened and abruptly said, "Okay, I'll be getting back with you."

A month later, he was given the power by state legislators to run the Chicago school system. The following February, Nelson Carlo arranged for the mayor to speak at a fundraising breakfast for us at the Drake Hotel. I walked in with Mayor Daley at my side. He went to the microphone to discuss his school reform efforts and, to my surprise, started describing elements of our program, such as "Peers Inspiring Peers."

Inside, I shouted, "Terrific!" We were now on a public platform.

I asked the mayor to give us funds to expand our programs in Chicago. He offered to fund us to the tune of about $250,000. I was hesitant to receive that level of funding, because it was going to be more than one third of our budget. Exceeding this formula could mean our vision and mission might be controlled by the funding source.

Also, he wanted to promote our Peer Mentor Program, the one that needs the focus: LIFE spiritual formation in the community to be strong enough to sustain our Peer Motivation Programs in the high schools. This would give us the trained Peer Mentors to guide the eighth-graders to make high school work for them. He would explain this program to President Clinton in April 1996 as the "pyramid of support" for eighth-graders to have college or a quality career as a viable option.

The mayor came to our fundraiser that year when we gave First Lady, Hillary Clinton, our "Guiding Light Award" and Kevin Garnett, of the Boston Celtics, our "Alumni Award" for his time with us at Farragut. With the public recognition, we were about to face a challenge the likes of which we had never had.

In Detroit our staff, under the leadership of Pat Trainor and his Development Director, Joan Duggan, negotiated a major five-year agreement to reinvent family life within two major housing projects. We would build a staff to engage street gangs and transform what was not working into what an intergenerational effort would make possible. It was a major task that needed a dedicated staff to do just that alone.

It was clear that God was the navigator of our journey, but among the staff in Detroit and Chicago, signs where showing that indicated we needed deeper training and spiritual growth. Our operations were becoming too "bottom-heavy," meaning we were working directly with too many young people under eighteen years of age and not having enough spiritually-centered young adults and adults over eighteen.

The problem is that when we get too bottom-heavy, we will have less to offer the younger people: less trained Peer Mentors, even lesser trained Adult Mentors. We had never had to face this challenge of possibly having too much money before.

This raised a whole series of interconnected challenges. We may not have the spiritual energy of forgiveness. We may lack leaders who were humble enough to make mistakes—while taking responsibility for them—and yet visionary enough to succeed in spite of what others may deem impossible. Could a spirit of competition rise up between Detroit and Chicago or the other sites? Could it be that we were growing faster than we could sustain? We just weren't sure.

But we did it. In 1998, we were doing great work in five cities: Detroit, Chicago, San Antonio, Tucson, and New Orleans. We had budgets that were balanced with boards that were able to plan the work and work the plan. Our National Board meetings were on-point. We were about to attract a major COO of a national for-profit organization to lead our National Board.

But what we had feared in Chicago--expanding before having the capacity to assure quality—was about to play out in all our sites. Among the staff leadership there was tension. Some were invested in programs for those under eighteen years of age and did not see the need for the inclusive spirituality of Life Directions.

Meetings became really tense. We tried to encourage people to envision our programs as resting on our focus: LIFE spiritually-centered retreats with the people who come through them to lead. Peer Motivation and Peer Mentor were not stand-alone efforts. With focus: LIFE, forgiving would be the response encouraged by staff and volunteers to make life grow.

We did not have our financially-supported staff working with eighth-graders. If the funds were cut, what would happen to those young people? We wanted to set up a way for the self-supported people to sustain the mission. We wanted self-supported volunteer Adult Mentors to mentor high school students. We wanted volunteer Peer Mentors to mentor eighth-graders. Our staff would be spiritually-focused with the knowledge and skills to see and to guide the paradigm shift from being a victim to becoming responsible for being a victim. We wanted the staff to know how to encourage a gradual growth into building balanced relationships based on talents and gifts that bring everyone involved into becoming excellent. We wanted to encourage multicultural and intergenerational, interdependent, community-based partnerships. All these aspects would take time.

After twenty-five years of leading young adults to be self-responsible and balanced, we were now about to do the same for Life Directions volunteers, staff, and boards. As I look back on the journey since 1998, I can see that we have put in place that which is needed for our succession plan. It is only by being faithful to our interdependent partnerships that we continue to respond with renewed energy to the intuitions that began our work. We do our best and gratefully pray to let go and let God do what only God can do.

Pat Trainor and I became a COO and CEO team as a national team. We set out to work with the five Directors in the five sites. It was clear that we were going to have to slow things down, maybe even downsize based on the spiritual rootedness we needed to sustain Life Directions.

By the end of 1999, tension was showing. We knew we had the challenge to reshape our selection and training of staff in a way in which we all embraced all three of our major activities and our foundation of spirituality. But to do so while producing outcomes that are fundable called for knowledge and skills which Pat and I knew we did not have to offer our staff.

Before setting in motion a change in direction, we needed to assess where we were in each of the sites, as well as seek counsel on how to respond to what we sensed we were going to discover. Pat did the assessing and managing of the directors. I stepped back for operations to find the resources we sensed we needed.

It was at this time that I came upon the Gallup Institute, which had a special training workshop for CEOs looking to be great leaders with great managers who make a vision work. I went to the Institute and returned from the training with two major insights. The first gift was the Gallup Organization which taught us how to develop the partnership between the CEO and COO. One, usually the CEO, is to lead the organization where it needs to be in the future, which can be painful, stretching one's skills. But more importantly, the COO is to manage the organization based on where it is, which is designed to be encouraging. The second gift came in the form of the articulation of the vision. The need for a clear vision is what makes it all possible.

I wrestled with this challenge. I was forced to put down the vision into ten words or less. It had to be self-explanatory and simple. By the last day of the workshop, I came up with the five words that I was to bring back to the board of directors and my fellow co-founders. It sounds so simple, but I well remember the pain of finding this pearl: "Peers Inspiring Peers Through Forgiving." It was simple and to the point. The first three words are about peers rooted in positive values to inspire. The last two words are about them doing so through forgiving. We want to inspire peers who lack either or both, often through no fault of their own. "Forgiving" is the decision to change the paradigm from victim-persecutor-rescuer to responsible-balanced-partners.

I look back now and see that this workshop would be the gift for all of us who wanted to pass on to the next generation what we have lived. The tension in the transformation of our mission was manageable because we remembered why we began the work—to get to the cause of self-destructive decisions.

We did not want to do the same to our work. The courage of so many is the reason we did not lose our way. The wisdom to slow down and the courage to excel came to us slowly as we turned our humiliations into the humility to see our enemy as the friend we are forgiving. Who would have thought that what would happen to the co-founders would be life-giving to all who choose to be responsible for his or her life direction? Who would have imagined that we would be healed of our hurts by the very gift that we offer—that when facing death, we found life?

I remember so clearly that I would wake up early in the morning and review the last workshop with the Directors. I would breathe forgiving toward each one. I believed they were sincere. I prayed to be given people with whom to work to find the way to the truth of how to internalize the vision and mission among financially-supported people.

I am convinced we made it not because of my intellectual grasp of the issues but the spiritual support we gave each other. We would all be honest with our struggles. We kept each other from seeing ourselves as victims and others as persecutors. We did not rescue each other. We kept our vision. In fact, we internalized it ourselves—in a way we never would have expected, through sharing how we felt—became aware of how we saw the issues, and were able to change our perceptions.

I shared the four "bones" in the spiritual life. The head bone—our intellectual IQ— is to think it all through; the back bone—our emotional EQ—is to feel it all through; the knee bone—our spiritual SQ—is to pray it all through. To keep all the bones together, keep our funny bone to keep laughing, remembering that it all began when Eve ate the apple or, to be politically correct, when Adam got it caught in his throat!

The amazing gift through it all was that the programs and retreats lived the spirit of "forgiving." They actually encouraged us as staff and boards to receive what we were giving.

THE PARABLE OF WHAT IT TAKES TO HAVE A PRAYER

A man walking through the forest saw a fox that had lost its legs; he wondered how the fox continued to live. Then he saw a tiger come in with food in its mouth. The tiger had its fill and left the rest of the meal for the fox.

The next day the tiger fed the fox again. The man began to wonder and said to himself, "I too shall sit by the tree and the tiger will bring me food."

He sat and sat, but nothing happened. He was hungry and asked the tiger, "Why do not you feed me like you feed the fox? I am doing what the fox is doing, willing to depend on you."

The tiger dropped the food he was carrying for the fox and said, "You have legs. Come with me and I'll show you how to do what I am doing. You can feed us and others with me!"

1. Take the situation of seeing a naked child, hungry and shivering in the cold. Some ask, "Why does God permit this? Why doesn't He do something?"

2. What would happen if we became quiet and heard God's answer? "I did something. I made you."

3. What meaning would you draw from this story as it relates to hope attached to leadership?

4. How would you call people to "walk the walk" and not just "talk the talk" of making the world a better place?

CHAPTER SEVEN
THE ROAD LESS TRAVELLED

In 1916, Robert Frost, the unofficial poet laureate of the last century, penned "A Road Not Taken." The poet eloquently made the point that the more commonly chosen path is good to take. To take the road less travelled is to follow a call to risk and to be open to failure. It captures the spirit that sparked the pruning which was both painful and purposeful for Life Directions. Our experiment to awaken forgiving within public life "has made all the difference."

We saw ourselves as pioneers, as described by Abraham Maslow, who wrote *The Farther Reaches of Human Nature* (1973). He wrote this book after his famous "five-hierarchy-of-needs" presentation. His work explained the nineteen meta-needs that creative people have. They are the needs that go beyond meeting individual needs. They are more a part of what leaves a legacy for the common good.

Frost and Maslow expressed the intuition that inspired our journey that began in 1973. It was a matter of integrity of the spirit that would be the "hunch", as Maslow called it, that we would follow when we knew not the way.

We knew we were taking the road less travelled and we knew it would make all the difference. M. Scott Peck centered on self-responsibility in the first of his trilogy of writings. We have used them as a set of source books for those who want to reflect on what inspires a choice such as ours. The other two books were *People of the Lie* (1998) and *The Different Drum* (1998).

But what has proven to be our best GPS (see Chapter Four) for our journey into the twenty-first century continues to be the Hebrew and Christian Scriptures. The complement to these works has been the Qur'an with its awareness of the need for "submission" to a Power Greater Than Human. The discipline of prayer, fasting, and almsgiving is also our interior discipline to follow what inspires us to lead as a team of five. It ensures that we stay committed to justice as the balance needed for all relationships. The destination of remembering "the least" is the motive of our challenging each other to forgive, because it is the way of those who love unconditionally. Without justice and peace, violence will continue to define our children's future.

Lyrics from a popular song by the Beatles surrounded us in our beginnings: "You may say I am a dreamer, but I am not the only one." As the five of us have remained faithful to the journey to bring hope out of the synergy of peers inspiring each other, we are finding others "dreaming the impossible dream." Alexander MacDonald put it best: "When I see what we are doing, I feel as lonely as a skull in the desert!"

In 1989, Fr. Bill Nugent, who had spent most of his life as a Redemptorist in the Amazon Valley of Brazil, told me "If what you are doing is more than the five of you, it is time to test it."

What follows is the way in which we continue to test our mission. Is it possible to be spiritually synergized as boards, staff, and volunteers to transform the way of life of anorexia to values and to inclusive spirituality into mature people of hope for the sake of our children's children?

Pruning Healthy Branches

As I mentioned, the call to go to Chicago went well. We began our work with the retreats among various neighborhoods, for which Chicago is best known. We had the seed funds to build our foundation with the spirituality of focus: LIFE. It was when we were recognized in March 1995 by the mayor's office and were given our first major source of revenue that the struggle to be faithful to the vision began. But we were unaware of the challenge, since the joy of being empowered to do so much more for so many was what we saw.

We were also unaware that the confrontations that would occur would be the catalyst to compose our framework to explain why we are who we are and how our vision works. We did not know that we would find what is essential and what is changeable in what we do. Each city brought these insights to light.

It may have been avoidable, but if it was not for people of integrity on all sides of the challenge, we would never have grown through the pressured question: "The money is here. Your mission is there. What happens if you hold to the mission and lose the money?"

A very significant moment happened in Tucson in late 1998. Pete Raskob and Sister Rosalie met because of Sister's religious community's involvement with the Raskob Foundation. Pete was intrigued with Sister Rosalie's presentation as was Dan Ranieri, the director of one of the largest intervention programs for troubled children in Arizona. What they both valued was how Sister explained getting to the cause of what becomes a cost-prohibitive intervention effort. "An Ounce of Prevention Is worth a Pound of Cure" was their takeaway line.

What Sister never imagined was what resulted from her talk: she introduced me to both men, and a very significant opportunity arose.

I shared with Pete the struggle we were having nationally in putting in writing our intuitive way of getting to the cause of dropouts. I remember saying to him, "You would think that after twenty-five years of doing the work, we could clearly and succinctly explain our work in writing."

Pete's response was the reflective wisdom that would be the defining moment in our future. "Have you ever been supported just to do that? I mean, have you ever been given the opportunity to reflect long enough to craft it for people like me to understand and want to support it?"

I told him "No," at which point he explained his grandfather's foundation that was begun due to an issue of injustice based on discrimination against Al Smith, the first Catholic who ran for President in 1928.

"Let me help you do what you haven't done. Let me help you write to our foundation for a grant to articulate your vision, mission, and values." He helped me write the budget as well. It was for $98,000.

I received a call from Pete four months after submission:

"Fr. John, how much do you think you got?"

"$50,000," I guessed.

"No," he answered. "You got the whole amount. Now go do it!"

It was the first time we had received serious money for anything other than directing programs. We never really had time to focus on anything other than doing the work. We had not had funding that would give us the space to create longitudinal studies, or analyze systemic change in our operations. All these issues had become extremely important because Life Directions was expanding nationally.

We knew we needed quality staff. We had put together our proposal for our National Training Institute in 1995. We included in the proposal the desire to become an Institute as part of a faith-based university. We knew we needed to "package our work" in order to replicate the model. We were a "not-yet" recognized organization seeking six-figure funding. We knew what we needed to do to support the planning and designing of the board, staff, and volunteer development. We knew we needed to free up a mobile team to work the plan needed to train and manage five cities at once.

We also knew it was essential to build up the spiritual foundation of our core staff, while keeping the "firewall" between our programs: addressing spiritual anorexia in those over eighteen years of age, and working with young people between thirteen and eighteen years of age in the public schools and their surrounding communities. We knew we would not be faithful to the vision without it.

When our grant was not accepted, we faced into the challenge of doing what we had designed but without restricted funding to do so. That we did as well as we did was a gift for which we are most grateful.

Selecting leadership would be our greatest challenge. We did not have a pool of candidates from our focus: LIFE weekends in Detroit to draw upon. Our long-term record-keeping did not keep our database updated. I once said that it would have been great to have secured everyone's social security number. We remembered the first recommendation of our 1978 five-year organizational evaluation: "pick people who 'see' with focus: LIFE 'eyes.'"

What became even more critical was the other recommendation: "build the board to sustain the programs." People were joining the board in all our cities, but we had not attended to their awareness of our vision. We did not take the time to ensure that they embraced the spiritually-rooted vision among those over eighteen years of age. We took for granted that they understood to be our inclusive spiritual vision and mission. Why else would people say they wanted our programs for young people in middle and high school?

We slowly came to discover our "non-negotiable" principle. We would not cut our "roots," even if it meant cutting what appeared to be healthy branches.

The Lesson of the Palm Tree

I look back and realize that many people are conditioned to cut their roots and start anew. It may be painful, but to have a better life it has to be done. That is what many people coming to the United States from Europe thought. It is part of the history of the founding of the "American Dream." The leadership and citizens of the thirteen colonies chose to cut their European roots to be free from tyranny and have a better life for their families.

But also in our history were the "Negro Spirituals" which served as the inspirational tracks of the "Underground Railroad." Being from St. Louis, I knew well the song "Ole Man River." A different cultural value resonates within the lyrics. Africans were made to cut their roots and lose their freedom to live where they wanted to raise their families. Slave owners brought them to America to do the work needed to build the country.

When I was growing up and our Catholic grade schools were integrated, I heard about the struggles of the slaves to survive. I remember during my college years in the early 1960s marveling at how they held onto their value of believing that they were chosen to be free. Even in the face of death, they would be free—"free at last, thank God almighty," they determined to be free at last. I remember 1963 and hearing Martin Luther King, Jr. give his "I Have a Dream Speech" in front of the Lincoln Memorial. Such unconditional love would inspire me to be true to the vision of our work, even in the face of being misunderstood and rejected.

As I look back, I realize where we drew our strength as a team. Sister Rosalie had a talent to know if people understood what we were saying. How she knew was never questioned. We just trusted her ability to discern. Judith MacDonald's way of thinking made sure we were faithful to our values, no matter what. She did not say what we were to do, but she would definitely let us know if we were *not* being true to the vision. Both of them challenged me, and I sense it challenged Fr. Alex and Alexander MacDonald to look at our "white man's" way of deciding "what to keep and what to lose." (Ecclesiastes 3:1ff)

When I thought of the assassinations in the 1960s—the Kennedys, Malcolm X, and Martin Luther King, Jr.—I knew the price paid for choosing to live a purpose-driven life when it was not a popular idea. When I would see how our two co-founding women would manage keeping their "center" in the face of disrespect, the two Alex's and I were schooled without knowing it. We were learning from our role models how to transform humiliations into humility that leads to truth. It is, as I see it now, the most powerful force sustaining us still. The "grandmothers" are the heart of our reflective pruning.

The lesson of the Palm Tree speaks of the way we sustained Life Directions as we were living through our own tsunami. The palm tree has roots deep beneath the sand. Somehow, the roots seem to know how to wrap themselves around rock that is far below whatever wind and rain can reach. The redwoods, on the other hand, are far taller and more majestic to see. They sway in the breeze from the Pacific with character and grace, but their roots are very shallow. They would never survive a tornado or hurricane. No wonder they are far from the shoreline, far from the edge of where soil touches the sea.

We were getting funded, but the funding was pressuring us to consider cutting our roots. Spirituality was *not* empowering our expanding work. It was a strong part of the fee-for-service work with faith-based communities. We also had two major training contracts. First, we did a ten-year contract (1979–1989) to research all Hispanic programs in the United States and to build and implement training materials that would best serve their people. Sister Rosalie was the lead person from our team. Then, we had a two-year contract (1989–1991) to implement the National African American Pastoral Plan in twenty-four faith communities in Detroit. Fr. Alex directed this contract.

We found ourselves developing our inclusive spirituality as a service. We were hoping enough young adults and adults would come to the focus: LIFE weekends to internalize "forgiving" as a result of knowing us from the contracts. We would promote this way of a deepening of knowing the power of forgiving to remove the cause of violence.

Simply put, the challenge from the late 1990s to 2005 was a struggle to sustain our inclusive spirituality as the core of our work. We found out that our "firewall" was not a wall to separate, but more "the foundation of our building." If we pulled away from our inclusive spiritual foundation, the first and second floor would collapse. We would become "rescuers" wanting to "save the kids" and "be the solution to their problems." We knew it would be less effective than peers inspiring peers and not sustainable. When the funding would be cut, the "solution" would create a condition for "those living in an environment of poverty" - a solution that would be worse than the one in which they are living.

We discovered how essential our spiritual intuitions were by events where they were lacking. We were especially aware of what happens when our spiritual roots were cut. We knew intuitively the results of rescuing kids and showing results to keep the funding. We would have many dependent people. We would not develop self-responsible, balanced people who would appreciate wisdom to influence their decisions for their lives and the lives of their children.

Pioneers that we are, we would need to internalize the lesson of the palm tree, and the Raskob grant freed us to do just that. When I went away for special training to be a CEO to understand the relationship of a leader and a manager, I had the opportunity to study our journals and review our manuals and workbooks. The painful confrontations that were happening would become the intuitions we needed to know what to write and teach. It was a simple yet freeing insight. I needed to surround myself with talents that complimented mine. As I lead, I am to remain at the center of the team as we all head into the unknown, no matter how painful it might be.

Sister Rosalie and Patrick Trainor were given the tools to become great managers, to break all the rules, and to accept people where they are. And we all would learn that a system grows to the extent the managers ensure everyone is moving together. It is the challenge to the CEO, I learned, to lead at the pace set by the managers, and not the other way around.

As we three were in training, I articulated the vision. The mission and values would be reviewed by this vision. The managers were given the encouragement they needed from me to walk at the pace of the staff and volunteers. And I would need to lead in such a way as to sustain our resources with board buy-in of *why* we do what we do.

In the summer of 2000 we had completed our work; we were ready to proceed. It was time to share the fruit of our training and development.

The Various Vines: Pruning with Purpose

At the beginning of the twenty-first century, Life Directions was on a roll. There were no violent acts in any of our programs across the nation—not anywhere or anytime. We were really enjoying the Peer Motivation and Peer Mentor programs in the public schools. We were having very good retreats in Tucson, which was a good replication of our work in Chicago.

San Antonio was facing obstacles as they sought to get the spirituality to be sustainable. At the same time, we could not get the retreats started in New Orleans. In both sites, we were dealing with growing our high school program *without* the beyond-high-school experience. Gradually it was not seen as intrinsic to the San Antonio board, and it was not able to be implemented by the team in New Orleans. It would be, at best, an after-the-fact approach.

By 2001, we were experiencing confrontation that we prayed

would bring life out of rejection. All three executive directors and two out of the three board chairs wanted to encourage programs and activities for young people *under* the age of eighteen to be offered by financially-supported staff.

In May 2001 the National Board made the decision to remain faithful to the roots of our work in the spirituality of "Peers Inspiring Peers Through Forgiving." The spirituality would guide the programs for those under eighteen years of age. The National Board decided to amend the bylaws to explain this way of doing what we do. The CEO and staff were charged with crafting a document that came to be called "The Framework," to institutionalize the total operations of Life Directions, its programs, and the training and development of boards, staff, and volunteers. Due to lack of financial support in New Orleans, the National Board suspended work in that site, keeping the local board in place with a plan to begin again. We amended the bylaws. We positioned the co-founders as Corporate Members with the challenge to appoint the Board of Directors and to approve the appointing of Boards of Trustees that would function under one 501(c) (3).

The impact of this major shift in leadership called for sensitive implementation. I knew we needed to build a succession plan. But the tension of "righting the ship," so to speak, would take incredible energy. It was then that I asked to meet Pete Raskob.

It was November 11, 2001, two months to the day after 9/11. Our deep desire of getting to the cause of violence met his urgent need to bring such a way of responding to the events of today in public life. Again he counseled me to write a three-year proposal to lay out a three-year plan of action that would result in a succession plan for Life Directions to live beyond the lifetime of the co-founders.

In May 2002 we secured a three-year succession planning grant from the Raskob Foundation aimed at putting a quality succession plan in place, based on lessons learned. In moving forward, we had to first look back. Looking back at the beginning of each site, we discovered various roots planted in each city. Some were based in spirituality but most sites were founded to meet an urgent need for those under eighteen years of age. Keep in mind, Life Directions' successful formula usually starts with retreats, then the building of a board. Once in place, we go into high schools, then middle schools, because we have our Life Circles to sustain our spiritual energy of forgiving as a response to violence. These are the basic steps we had designed in 1990.

When we were given the opportunity to go to Chicago, we were able to follow this formula. We were given a retreat house in the suburbs but found a way to reach the young people in their high schools in the city where we wanted to serve. The bottom line, however, was that our spirituality led to the opportunity.

As I said earlier, we went into San Antonio for different reasons. Fr. Alex, who went to improve his Spanish, discovered a need that related more to middle schools. It was almost like he was given an invitation to start Life Directions at its end point and not at its beginning with older students who we would help become peer mentors for younger students. He started with the branches not the roots and he started alone.

San Antonio also had a unique situation in their public schools. There are sixteen separate school districts. To be accepted in one district did not translate into the ability to move into other districts. The way in which people chose to be in which district was challenging to understand. It seemed more than geographical, but it was not all that clear. For sure it would make for difficulties in staffing and city-wide programming. Coupled with the challenge of being near the border of Mexico we knew we had major issues to address in order to move forward in a balanced way.

Our entry into Tucson was in response to an invitation from a Native American tribe, which was a new and different approach for us. The tribe was concerned about their children who weren't getting through high school, and we started to relate to that need. Peer Motivation was the entry point.

Sister Rosalie found a Catholic high school, Salpointe College-Prep, with a spiritual program to ready young people to make college work for them. She was able to find enough graduates from there to put together the focus: LIFE retreats. We had a combination of the Yaqui Tribe, focus: LIFE weekends, and an owner of a MacDonald's franchise to be our "Barnabas" who joined Sister to start the board in Tucson. The owner knew of our work and activities in Chicago and was happy to do what he could to get us up and running.

Later, we were able to connect with Sunnyside High School through the principal who knew the owner. In 1997, Sister went into Sunnyside High School. Raul Nido, the principal, focused in on what she had to offer. Nido eventually became the chair of the board of Life Directions in Tucson. It was our first board led by a high school principal. This was the school where Pete Raskob met Sister Rosalie. He also knew Principal Nido well and had read the results, which were amazing to him, of what Sister Rosalie was doing at Sunnyside. But we never had a sustainable funding source. Of the six School Districts in Tucson itself, Sunnyside was known as one situated in "an environment of poverty."

Near the beginning of our programs in Tucson, the Redemptorists community requested that Life Directions go into New Orleans high schools. A Redemptorist, Fr. Binh Ta connected with Sr. Gilda Marie of the Blessed Sacrament at Xavier Prep High School, where she had worked in New Orleans, who was open to working with him.

Fr. Binh knew about our Peer Motivation Program. Sister Gilda Marie was part of Xavier Prep High School in New Orleans. Both were spiritually-centered and committed to getting a retreat program up and running.

They did something culturally unique in New Orleans by creating a rapport-building program just for African and Asian Americans.

Fr. Binh and Sr. Gilda Marie looked to bring the two cultures together. They discovered a disturbing and challenging aspect in the city. There seemed to be profound racial resistance that prohibited the sharing of cultures between African and Asian Americans. The two cultures simply refused to interact with one another.

The need to bring our volunteer board up to speed with the programs and inclusive spirituality became our first priority. Some members took to it well; others were confused. Some walked away. At the same time, New Orleans was unable to secure funding and had to close operations.

What we learned was to insist that we have the funds in the bank needed to start before beginning any new site. This way we would have the money to support building our spiritual foundation. The best way to get funding such as this was to ask major donors who would see what we do and decide to support the start-up costs of doing business.

We found a person who was politically-networked in Marion County, where the state capital of Oregon is located. My brother Ray introduced us. Because of their professional relationship, he agreed to study what we had built that was working in other cities. At the invitation of our new supporter, a group from the judicial system visited our Chicago site. They saw how the Peer Mentor Program worked. They read the evaluations; they saw the data and the facts sheet on outcomes. They were so impressed that they went back to find major donors.

As people in Marion County began to invest in start-up funding for Life Directions, one of the criteria of the Raskob Foundation Grant was being met. We needed to have a major source of new funds in the first year of our three-year grant. It was a natural fit with new funds coming from a new location. But as we found out, the major donors were not focused on the infrastructure of our spiritual rootedness. They were more interested in our school-based programs.

After our first year of the three-year grant to build a succession plan, we stepped back to assess each site, beginning with the last to be launched. A juvenile/judicial need brought us into Marion County. A Redemptorist need to reach "those living in an environment of poverty" was our entry into New Orleans. An Adrian Dominican need called us to be with the Native American tribes in Tucson. The Passionists supported the need we found to serve middle school students in San Antonio. A Redemptorist need led us into Chicago. All reasons were good. What we discovered was that we did not assess Life Directions' vitality to determine the ability to expand.

Life Directions' branches were actually becoming separate vines. They were spreading across the country touching on various needs, but it concerned us deeply that all was not rooted in spirituality. The importance of spirituality became more of a center piece in our dialoguing and articulation. Still, we faced the challenge of discovering who we really were and how deeply our roots were planted.

Breathing Forgiving in the Midst of Conflict

The National Board decided to deepen our spiritual foundation. Pat Trainor returned to Detroit as its executive director to revitalize the site's spiritual rootedness. I returned to Chicago and chose Tom Howard to fill the position of executive director. Fr. Alex had moved into a position within his Passionist Community and was not available to return to San Antonio. It was painful to let go of San Antonio, but it would be irresponsible to overextend ourselves.

In the summer of 2003, the co-founders completed the board mandate for a document to outline the work of Life Directions. The thirty-two-page document was called "The Framework." It explained in detail the vision, mission, and values of Life Directions. It was written and rewritten by the corporate members and the chairperson of the Detroit board.

The document set into place protocols and standards. It explained exactly what board members and donors needed to know as far as becoming part of a spiritually-founded, value-centered organization that has a proven track record of not crossing the line between Church and State. The first twenty pages detailed how values and spirituality unfolded in Life Directions. The next set of pages detailed each of our programs and how they were all interdependent, resting on the foundation of the inclusive spirituality of focus: LIFE.

Laying all this out and putting it in print were essential. It was the culmination of a more than twenty-five-year journey of learning. M. Scott Peck's book, *The Different Drum*, explained what we were experiencing. In it, Peck described the growth process of a spiritually-centered organization. There are four painful stages, he said. First, we know each other, but only superficially at the board and staff levels. Second, something happens that causes the group to go into "chaos." Simply defined, chaos is the result of two or more individuals or groups certain of the answer and totally opposed to the others. Third, after seeking to "fix the problem," there is emptiness when all agree that there is no solution. Fourth, in prayer and reflection with the integrity that only humility can give, common ground is found and community is built.

Having such a "map," we were able to avoid getting distracted by grudges and egos. Seeking to constantly learn, we once again discovered the power of breathing forgiveness in the midst of chaos and emptiness. This insight taught us that if we continue to forgive in the midst of conflict, the ones who lose at first may be the very ones who give birth to what all sides need. In the end, we all win. We leave nobody behind except those who choose to walk away. It is a spiritual intuition of ours to believe "when you lose, you will only win, especially if those who won because of your losing are free for you to win as well."

I'll never forget being asked in the fall of 2004 to explain "forgiving" as we did on our first weekend of 1974. Without knowing it, one of the participants saw the woodchips and asked what they meant. I said, "They are chunks of wood to remind us to remember the Cross and not to make it into a double cross. That is how life is reborn. It is the symbol for our weekend. We put it on a string so you can put around your neck or as a keepsake in our room or car."

Our music minister, Larry, created our woodchip symbol in March 1974, during our first weekend. Since we did not have any money, he suggested that we could give a woodchip to remember the cross caused by the Master wanting to forgive. The way Larry put it, "if you have the vision, you'll know what it means." It is not a religious symbol only; those who were together on the retreat would remember its meaning.

Toward a Gentle Spirit

By May 2005, we had completed our succession plan through the support of the Raskob Foundation. Immediately our plan was put to the test. The Redemptorists called me to take on an important institutional commitment that our congregation needed me to manage. Sr. Rosalie became the logical choice for CEO by the Board of Directors. The reason was that the staff's priority was to focus primarily on quality spiritually-centered programming. The National Board saw that the local board had enough potential to generate the sustainable funding for growth without heavy involvement by its executive directors.

In the four years between 2005 and 2009, the work of Life Directions in Detroit, Chicago, Tucson, and Marion County was spiritually-centered and growing within the communities surrounding the schools we served. This was the good news. And it was encouraging to the boards and the participants of our work.

What we discovered was that the boards of the sites and the National Board needed a full-time executive to be the "face" for fundraising in Life Directions. The person would be called upon to lead both the securing of the resources and the delivery of spiritually-rooted work. Sources of revenue needed to be managed more closely than a volunteer board with administrative support could do.

This awareness came at the very time the economy of the United States went into a profound recession. The funds in Marion County Oregon and Tucson Arizona resting primarily on major donors became unsustainable. Both sites had to suspend operations with their respective boards having a representative of their site on the National Board.

The Redemptorists freed me from the responsibilities I had assumed so that I could return as CEO of Life Directions in the fall of 2009. I was to take up the challenge of refashioning the role and responsibilities of the CEO to relate to fund-development and image-building. We had made clear and purposeful choices, intent on building one cohesive effort with four sites functioning as unique contributors to the other. Now we were setting out to put the leadership at the board and director level in place.

I was grateful for the spiritual growth of our board, staff, and volunteers. We were conscious that our work is a walk in faith. Together we would decide the sustainability of our work. Each of the sites decided for the sake of the common good to suspend programs in Tucson and Marion County. A representative from each of the boards continued on the National Board. We decided that I would be the CEO working with Detroit and Chicago to design and implement a succession plan with proper funding and staff.

As I would reflect in our journal, to be financially supported would challenge the character within each person in the crucible of humiliations. The result would be a gentle spirit among board members. Everyone knew there was a responsibility to build with the staff a quality work for the young people we wanted to reach.

I noted in the journal that to be a self-supported volunteer would call for the integrity of perseverance. The staff would invest in their training and development with an eye on our succession-planning for program delivery flowing from our spirituality. What we did not know was that our "gentle spirit" was about to be rocked by catastrophic events that would impact Life Directions and the world.

September 11, 2001, was the beginning. Hurricane Katrina in 2005 in New Orleans was the next major challenge. But the recession that started in 2008 would be far more lasting to the people we were dedicated to reach. Detroit would be sliding into bankruptcy. Chicago would experience the rush of stimulus funding for public schools, only to watch violence escalate and the fiscal challenge forcing one of the greatest cutbacks of public schools in the country.

Within our two cities, within which conditional love had been increasingly birthing fragmenting families, the loss of hope would permeate the lives of young people and young adults to whom and with whom we are sent to serve. Discouragement would dampen the dream that "all may be one through the young with the adult."

"Together as one," was our mantra in our beginning. We would remember. It would serve us well in creatively responding with a spirit of joyful hope to spark peers to want to inspire their peers— to let go by forgiving and let God do what only God can do.

Inclusive spirituality was our foundation. We had not compromised our values to keep the funds. Now that the funds were less and more challenging to secure, we were rooted and ready to create. We held to the hope of knowing we were doing what was life-giving with God's people. We looked forward to God making a way for His people to thrive.

"Partners for Peacemakers" – Gardens of Forgiving – focus: FAMILY

Two factors began to work for us. First, we were not spread so thinly. There was a five-hour drive between Chicago and Detroit. Second, the Raskob funding had given us seed funds to secure a CEO to be the successor who would work with the boards and staff to do what we knew would work. We had been able to protect this resource throughout our downsizing.

It was time to create new ways to offer spiritual development among young adults who were to start into their college careers and begin family life. We had fewer funds, so our work would need to be primarily done by self-supported people.

New ways to do the inclusive spirituality of Life Directions came forth. Our weekend retreats would be done by teams and offered to people from both sites. Within Chicago and Detroit, we designed one-day workshops called "Partners for Peacemakers" with ongoing growth kept together through creating and maintaining gardens.

The world in which we are living is fragile and unpredictable. What a perfect place for understanding that walking creates the path for those who let go of being in control and let God do what only God can do. This is the genius behind the Partners For Peacemakers Workshops. A five-step way of moving from victims to self-responsible people opened us up to be balanced in our relationships, seeing each other as partners on the journey.

This is how it works. First, what is the "mess" we are in? Let the people create their own poster board. Now it is right in front of us, Step two is what is the "mess-age" that comes out of it that we want to give to the next generation? It is amazing how dreams come back to life! Step three, who are the messengers? Hello! We are together. Step four, we need to take ourselves where we are and decide what to do. Examples are to build gardens connected to public schools, to build a youth board of teenagers to paint a mural or work on a garden, to have programs of enrichment for young families and activities where all the people they know can come for an intergenerational way of celebrating life. Step five is the critical moment to determine sustainability by the volunteers. If it's sustainable, then the self-supported will lead the circle and work with whatever resources are available from staff. This is the model that worked in the 1970s.

We designed a way for financially-challenged families with children less than five years of age to be spiritually strengthened. We redesigned our Neighborhood Enrichment Program by creating "focus: FAMILY," a program we tested in 1977 but discontinued when we still had full-time youth workers. Now it would be a guide for young families to turn their obstacles into opportunities from fellow peer families.

We had no idea that we would be stepping into the struggle of immigration. We brought together families who were seeking to be in the country legally. When one family shared how one of their friends was sent back to Mexico with no warning, we knew we were dealing with young adults who had a different set of challenges.

I remember how the families wanted to make sure they were doing what they needed to do. They wanted to get themselves ready to raise their children here in the United States. They needed to learn the reality of our country. It was amazing to see those who have been in Detroit teaching others how to relate to people of different cultures and languages.

They focused on their strengths, their family life, and their love for their elders. These ways of seeing their life as a gift put a smile on their faces and hope in their talking through their challenges. Their getting to know people who have been here gave them a path to walk.

Creative ways to "make lemonade out of lemons" is what Life Directions does best. As traumatic events led other agencies to paralyzing analysis, the recession led us to rigorous downsizing, cutting our programs by 80%. Through it all, we worked in schools and neighborhoods, touching lives effectively and efficiently.

Comedian Bill Cosby was once asked if he saw the glass as half full or half empty. He gave the answer his mother taught him: "It depends on who's pouring!"

We saw the glass half full because we knew God was doing

the pouring! Judith's mantra was oh so relevant: "Build with a foundation of self-supported people, so when the funds are cut, the children aren't lost."

We remember, and we radiate hope. Major funding drew us off-mission. It also made us aware of our need to manage by talents within us more than by objectives beyond us. 9/11 opened us up to the Raskob Foundation to build a succession plan. The stimulus money that we never received was the gift we did not see at the time. We never expanded beyond what we could maintain.

A major growth made it possible for so much to be accomplished with so few resources. And our boards of trustees were, and continue to be, integral to the response. They have been leading us to build visibility through expanding our support system of donors who believe in the "ounce of prevention" approach to life. They have ensured that we keep our eye on the growth potential in social media. It is amazing what more you can do with less with which to do it.

Our journey since 2001 can be described as a "Pearl of Great Price." The fragility of our efforts to reclaim our roots was all part of the dynamics of our journey. We prayed to listen well and follow the path of our Master. Out of listening was a flow of understanding that brought about tough but vibrant transformation.

THE PARABLE OF WATCHING THE HAND

The master was asked by two young people to teach them how to be aware. They wanted to know in order to make and keep a permanent commitment. The master invited them to discover their level of awareness. He took a glass of sour grape juice. He asked them to do exactly what he did. He put his finger into the glass. He put his finger to his tongue. He did not react at all. The two did the same. When they put their finger to their mouth, the taste was so sour they spit it out.

"You did not do what I did."

"Yes, we did. We put our finger in the glass and then into our mouth!"

"I put my first finger in the glass and my second in my mouth."

1. What does the story say about focusing on the other person and putting aside what you think?

2. What does it take to forget about oneself, concentrate on the other, and be fully aware of the other?

3. What does such an attitude say about making a permanent commitment?

CHAPTER EIGHT
YOUNG ADULTS: SHIFTING THE PARADIGM ON PURPOSE

To respond to violence is the litmus test of love. To paraphrase Gandhi, it seems that everyone knows what Jesus stood for except those who call themselves "Christians." Gandhi said he likes the Christian teaching, but has yet to meet a Christian.

Being a Christian, I took his challenge personally. I could not change others, but I wanted to know if I could change myself, not only to remember what Jesus did but also to do what I remember.

I was once told *not* to tell our story until I was seventy years old. The advice came from that very wise priest, Msgr. Clem Kern of Detroit, who had helped us get started with raising support. Judith MacDonald had said that it would take forty years before people would believe us. Now it seemed to be the right time to tell our story. In July 2013, I was given the opportunity to go to the desert in the Middle East to put into writing our journey to encourage young people to find hope within their own journey. When I arrived, the Islamic people were a few days into Ramadan, their month of prayer and fasting. I would live within the community seeking to understand their path to perfection.

Mark Twain wrote a small book called *The War Prayer* in 1905, as the world was about to launch its first world war at the time he was told it was not the right time to go public with the message. It was published posthumously in 1916 in *Harper's Weekly*. It told of a group of Christians praying in a country church in Middle America. They were praying for our soldiers to kill others and save their own. Jesus walked in, dressed as a German soldier and shared his dilemma. The other side was praying the same prayer. Whom should he answer? Which side should he save? Twain's adventures of Tom Sawyer and Huckleberry Finn were selling well at the time. It was not the time for this message. When I read it recently, I was also encouraged to wait—the vision has its time. Is now the time?

I thought of how other people see suicide bombers causing violence. But I have been with people who believe in the compassion of Allah written in the Qur'an. I know how easy it is to judge a book by its cover. I was grateful to be there where no one would know my life by just seeing "the cover." I would look like an ordinary person from the United States on a temporary visa. The gift to listen in silence was the gift that made possible "remembering."

I found myself living among neighbors and people like my friends back in the States, except some of them had the titles "The Taliban" and "Al Qaeda". As I went through security and check points at the airport, I discovered why I was there: to listen to the streets of Detroit and Chicago. I remembered what Pete Raskob had asked, "You can get to the cause of what led to 9/11?"

After forty years, I was about to tell how we had found the cause of violence. I was about to put in print what I promised to share. It lies within our story, our journey to find hope within despair. And I knew most of us could find the cure, if we would only want to take the time to know.

Life—this is the focus of my journey into forgiving. I am aware of my gender; men are seen as the aggressors. I turned up the stereo—the "stereotyping" that surrounds me. It is my cover, if you will, hiding within the unopened book. My race is Caucasian. We designed most of the international acts of violence in the twentieth century and before. My cultural roots are a hybrid of the Irish— both Northern and Southern Ireland and the English from Wales. Ann Wilson Schaef, author of *When Society Becomes an Addict* (1988; new edition, 2013), looks at our addictive culture as an all-encompassing societal matrix of white male conditioning and influence. Do not judge the book by its cover. My career has a Roman collar. I found it interesting that, as I came to the Middle East, I knew *not* to wear it. It would be no different from my experience in the public schools. Before arriving, I had practice about which most people would never know.

Neurologist, psychiatrist, and Holocaust survivor, Victor Frankl understood that the gift Solomon sought, more than all others, was "logo therapy." He found this way to wisdom in a concentration camp. He was set free in 1946 only to find that the love of his life had died in 1942, the year I was born. But he knew she was still alive within him. His memory of her was the reason he lived to tell the story: "if you know 'why', you can endure any 'how.'"

As a child, I was never to enter a public school, yet I remember my father saying to my mother, "Margaret, the Catholic Church has got to get out of the school business. It costs too much."

I went back to my home town of St. Louis, "the Gateway to the West," just two years before the 150th anniversary of the Dred Scott decision. I was to be the pastor of a beautiful community of African Americans at St. Alphonsus Liguori "Rock" Catholic Church. My parents grew up there, when it was segregated. My Redemptorist history professor, who was pastor for about a year, integrated the church in 1943.

I came to the "Rock" as a Redemptorist, part of the group of men in our Church called to encourage forgiving as the way to be excellent. I opened my album to share some pictures of my past. I saw the soccer team I was on when I was five—all white like me. I wondered why. I knew our Catholic grade school was integrated. Is this why our sports programs were parish-based and not school-based? I kept the picture secret—only to be at my night stand. I wondered if I would be judged by the "cover."

Being judged by my "cover," my Roman collar as a pastor, was the same reason I could not go into Vashon Public High School in St. Louis. I was out of position. I could go as the CEO of Life Directions, but I would not be acceptable as pastor of a Catholic Church; I would be judged as having a hidden agenda. It would be seen as illegal to do anything as a pastor.

"Mine eyes have seen the glory of the coming of the Lord" was sung in 1968 as Bobby Kennedy's body rode to his gravesite. His was the last of the four high-profile assassinations of the time. It was three weeks before I was ordained a priest.

As stated earlier, a coincidence is God's way to be anonymous. It is no accident that I worked in a public school, unable to network with the Catholic school system. It is no accident that Life Directions became a not-for-profit to ensure we could live on both sides of the "separate-but-equal" wall of Church and State.

Why? I believe we were meant to lead the walk to gradually bring forgiving out of violence. I know it works; it is my story. I am well aware of being disrespected. I am also conscious of the moments when I did the same. No rescuer can erase those moments. Depending on the depth of the hurt, the memory is profound and irremovable. My scars, once healed, are the gift that opened me to focus on life that comes out of death.

I discovered that no one will take away my joy as I grow in forgiving those who want to kill me, in the various ways we, as a people, encourage violence. I sensed my mission was to wake up others to the energy of forgiving as the way out of violence. I remembered what Jesus did, and I wanted to do what I remembered.

I began with myself and my siblings. I continued with my gender and culture. I faced my faith community and peer group. A path of self-destruction is labeled as addiction or sin, depending on what side of the "wall of separation" you are on.

Knowing my own story and remembering those whose love continues to heal me, I am so grateful for the forty years of stories of people shifting the paradigm. It is no accident. Its purpose is clear: the needle threads the quilt of our torn lives, one stitch at a time. All are included, except those who say "no." The decision is for each of us to make: either end up as Judas Iscariot or continue as Simon Peter. Jesus did his best; He gave his life for both of them, as he did for all of us.

Why is it that when we put our words into God's mouth, we justify violence? We may call it a "just" war, but when God put his Word into our mouths, He killed no one. Why did He not start a "just" war, when His followers were being killed? Why did He transform Saul into His apostle? Amazing how God killed no one. Why not?

Why is it that excellence cannot seem to include everyone? It does in the Special Olympics. Just to get to the finish line is to win. It takes keeping faith within and fighting the good fight. For most, if not all, a spiritual bypass will turn the hardened heart into a heart of flesh pumping blood into the body and all its parts. I wonder if we can learn to know this by heart if we are willing to practice seven times seventy times.

What a privilege to be chosen to be sent—a white Catholic Christian priest and a citizen of the most powerful nation in the world to follow the legacy of unconditional love for those who often judge me by my cover. I was trained to forgive by those who reject me. What a privilege to be trained for such a marathon, not for the silver or gold, but for the crippled to walk.

And to be telling my story while living during the second term of the first African American President and doing so during the fiftieth anniversary year of the "I Have a Dream" speech. What a privilege, for which I am not entitled, so others can have the same gift for their children's sake. Just act tenderly, lovingly, and humbly while walking—it is the message of Micah (6:8) that never stops for-giving. Each of us decides to give *or not* for the sake of the one who violated us.

I noticed the Bible could not be found in the public school. I saw its absence as a type of non-verbal lesson. Since it is said that more than ninety percent of all messages are non-verbal, I paid attention, as Mary of Nazareth did. I reflected on it in my heart. The Bible was not in the public school library. Young people in public prisons were allowed to have one. I reflected on this teaching in my heart, unintended though it may be. Bibles are okay in public prisons, but not in public schools. Why is this so?

I was asked to lead a prayer at Wendell Phillips High School, when it was on the verge of closing in 1991. I stepped on the stage where the ministers were sitting. I looked at the students, all African American, clapping for me as they sat in the auditorium. Juanita Tucker, the principal, asked me to pray. I went to the microphone. "All who can legally pray, please stay." There was a hush. "Ms. Tucker, the school does not have a prayer ... from me," I said. "It is against the law."

Ten years later on September 12, 2001, I noticed a "God Bless America" banner on the school's wall. Fear created a bridge between Church and State. I wondered if it was noticed and if it was intended. I was grateful we had found a way around the "separate-but-equal" law. However, it took violence to make the "way out" of what some considered "no way."

Why is it that 9/11 made possible what was not permitted before?

Be Free – The First Discovery

It was at a focus: LIFE weekend where the drama of a family fight was acted out by six young adults who did not know each other. One of the adults, Mary Ann, had brought up a situation that happened four years before as the story she would use. Her mother was an alcoholic who did not want her child around. Mary Ann was angry and took it out on a teacher. She got suspended for five days. Her mother never came to the school. Mary Ann remembered getting back in the school, but not *how*. But she never forgot what her mom did to her. During the role-playing exercise, she was asked how it had felt.

"Felt? It still feels … feels like I am dirt," Mary Ann replied. Her friend started to cry. Mary Ann was stunned.

"Why are you crying?" she asked the friend.

"Because I want to understand," was the response.

There were about thirty of us on the weekend. We all debriefed what happened. The way we taught each other was amazing. It was like watching a quilt being stitched together with each person on the week-end being a piece speaking "freedom".

Watching the smile come across Mary Ann's face, as her tears started, was not as amazing as her saying, "I forgive my mom. I am only sorry she's dead."

Learning coming out from the stories of each other cannot just heal wounds but it can also lead others who were wondering which direction to go in life. From that weekend came a person who went on to become a police officer. Another became a teacher, and one studied to be a social worker, while another became a minister. It is what happens when the climate to explore knowledge is open to involve each other.

Mary Ann is but one of the thousands of young adults who came to discover forgiving from violence. As I look back over the thirty-nine years of focus: LIFE weekends, I am so grateful for all the learning that has been given. I am grateful to have discovered that the mystery of life is so close—it is one question away from being opened, but it will happen if the one asking sees the answer lying within the other.

This is the way we discover how to awaken a hunger for the Power Greater Than Human among people who were spiritually anorexic. The question is the key, but turning the lock takes "forgiving others and myself, and letting God do the rest."

If we do not sow the seeds of forgiving, we will know why we left the world we touched bankrupt of vision! The inclusive spirituality of Life Directions centers on changing the paradigm of victim and persecutor to responsible partnerships. The very person who I have seen as my enemy is the one who needs my forgiveness to know the freedom that is only mine to give for their sake.

The life and legacy of Dr. Martin Luther King, Jr. also served as inspiration that complimented the work of Paulo Freire *(Pedagogy of the Oppressed)* and Dietrich von Hildebrand *(Fundamental Moral Attitudes)*. Our "team of five" was particularly drawn to King's 1963 book *Strength to Love.* We saw it as a guide to forgiving as a way to life. King started writing during a fifteen-day stint in what he described as a "dirty, filthy, and ill-equipped" segregated Albany, Georgia, jail cell. He penned a series of sermons that chastised a world that was wasting human life due to racial hatred, poverty, and violence.

King prescribed love as the potent social and political force for change. Personal transformation is at the root of achieving real and true worldwide social justice, he maintained. As I prayed over what he said, I was encouraged to stay the course. I may not see change through peace-building, but I believe unconditional love will overcome evil someday. By reaching beyond ourselves and tapping the transcendent moral ethic of love, King believed we shall overcome evil.

We also took great insight from the *U.S. Catholic Bishops' Statement to the Native American People* (May 1974). When they wanted to focus our attention on segregation in the United States, they mentioned the deepest wrong, as they saw it. The enslaving of African Americans was wrong; the oppression of Hispanic Americans was wrong.

But, perhaps, an even deeper wrong was the way Native Americans had everything taken from them, including their land and language, with broken treaties. To "face into all injustice," the Bishops' Statement said, will call for a humility that will set everyone free.

Our work in Tucson among the Pascua Yaqui Tribe faced this injustice. We wanted to encourage the Native American people to do what they could to make high school work for them. We found families who wanted to pass on their values and not let the burgeoning casino business destroy them through greed or addictions.

Having family gatherings after the focus: LIFE weekend retreats would lead to sharing stories from their past. Young adults would hear the elders remember the past and celebrate their ancestors. We wanted to spend time together as Hispanic, Native, and European Americans. It was healing and enriching to all. It was a powerful witness to the importance of mutual respect and encouragement of being peace-builders.

Be Excellent – The Second Discovery

How to awaken a hunger for what money cannot buy and without which people cannot live is the question that opened us up to seeing the importance of respecting each culture and ethnic community. We set up conversation groups, asking young adults to name their culture. They responded rather easily. But when we asked them to explain their culture, the responses were very different.

Francisco, a young adult who had been on a focus: LIFE weekend became part of leading a neighborhood group of mixed cultures. They had been together long enough to start to trust each other. An African American young man, who had been rather quiet, spoke up and confessed that he wanted to find a way out of the gang he was in. He did not know how.

From nowhere, it seemed, Francisco spoke up. "Do you want to get out? If you do, I am willing to walk with you. Someone helped me to get my act together. It is time for me to do the same.

"People talk about the problem but never fix it. They say the problems cannot be fixed, but I say why talk about it and not fix it? My parents had to leave their country to come here and make it for us kids. I woke up one day and said it is time for me to take charge of my life, before I lose it.

"I do not judge you because you're in a gang. I want to judge you because you want to get out and make something of yourself. You're the driver of your car and not a passenger. What you want for your family is the decision to make."

The group got real quiet. They heard stories of people wanting to get out of gangs. They knew Francisco's challenge, and his willingness to walk with the young man had changed the dynamic. It took time but it worked. Why?

Francisco had gotten in touch with his own worth. He wanted something better for his future. He did not want to mess it up. But he went further. He cared about someone who was in a mess like he used to be.

The group had begun by talking about the externals—food, clothes and music—but this issue was much more challenging. It was getting into values. It pushed them to explore the core value of being men or women and remembering their roots. These kinds of confrontations to take charge of our lives are life-changing. It takes a lot of time to build the trust that makes it happen.

When we tie it into culture and the struggle that people have gone through, the present challenge looks different. It is then that wanting to connect with a Power Greater Than Human is real. We pretty much know they will need something more than what we have to make such a change. When something this real surfaces, we explore our relationship to a Power Greater Than Human.

We approach faith traditions with a sense of reverence. We see each community of faith as a gift. It is the genius of the Creator. It is a joy to encourage the same path of discovery of creeds that we use with cultures. On the weekend that focuses on "Life" we awaken a thirst to *want* to know more about the Creator.

We encourage each other to follow that thirst, knowing it will lead to a way of seeing life that goes beyond what money and power can offer. We do so in seeking the power to see that forgiveness to overcome violence is integral to all mature faith-based efforts.

We strive to encourage all people to be excellent. We picture the quest for excellence with asking "why" we were chosen to know the Power Greater than Human as we do. "Whatever culture you are or whatever creed to which you belong, be excellent." With this mantra, we reinforce the diversity of culture and creeds and the importance of operating at the same level of respect.

Beyond Our Control – The Third Discovery

Recently, at a conference in Birmingham, Fr. Alex heard Paul Tough, the author of *How Children Succeed*. Since we work within public schools, I read Tough's book as it centered heavily on the results of school system reform in Chicago under the leadership of Arnie Duncan and his succession as CEO of the city's public schools. What I found, however, was a professional study that explains what makes the focus: LIFE process so important. The CEOs were working to create "cultures of calm" within the school. They were working to reduce violence. They failed, as the study verified.

Simply put, public education is doing what it knows best to do: academic development. What is lacking, and what we believe schools are *not* designed to do, is to build ways for long-lasting and mature life choices. This is beyond the scope of schools and is best engaged in the community.

The efforts at reform have not made the difference. It measures the outcomes it sought to achieve. Test scores showed improvement in a number of areas but to see character development as a life-changing result was not one of the outcomes shown. To expect to get to the cause of violence that is crippling so many is beyond all that was designed and implemented.

What the results showed is that Life Directions is engaging the right issues and doing so in the right setting—the community, with the families and the young people who live there. If what is needed is alive *within* the community, it makes the difference in the life of the schools.

In a study conducted by the University of Illinois at Urbana-Campaign, Brent Roberts underscored what Life Directions does best as far as character development in young people. We focus on the development of EQ (Emotional Quotient) and SQ (Spiritual Quotient) that was explained in the introduction. Simply put, we work among young adults over eighteen years of age to motivate those in high school who will follow their example of doing positive actions when surrounded by the negative. This frees them up to choose to faithfully grow their SQ.

The study looked at what is emerging to encourage SQ, namely "organizational psychology." As I studied Paul Tough's work, I realized that approach of psychology does not hold much influence in prestigious universities. It is usually seen as valuable for consultants or human resource managers in large corporations with very specific needs. It is far removed from esoteric academic debates. It is called up in corporations who want the most productive, reliable, and diligent workers they can find.

As I was reading the findings, I thought of the course I received from the Gallup Organization. What I gained was in harmony with what the study promoted as integral to a mature and productive life: "talent-matching and strength-finders work for life."

The outcome of Roberts' study in Chicago points to one indicator of a mature person, namely "conscientiousness." The profile of such a person is to have *grit*: the energy to see "failure" as but a challenge along the way. It takes *self-control*: learning from failure and looking for another way; *zest* to live after searching for another way; *social intelligence*: enjoying the diversity that opens new ways to seeing. *Gratitude* becomes a way of life for those who are thankful, knowing life is a gift to be reverenced. *Optimism* is grounded in believing in the "not-yet," and *curiosity* is the spark for the journey into hope.

Amazing Studies Tell Why Forgiving Is the Way – The Fourth Discovery

My two-week course with Paulo Freire helped me discover that our team of five was revolutionary leaders in our own right. We do not think *about* the people or *for* the people. We five seek to think and feel *with* the people. *Pedagogy of the Oppressed* is where Freire proposes a new science of teaching. The book is widely considered a critical foundation of effective teaching. Freire, a renowned international leader of oppressed people, introduced a new manner of inductive learning.

He positions people who are going to learn to begin with what they know, not with what the instructor knows. We found that this method is essential when encouraging young adults and adults over eighteen years of age to reflect upon their experience of relating to their spiritual journey.

Freire invited professional educators to look at the traditional model of education. The "question" was key. Did we see the teacher as having the knowledge? Do we see young people as having to know what teachers know? What would happen if our learning together began with what young people know? What would happen if the teacher learned what young people know by the questions they asked and the answers given?

This method which begins with the teacher is known as "banking knowledge." The other way is "inductive learning." "Banking" sees the student as an empty vessel. The teacher is to fill that vessel like a person is a piggy bank in need of coins (or knowledge) that they do not have. Students go to school to get their grades based upon remembering what is been "put in the bank," what the teacher told them to remember. If, after graduation, they do not have answers that work, they are considered bankrupt--maybe in more ways than one.

This method puts the priority on what to think and remember. It does not encourage the integration of new information based on what the student already knows. It does not encourage people to think for themselves and to learn how to build on their experiences in life. It does not address knowledge from where a person is-how they learn to think through what they already know or how to add more information to it.

This way of approaching others can lead people to think they have little to offer others. They are meant only to receive. What little they have is not worth as much as what the teacher will give. When oppressed people are treated this way, they may feel unqualified to even think for themselves. As a result, repressed anger can build up. Consciously or subconsciously, they see themselves systematically denied their own dignity. This can actually lead to violence.

Freire believed that the learner should be treated as the "co-creator of knowledge." His inductive method freed people who were less literate and helped them gain a sense of their own worthiness based on what they knew.

I had the pleasure of taking a two-week workshop in the summer of 1971 presented by Paulo Freire with Father Dan Berrigan, a prominent Jesuit priest in the Peace Movement of the '60s. Through them, I learned much about freeing people to discover what we know is worth knowing and a way we can open up to gain new information. This is done by giving what we know and receiving what we do not know. In fact, it was amazing to see how people themselves discovered what they did not know and now wanted to learn.

Remember Bill Kilburg, the young man who was so confident that his basketball talents were the end-all and be-all of his existence (Chapter Two)? A "Trust Walk" with a paraplegic was the beginning of his transformation. Once Bill discovered that his talent was a gift, he was able to move away from feeling like he was entitled to be recognized, to a place where he felt humbled that he was given a gift to share with others. When he could learn a new way of seeing his abilities, he understood himself in a way he would never forget. It was built into what he knew.

Forgiving Has Its Own Time – The Fifth Discovery

With people who feel oppressed, Freire's pedagogy is amazingly profound: before speaking *for* the oppressed, make sure they agree with what you're saying. After all, they are the ones who will have to live with the results of your words and actions. The *Pedagogy of the Oppressed* served as a way to awaken a hunger for people to understand themselves.

This discipline for the less literate served us in helping the socially, economically, and spiritually oppressed, especially those who were not aware of the oppression. Awareness came as they listened to their own stories and heard themselves put into words what had happened. I was grateful we could begin to open them to new ways of responding. It is the miracle that happens, when the other knows you know and you receive them just the way they are.

Dietrich and Alice von Hildebrand expressed the inclusive spirituality of forgiving as a response to violence. They were engaging issues such as world hunger and world wars. Their meaning of reverence was their primary Moral Attitude. They wrote as German citizens reflecting on the world five years after World War II.

Dietrich and Alice von Hildebrand's assertion that we should respect and reverence moral values as the highest of natural values resonates with us. When we seek to make concrete abstract values like goodness, purity, truthfulness and humility, we focus on what "sparks us", what excites us. We then say that is our life direction. We ask people to *want* violence to end and to respect each other. We ask that they consider the damage that comes from what people say about others and how humility grows through humiliations. When we have more than five or six people, there is a lived experience of each of these values.

When I studied von Hildebrand, I found myself wanting to find ways to show how building a burning and selfless love can be more significant, more important and eternal than all cultural values. I agreed that negative moral values are responsible for the greatest evils—worse than suffering, sickness, death, or the disintegration of a people. We too believe the alternative to negative moral values and its results is to focus on and develop positive moral values through forgiving.

Dietrich and Alice von Hildebrand's work drove home the integrity of values based upon spiritual rootedness. They were inclusive European thinkers who pushed the envelope to encourage all people of goodwill to want truth and full integrity to be reverenced. In other words, everyone must be included in what they were bringing forth as *their* truth.

We held fast to our belief in the value of each person keeping his or her balance in relationship to everyone else through forgiving and walking with others, who were following the "law of gradualness." (See Chapter Two.) We know the value. We live the value. If each person seeks the way to the truth that centers on including everyone, we will all find *the way* some day.

Losing Control with Self-Control – The Sixth Discovery

We were getting to the heart of violence: thinking it impossible to forgive…just because. We were getting to the core of the resistance: we want a reason to forgive. The reason would be conditional love that makes forgiving more a masquerade than the mystery that it really is.

As I mentioned earlier, Ann Wilson Schaef, the author of *When Society Becomes an Addict*, discusses our addictive culture. The root cause of society's addictions, according to her, is based on the belief that we are in control of who we are. One of the illusions of our society that also leads to spiritual anorexia is the teaching that anyone can be anything they want to be. This is simply not true. I do not have Michael Jordan's basketball talent or skills. No one can just step up and decide to become an Einstein. These are special gifts.

A symptom of spiritual anorexia is the idea that we can control God or the belief that "I am going to control the Creator's way of relating to me." Seeking to control God is what fuels addictions to sex, drinking, drugs, defaming others, gambling, violence or any form of self-destructive behavior. In fact, many end up taking their own lives because they tried to control the One who gave them life. The more we try to control life, the more we are going to kill it.

However, once an individual relinquishes control, they can discover that they have been *given* skills and talents. They can enter into a real relationship with the Creator that connects them with all His creation. They come to realize that they are not entitled to life but that everything is a gift from the source of life.

Relinquishing control of external factors can actually help individuals take personal responsibility for their own lives and choices. Dr. Leo Rasca worked with us in Marion County, Oregon. His doctoral dissertation studied African, Hispanic, and Native Americans who complete college. According to his study, only ten percent of those who begin college will graduate. The two values they had in common: they may be the first to graduate in their families and they have a spiritual rootedness to survive the challenge. He tells the story of Myra, a young woman who was a team leader on our retreats:

"Myra had come to one of our focus: LIFE Retreats and at first regretted her decision. She arrived on a Friday, hands clenched and filled with anger. But, by the next day, something happened. There was a transition in her attitude. Myra realized that her life was chained by the hurt she had received from her father. She told of his leaving her mother, younger sister, and her to make it on their own.

"She remembers forgiving him during the retreat. She made a conscious choice to let it go. She wanted to get on with her life. She was not going to hold on to his not being there at her graduation. She was going to let go and let God do whatever He does.

"Myra finished at Chemeteka Community College," Dr. Rasca continued. "She was very active in the Life Circle. She went on to Willamette University in Oregon. In 2007 the Board of Trustees of Marion County nominated her to receive the Governor's 'Young Adult Achievement Award' given annually to an outstanding young adult who had turned his or her life around. Myra received her award with a standing ovation from all of us.

"Myra married Ricardo Larios. They have one child, Ricardo, Jr. Myra works in the juvenile court, and Ricardo teaches at Waldo. He opens his classroom after school to do the Peer Mentor program that he learned eight years ago. They are truly a shining beacon of hope."

I am thankful for our co-founder, Judith, for teaching us to know the reason why we do what we do and build it with "self-supported volunteers." This way, the mission continues without funds, which is happening through Ricardo.

The key to Myra's turn-around was taking responsibility for her life. Self-responsibility is achieved when awakened young people decide to turn away from seeing themselves as being "victimized" by external factors. Through peer-to-peer inspiration they are moved to declare, "If I want to be, I am in control of my responses to whatever happens to me, both good and bad." "

It is the essence of what we promote. Recognize that you have a unique gift that is meant to be given to others. It is then that you understand a way to express unconditional love and forge relationships based on forgiving.

Awaken the Gifts for the Next Generation – Yet-to-Be Discovered

Education can either condition generations of young people to accept society's status quo or encourage them to be different. To dare to be different gives us the freedom to deal critically and creatively with reality and discover how to transform our worlds.

Life Directions has designed a four-plateau approach to walk the mountain of forgiving drawn out of violence. The *first plateau* is the Peer Motivation and Peer Mentor Program, where high-school-aged young people become CPAs, "Certified Peer Achievers." The *second plateau* is focus: LIFE One, for young adults after high school to move from seeing themselves entitled to life to knowing their "spark" is their talent, the gift they have received. The *third plateau* is focus: LIFE Two, for young adults and adults who want to see how their talents can be gifts for others. The *fourth plateau* is to see how unconditional love can transform F.E.A.R. as "False Expectations Appearing Real" into the beginning of wisdom as "Forgiving Excels Always Redeeming." Seeking to live this value is to be a "Gift for the Next Generation."

Each person is free to climb the mountain…or not. All we do is invite and wait. The invitation gives people the ability to respond. It is then their "response-ability." Focusing on redemptive and unconditional love never forces anyone. The most natural place to receive unconditional love is from the bond between the two who birthed us. But even if this is not how our life began, this invitation to see may be a way to find the God who makes a way out of no way.

The first plateau centers on discovering my talents and what sparks me. Activities like gardening can give everyone a chance to discover that talents are like seeds. They are planted in us, but they need to be watered and nurtured along. This is what the discipline of getting ready for the adult world is all about. To be a Certified Peer Achiever (CPA) is to want to be ready to make college or career viable options. Once young people complete high school, they can go on with their lives.

Tim, the young man I mentioned earlier in this book whom I met at Southwestern High School, enjoyed our Peer Motivation Sessions. A Palestinian Muslim American, Tim especially liked our way of encouraging people to share the richness and diversity of cultures. He was comfortable explaining the ways of living values within his culture and appreciating those of other cultures.

Tim graduated from our first plateau and went on with his life. I was honored to be invited to his wedding in Dearborn, Michigan. I was even more grateful when I heard he had become a lawyer and was interested in having a Jewish partner. What a gift his roots are for people who are different from him and, likewise, others are a gift to him.

The second plateau opens our eyes to see that we were not entitled to be born. We had nothing to do with that decision. Being out-of-control was the way we began life. Since birth, we may have used others through seduction or deception to gain control because we are conditioned to want to be in control. We may have hurt or violated others. If we want to move on with our lives, we must forgive ourselves and others, for such a way of treating each other; it is our decision to make. We discover our strengths that we may never have known are within us. We are responsible for our own lives, striving to use our talents as the gifts they are.

It will be important for us to want to discover *why* we were given the talents and gifts that we have. Do we want to know how we are meant to be a gift for others as others are meant to be gifts for us?

We are like animals in the sense that we have a body and a brain. What makes us human is our power to reflect and find the meaning—the "why" behind the "how." What makes us more than human is our ability to forgive and cherish life beyond our own lifetimes.

This is what philosopher and theologian, St. Thomas Aquinas, meant when he described humans as "rational animals made for others." The last part of the quote seems to get dropped as societies moved into individualism. We may want to see no value in others unless it serves our individual interest. But if I exist for somebody else, I am an individual person "made for others." As I mature in my awareness of our interdependence on each other, I want to relate to all of life. I do not want to destroy anyone or anything. I may be destroying myself in the process.

In Detroit many know Hansen H. Clarke, the Democratic U.S. Representative for Michigan's thirteenth congressional district and the first U.S. Congressman of Bangladeshi descent. Born in Detroit, Clarke's father, an immigrant from India, died at an early age. Clarke's mother, whose heritage was Afro-Caribbean and Native American, struggled as a crossing guard to support her family. When I met Hansen, he wanted to attend college but saw no way to raise the money to pay for his education.

I basically challenged him to wake up and not see himself as a loser. He came on the focus: LIFE retreat in the early 1980s. He was personable and connected well with others. They encouraged him. He heard it by his encouraging others. Hansen completed the second plateau. He sees Life Directions this way: "It gave me hope when I had no hope." He is grateful to see the value of taking responsibility for his talents that were much needed in public life. This is what led him into higher education and a career in politics.

Our third plateau explores life as less than human (violent) and as more than human (forgiving). We share how we connect with the Creator. We encourage all of us to be excellent in prayer and fasting and almsgiving—the disciplines that sustain life that is greater than human.

I mentioned the co-founders, Alexander and Judith MacDonald. Patrick, their second oldest of eight children, completed his education enough to know he was a born skilled trades person. His "spark" is to work with his hands, and he does it very well. I asked Patrick to be an Adult Mentor. He came to know us when he was nine. That was thirty-eight years ago. He had attended a focus: LIFE Two weekend and faced the challenge to see his talents and gifts as bringing meaning and life to others. I asked him to encourage high school students to mentor eighth-graders.

He really got to like it. He made time to be with the mentors assigned to him. He wanted to give back. When I asked Patrick to join our Board of Trustees, he said "yes." Even after having second thoughts, he sees himself as the next generation of young adults. It is now his turn and his peers' turn.

This book is a representation of our fourth plateau: "Our Gift for the Next Generation." Basically, you and I are the gifts for the next generation. This book has not been written for me or those associated with Life Directions exclusively. It was written for others who want to follow us. We have written this book for others, remembering those from whom we received what we gave.

The fourth plateau is the one that will continue our way of encouraging forgiving to get to the cause of violence. To step up to this challenge takes a person who sees the value of being an elder—a wisdom person who wants to stay the course for the long run.

Tom Howard is such a person. As I mentioned in Chapter Six, we met in October 1990 at Farragut High School in the middle of the mess I spoke of when the Mexican grandmother cried for her murdered grandson. Tom came to know our work. He left his job and joined us. He was promoted to the role of executive director of Chicago.

He took a turn in his career to deepen the challenge of excellence within his family's culture and faith community. As his children are completing their college careers and moving on with their lives, Tom is now one of the corporate members of Life Directions. He is one of the people willing to do his best to give to the next generation what was given to him and his family.

Gifts Within – Grateful Discoveries

When Annette called me in 2010, I could not remember her at first. She said she wanted to make it possible for the next generation of young people to have the experience she had. I had just come back into Life Directions seeking to build up the board and the staff looking to do whatever it would take to implement our succession plan.

"Fr. John, let me tell you," Annette began. "I have been all over the place seeking to help troubled youth. I was a probation officer for a while. My degree in social work gave me the tools I needed, but it did not give me 'that seed' that was planted in me back in 1974, when I was sixteen years old. I am now a foster parent with two adopted teens. I have seen it all. I want to write my story."

"Annette, weren't you in Will and Tina's circle?" I asked.

"Yes, I was one of the ten in the circle; they were great, and the circle was the landing strip after the 'mountain top' life-changing focus: LIFE, as you call it now. Most of us went on to college. Joel is a state policeman. Linda is a judge. Carl completed Notre Dame and is doing great."

Annette went on with what she had been doing with her life. We talked for two good hours discussing her life struggles, the traumatic shooting near her home on the west side, her spiritual journey through a Protestant seminary and her recent challenge to face her younger sister's passing.

I sensed Annette wanted to stay connected. I asked what she was doing and she explained it in such a way that I could hear an opening to partner with us.

"Would you be open to working part-time with me at Western International High School?" I asked. Within a week, Annette came back to say "yes" to my offer. The trust that set her free and the "forgiving" that keeps her alive would be part of the building of our foundation.

Most of these alumni stories of spiritual awakening happened without us knowing it. That was the beauty of it. It was not like they were learning the Life Directions' way of becoming excellent. They learned that they had their own way of becoming excellent. They had to find it for themselves. It was their quest. We were not responsible for the decisions they would make. We just challenged them to be responsible for those decisions.

"Discernment" is a value upon which many do not reflect. For us, it means the Creator has given us what we need for our life direction. He gave us the talents and gifts to be excellent. But He is not going to force us. As we find our life direction, we will know the joy that comes with discovering who we are and why we are. We will live a full life and be open for a wonderful life beyond time.

If we allow ourselves to consider ourselves as true gifts for others, we will value our talents and skills. It is all going to click. Everything will fit together. We will be amazed at how many connections will suddenly happen.

Peers can inspire each other. Forgiving can give peace a chance. At the end of the day, each of us is free to respond and to decide our Life Direction.

THE PARABLE OF THE BRAKE

The young man wanted to drive the car. It looked great. The dealer gave him the keys. He showed him the petal. He explained the automatic shift. His father told him he could not drive.

"Why? I have gas, my driver's license and insurance."

"You do not have a brake. It is like life. It is one thing to know how to drive. It is another to have the *wisdom* needed to put on the brake. I need to give you a brake and show you how to use it, before you have an accident."

1. What is the reason why knowledge is given without the wisdom to understand?

2. What is the challenge that people of wisdom need to face to give young people a brake so they can drive responsibly and not by accident?

3. What is needed in life to know when to drive and when to brake?

CHAPTER NINE
TEENAGERS: MORE THAN WHAT WE THINK WE ARE

We remember how we would challenge each other not to think we are inadequate. I still say, "Kids are dying. I have been chosen to wake people up before it is too late. And I know I'll do more than I think I can, if I just let go and let God help them do what only they can do, using me." Then I say, "And you too!"

Walking into Western International High School in 1973, I saw the faces of cocky bullies and quiet nerds. I remember seeing the "fear" in their eyes. I would meet them on the streets. Blank stares would hide their isolation. It was not much different from what happens in prison. Survival is to have secrets and to know how to keep them.

At Western we found a way for young people *not* to be so afraid to share their light and talents and to give each other permission to do the same. The insight that made it possible to do what we do best continues to be the genius of our work.

We see the young people as integral to the solution to the problems they and their peers face in their neighborhoods and schools. What they may not know is that when they look to their future they "... are powerful beyond measure!" Maybe that is why Nelson Mandela was the first President to change the paradigm?

Who's Making Money on You?

This question is a deal-changer. It raises the awareness of being an anorexic to values. It is not how we begin a conversation. But eventually we raise the question by having young people talk with each other about being consumers that older people make money off of producing and profiting off what they think they need and want. It is a question that turns on the light for many who do not know they were walking in the dark.

Addictions have quite a power in the lives of many in our world, a power that is even more seductive in poverty communities. Usually you need money to feed it. Crime and violence is a constant challenge. Addiction is simply defined as doing or taking something that achieves three things: first, it "feels right"; second, "I cannot stop", and third, "I am on self-destruct."

There seems to be seven kinds of addictions that impact the lives of young people with whom we work. The three "surface" types, as I call them, are sexual activity, drinking and drugs. The three "substantive" types are destruction of people's character by gossip (bullying—with or without social media), gambling and violence. The final addiction, where all of the above may end, is suicide, taking one's own life.

Dr. Patrick Carnes' book, *Out of the Shadows: Understanding Sexual Addiction* (2001 edition), gives us an up-front explanation of the path into and out of sexual addiction. His book gave me an understanding of what seems to be moving a person toward mental enslavement and what it will take to break out of such a lifestyle.

I was at Southwestern High School for about two years when there was a house fire that took the lives of five people—four children and their mother. There was one survivor; I'll call her "Tina." She told me she wanted to get out of prostitution but "they" would not let her. She was fourteen at the time. I remember her whenever I wonder if what we are doing is worth the effort.

Tina joined one of our groups at school. She was also getting professional help. But the group became for her the support she needed to get her life back in order. We finished the year. I never heard what happened to her, but I haven't forgotten her desire to be free.

Some people have described our Peer Motivation and Peer Mentor Programs as doing what gangs do. The only difference is we have "gangs for good." The needs that we inspire young people and adults to meet are the same types of needs that gangs offer. We are aware that the need to "belong" and to do what we do best is in all of us. To want to make a difference and find my way in life are what gives meaning to life.

Knowing the situations young people are in is not as important as finding *a way* to respond before it is too late. To meet "Tina" at her funeral is too late. What we do, and what we are grateful to have found that other community-based organizations do, is act. We want young people to wake each other up to values that are life-directed. By this we mean to want to choose positive ways of living that are responsible and balanced.

Values that build friendships and partnerships that complement our own talents and dreams. And to keep in mind that our lives can make a difference for the next generation. What is unique about our way is that we see the potential for these values in the lives of the young people themselves. All they need is to be given a chance to take charge of their lives. What we found that works best is for young people to wake up their peers who do not find such values important.

"Anorexics to values" is the phrase we use when young people who do not see positive values as more important than they see themselves as victims of the system. If they remain anorexic, they are at risk of the addictive way of life that is accessible to anyone in our society today.

What is the Problem with Young People and the System?

We have been told that for every one hundred kindergarten children, ninety will get to ninth grade, with forty finishing twelfth grade. Of those forty who finish, ten will sign up for college and only one in two will make it. Given how statistics have a strange shelf-life, we haven't spent a lot of time verifying this data.

In our effort to wake up young people to self-responsibility and freedom from violence, we do not need to spend time on in-depth analysis. There is enough evidence where we work that the majority of people in poverty are not graduating from college or ready for a quality career.

People like Jeff Nelson, CEO of One Goal on Chicago's south side, have done the math. He is responding to the challenges he sees. His way of engaging young people hopes for the following three outcomes: first, young people will learn how to think deeply; second, they will develop internal motivation for life; and finally, that they will want to persevere when facing difficulties. These outcomes speak to us. It is our desire to develop a "hunger" for such a way of looking at ourselves and to do so among anorexics to such values.

Most people know the system is not working. The challenge is what can we do to wake up young people before it is too late for them? That is the question we are living.

Let's revisit the conversation I had with Mayor Daley in March 1995, when he asked, "Father, what would you do if I gave you Chicago Public Schools to break and fix?" What I did not know at the time was that he was about to set out to do just that.

"There are 400,000 kids in the schools from K through 12. Only 200,000 make it through to graduate. There are 65,000 that go to college, and 70,000 go into the prison system," Daley said. "You can add and subtract. But it is about right. What would you do?"

I responded without having any foreknowledge that I was going to be asked this question. I said to make the young person the customer and the teacher the producer. Make sure both student and teacher are ready to meet each other. Make sure the teachers know what they cannot do and what the community is called to do. I explained what our team does in that dynamic.

We want to do what the school system cannot. We want to add value to it with a pyramid of support beginning with adult mentors from the neighborhood and the business communities. We want to ready them to coach high school peer mentors who are Certified Peer Achievers, wanting six social values to direct their actions. We want them ready to mentor eighth-graders to make high school work for them.

I focused on young people being integral to the solution and explained what we do. It is below the radar of major programs. The outcomes are verifiable. I then asked that all programs working with young people would be seen as a matrix of services that create the synergy needed for everyone to become productive adults. I ended by asking for all programs to have a common way of being evaluated with evidenced-based outcomes.

As I mentioned earlier, a month later, Mayor Daley was given the responsibility of Chicago Public Schools. Within a few months of that announcement, he promoted our Peer Mentor Program and raised our visibility as being one of the components he supported as part of his school reform.

We are still in the school and the community doing what we do. We applaud others who see young people as integral to turning obstacles into opportunities to get ready for their futures. It has taken generations of broken values from marriage to family, from jobs to gentrification, from abandoned neighborhoods to school-closings to get here. It will call for dedication and perseverance to put a solution-based and positive approach to revitalize the values to make it possible for everyone to have a chance.

What Do Young People Have to Do with the Solution?

What we have found that works is to find values that we all have in common. Approaching young people for whom life-giving values do not guide their lives to help them wake up before it is too late to show them another way. Those who can influence them are peers that have life-giving values. With the right setting, the addictive cycle can change. We have stories to tell.

I remember Angela telling me her story after she had become a Peer Mentor. That was in 1992. Meeting her just recently and hearing what she is doing is worth all the work it took to have her wake up, before it was too late.

What she told me then was that she had come to a group session because her teacher sent her—that is how she described it. We do not want to know *why* anyone comes. We want to approach each young person the same way. After a month, the teacher told us her attendance and grades were improving. "Whatever you're doing is working. Keep it up," she told us.

At the end of the year, Angela received her award as a Certified Peer Achiever. We went to her home to meet with her family since she said she did love to mentor eighth-graders. It was then that she told us her story:

"I had been arrested six times for loitering, hanging out with the wrong people, getting into trouble. A neighbor next door to us told my mom about Life Directions. She said her granddaughter liked it. I said I did not need any help. My mother said 'it is for young people to tell each other how to make things work for them.' I told her I'd try it. I asked my Social Studies teacher if I could go. I remember she looked sort of suspicious, but said 'as long as you get your work done.' I said 'okay.'

"I was surprised at how we all started opening up. When you asked us to write down where we wanted to be in twenty years, I cannot remember what I wrote. But when others shared what they wrote about that and other things, it got me thinking. What about it? Will I even be around?

"Then you put us into skits about real-life stuff going on. We played different parts as grandparents, parents, and young people. It got me out of myself. I started to think like somebody else.

"Then it hit me. The biggest problem I had was that I did not know I had a problem. I finally saw the problem I had. Nobody knew I was looking at what was not working in my life. All I knew was that we were giving each other ideas on how to deal with stuff, like boyfriends, homework, screaming parents, no money, gangs—you name it.

"What happened was that I found a reason to stop doing some things and I started to go in a different direction. I must admit it took time. But when I heard what people thought would work, and I tried it and it worked--Cool!"

Angela not only became a Peer Mentor back in 1992. She finished high school and went to a community college. She got a job working in southwest Detroit for an organization that helps people find jobs. She got married and has three children. Her husband served in Afghanistan. She has decided to take college courses and get a Bachelor's degree. She and her husband are starting a construction business. She said someday she may have time to be an Adult Mentor like the one she had with Life Directions.

Freedom to Discover

Another major component of Life Directions is *how* we free young people to discover positive values while surrounded by the opposite. We know young people have different values from each other. They come from their home and family and friends. In the right setting, we believe the "good values" will become greater, and the "negative ones" will become fewer.

We see life as something everyone wants to win. If the light to do so comes on, we all will go toward it, but it takes someone rooted in what is important to challenge others to see its power. Rather than "the bad apple destroys the bushel," we see "leaven giving rise to the dough."

Sister Rosalie explains it this way: "There is that old saying about a person learning everything they need to know by the time they are six years old.

"When we work with young people the goal is to wake them up to the values that often are already in them. Through the processes we use, they remember certain things, and when they remember, so do others. It is like, 'ah, yeah, that is what my Mom used to say.' It is a reawakening of the values inside.

"But it works only if you ask open-ended questions or use approaches that encourage sharing personal stories that invite others to come forward. The open-ended questions spark really beautiful stories and expressions of values.

"I remember when this young man, Jeff, came to one of our groups at Sunnyside High School in Tucson. He was made to be there. He said he did not know why. Immediately one of the young people set him straight. 'You do not know why? I remember how you came late and did not want to do the work.'

"I stopped the discussion, not knowing Jeff at all and not knowing how he would respond. I knew the question Jeff asked was not the right one. I said, 'Jeff, I would like you to sit in the middle of the group. Before you do so, I want everyone to write down one good thing you see in Jeff. You all seem to know him. As Jeff moved his chair, he just stared at me. When I asked everyone to read what they wrote, it was amazing to hear: 'strong leader, good in sports, does not give up, takes care of his little brother'… the list continued. I asked them to give him what they wrote and to sign their name.

"Then I asked someone to go to the chalk board and list all the bad things Jeff does. This list was just as long as the good list. I stopped everyone right there. I asked the group to say what would happen if Jeff erased the chalk board for real. I asked Jeff to do so.

"The group kept meeting through the semester. Jeff's grades got better. He graduated, and I never saw him again, until four years later. We were at a fundraiser at the Double Tree Hotel. And who comes out of the kitchen? Jeff, the chef! 'I want to thank you, Sister, for what you did for me, he said. 'I copied that list and still have it. Now I am a chef.'"

"Values formation," Sister Rosalie adds, "means reconnecting with what we were taught as children. In group sessions, young people who have such values can give them to others, who may never have heard them. In fact, they may not ever know who their father or mother was.

"My mother disciplined us but it was not with whips or abusive language. It was just by talking with us, and she talked real low so we had to listen. I am able to reflect on that when I see the way some adults discipline their children—with yelling, screaming, whipping, and a lot of anger. What is sad is when we find young people who do not have such an experience. It is a real gift to make the space for young people who received discipline to encourage their peers to want to follow them."

Helping young people form their values amplifies the vision of our work. Our priority is to develop a hunger in them that will lead to their thinking of their future before they react to what is happening. Often the reaction is violent, which leads to self-destruction, both personally and as a people. In promoting this hunger for values, we are also aware that as excellence rises, mediocrity coalesces to kill it. It will be a challenge for a young person to stay positive.

A support network, if it does not exist for the young person, must be encouraged. Finding ways to belong to positive peer groups is an excellent complement to what we do in the schools. We build up our own called "Sparks Initiatives." We also connect with other organizations and groups who have the value of believing in young people.

Asking the Right Questions

Teachers know what students relate to them within a day or two of school. We ask those educators who are open to a "partnership with accountability" to motivate young people who are potential dropouts to stay in school and make it work for them. We share that, out of a class of thirty-five students, there are those who need intervention, social workers, psychologists, law enforcement—whatever. We know there are those moving on a track which has its own life, and they do not want to be with people who may need motivation. But the middle eighty percent of the class can go either way. We ask for a "time-out" period of one session per week for twelve weeks. The outcomes are better attendance, better participation, and better grades. All the educator needs to do is select one young person who listens to them and two who do not.

Tom Howard, our Life Directions staff person, was at Farragut High School in 1994. He remembers Michael Wright, who was in the ninth grade at the time. His basketball coach suggested he should go to Life Directions. Tom said he remembers Michael not speaking much, staying to himself and sort of shy. Basketball legend Kevin Garnett was connected with the group; maybe that is why he stayed. Tom was not sure.

It was six years later when I called Tom about Michael. I was in Tucson. A donor asked me if I knew Michael Wright. Michael was on the team of the University of Arizona which was going to the Final Four. Tom said that he did not know if Michael would remember Life Directions.

I went to the locker room with very low expectations. Michael walked into the room where I was sitting with Josh Pastner, assistant to Lute Olson the Head Coach. Josh introduced me to Michael. He spoke up right away, which was not his style, "You're from Life Directions," Michael said, adding, "If it was not for Life Directions, I would be dead."

All of us in the locker room were stunned. Michael went on to say how much he got out of listening to everybody's challenges. He wanted to know if there was anything he could do to encourage young people to come to Life Directions' groups and get involved in the community. Josh said he could go and talk at Sunnyside, but that his schedule would not let him do more.

The *Tucson Citizen* newspaper did a story on Michael's visit. What an impact he made on the student body. Kevin Garnett was playing professionally already, and Michael was moving in that direction. When he finished talking at the school, we had lots of young people wanting to connect with us.

Peers Mentoring Peers – It Works

Emmanuel was the tenth-grade Peer Mentor for Roberto. They did activities and had "cool-downs," talking about what they learned from field trips and other things. They got into the subject of grades and what worked for Emmanuel in high school as compared to when he was in grade school. They deal with the change that happened as they make high school work for them.

Roberto had dealt with violence and bullying throughout the eighth grade. He told me how nervous he was when he was first entering high school:

"I walked into Western and freaked. I did not want to go into the cafeteria. I figure I'd eat my lunch in the bathroom. Then I saw Emmanuel. He waved me over to his table. That is all it took. He knew me. Now seven months later, I have got a 3.4 GPA and I am going into tenth grade. And I cannot wait to be a Peer Mentor."

Dr. Phil's book *Life Code* describes a growing group of people who would be just the opposite of the young people needed to mentor their peers. They are the ones preventing them from moving forward with a positive approach to life. Dr. Phil describes ways to handle words and actions of disrespect.

What the Peer Mentors are encouraging is to have a plan for our lives and make sure we surround ourselves with people who support us to get there. What it does is create a win-win climate, moving past the potential violence that could destroy someone's future. Given the social media that is expanding, this way to build support is even more valuable.

We hold to the value that peers can influence peers for both good and bad. When it is for the good, we see our vision coming to life: "Peers Inspiring Peers Through Forgiving." Peers who are rooted in life-giving relationships can encourage their peers to let go of past hurts, take control of their lives, and claim a future based on values that lead to Life. In this way they *choose* to be responsible for themselves and to be directed by positive values.

We have developed discussion and role-playing exercises with a series of key questions that unearth the value of belonging through sports, the value of family or extended families, or the value of cultural belonging within family units. What value can be found in the safety and security of neighborhoods, homes or within young adult circles? What are the values found in "academic competence" or through their own skills? What values can be discovered when one defines their own meaning through positive action in school?

Again, these are the "right" questions to help young people discover their own answers; the values they already have or are encouraged to find by their peers. But sometimes, the "right" question is a statement or follow-up reflection as Sister Rosalie remembers in the story about a young girl's wanting to get vengeance:

"During a session, this young lady expressed her desire to find a way 'to get back' at this other family. A young man in the group, who happened to be a football player, looked at her and said 'that is stupid!' I asked him to explain. 'Well, our coach says that when we come on the field and we are mad, everybody loses.' With his saying that, I saw the young girl sort of turn within herself as if reconsidering what she had just said. It was something said by a peer that caused her to reflect on her own values."

We do a series of different goal-setting exercises looking to where we want to be twenty years from now. We brainstorm things that would cripple their plans in the next six months. We identify those situations and we begin to coach through peer-to-peer intergenerational role playing. Their imaginations are their greatest assets. They inherently take to the roles of grandparents, parents, or teens. What surfaces in the plays, and the discussion that follows, are values that challenge them to think and decide what to do.

Sister told me about the time she asked a group of teens where they wanted to be in twenty years. The young people sort of played her off, not taking the question too seriously. But one student turned her chair around to face Rosalie and said, "Sister, they are just playing around because they think somebody's going to embarrass them or something."

With that acknowledgement, the whole climate in the room changed, Sister said. The young people started talking seriously about her question because a peer, with whom they had a trusting relationship, made it okay.

Our pre-and post-assessment lets us know the difference that *hearing* each other makes on what young people choose to do in school, at home, in their neighborhoods, or with the activities and organizations they choose to join.

The heart of it all is that young people have a decision to make. Do they want to see themselves as victims with no choice or not? Once they decide not be victims, they are ready to talk about their decision. They may never have considered deciding not to be a victim. The light of taking charge of one's life goes on. They want to decide what to do. They are open to hearing their peers and others giving those ideas, inspiration and motivation.

Where Do Adults Fit?

If you want to create boredom, give an answer to a question that was not asked. Starting with *your* agenda can often disconnect with the young person who either isn't interested in what you are saying or never had thought about it. The opposite way to create enthusiasm is by asking questions that young people enjoy answering.

The adults are needed to craft questions that look to life-giving values where the young people sense they are gaining control of their lives. If needed, they will find a way out of the mess they are in, that they may or may not have made. As they see themselves in charge of what happens and are responsible for doing what is right, they'll turn to adults for ideas. And they will want to listen because adults listened to them first.

It may seem obvious, but it is not the normal experience for young people to experience adults really wanting to listen to them. We remember this as we go into public schools to wake up young people to being self-responsible. Less-achievers are reactive, not reflective. Often they are "anorexic to values," disconnected from values that may have been given to them at an early age. When their achieving peers engage with them on issues and activities, a desire to connect can happen. Life begins to take on a real value and meaning for them. Everyone begins to feel they are winning.

When a person wakes up to being an anorexic to values, they may get angry or hurt as they start to see what happened to them. They can easily blame someone for their situation. It is then that the adults who are talking with them need themselves to be grounded in forgiving as the way that is working for them in their lives.

To think of ways to let go of what happened to the young people, the adult wants to open up ways of forgiving. I once attended a workshop for teachers conducted by Sister Gail Trippett, a Sister of St. Joseph of Carondelet. Sister Gail's basic formula centered on the added value of responding rather than reacting to someone or some event. The core message was this: "I must change my vision of the person or the experience before reacting." The lesson stressed the importance of listening well and deciding how to proceed from there.

Adults can use examples of how they have done so. They can even encourage role-playing where the adult is in the situation of being hurt and decides to forgive. All they do is raise the positive ways to respond. They want to remember they cannot rescue the young people, and they cannot fix their situation. If they try, they will actually get in the way. They may become like a co-dependent or an enabler of dysfunction.

We are constantly aware of the EQ (Emotional Quotient) that is underdeveloped due to what happens when anyone makes a negative judgment without knowing the person at all. For instance, to see a teacher and to feel scared usually leads to wanting to avoid the teacher. This will not make the relationship work. Until the young person sees he or she is free to see differently, they are stuck. If the way the young person sees the teacher does not change, it could get worse. It calls for a gentle and humble approach to open eyes among people who are in the dark, so to speak, to anything good in the teacher. It takes a period of adjustment to the light.

Take the situation where Roberto saw older students and felt afraid. When the adult mentor encouraged Emmanuel to talk with Roberto, the adult mentor was able to brainstorm ways to ask questions that would free Roberto to be the solution to his seeing the older students as a threat. As Emmanuel asked Roberto questions for Roberto to find out where he got this idea, it was great to listen to how fear just left him.

What Emmanuel did was mentor Roberto into a stronger EQ.

They did not say the words. They followed our on-the-spot training. First, know "why" you are in school. Second, decide you will do whatever it takes to finish. Third, forgive whatever got you to be where you are—accept what you cannot change. Fourth, change what you can—the way you *see* the older students as a threat. You begin to *feel* positive. You start to think of what to *do* that is positive. And you get what is positive, like you did. And you know what? You do not have to hide!

Partnerships in Diversity Need Intergenerational Learning

When violence happens in any community, the action bleeds the soul of a people. This violation has a severe impact on people, especially young adults within hard-pressed, disadvantaged communities. Peer pressure can easily lead to the cutting of one's cultural roots. The anchor to values from one's heritage becomes less important in the face of negative peer pressure. What often happens is a weakening or even an elimination of reverence for one's family, history, and culture.

We wanted to encourage ways to be proactive and prevent losing a life-giving community. In response to what we found, we developed an organizational framework led by our staff and trained volunteers aimed at encouraging the value-sharing of multiculturalism and interdependence. We discovered that those cultures that explain their values and ways of being faithful to their roots offer a framework within which to discover new meaning.

Without such a structure, the analysis flowing from looking at "reality" may paralyze or stop young people from thinking of ways to turn obstacles into opportunities in their families and community. We want to partner with young people to search for the values in their culture that call for excellence. As they become aware of their values, they are encouraged to mature into responsible, productive adults through self-determination.

We crafted a process called "partnership in diversity." It brings together adults, young adults, peer mentors, and mentees in eighth grade. Through a series of inter-active games, everyone talks with someone of a different generation within the first half-hour. What we encourage is to teach what only each person knows. We present the challenge. "I am a person who wants to see differences among cultures and creeds as an opportunity to reverence diversity."

We ask each person to be with someone of a different age whom they do not know. We start the conversation with this request: "Tell me something about yourself that I would not know." When one finishes, the other speaks. There is only one rule; you cannot repeat what the other person said.

Then we share food with one another. We sing or play music we like. All we ask is that it is the music "you" like, and we assume each generation will be different. It takes a lot of planning with the young people who are part of our group work in school. The results are amazing and lead to a way of discovering that "community" does not stop with the gathering. The climate for mutually-enriching and learning from each other has really just begun.

Nelson Mandela's experience of overcoming apartheid and Paulo Freire's way of educating the oppressed are rich in wisdom for young people, young adults, and all of us. It is empowering for those coaching young people to have the information that Douglas A. Blackmon brings forth in his book *Slavery By Another Name*. The author gives in-depth understanding of the destruction of young men—mostly African American—who have been denied education from the years 1866 to 1941 and beyond, that would have helped better their lives.

Our young adult peer mentors have a right to know and will be freed from misguidance if they listen to the lessons Carter G. Woodson shared in *Mis-Education of the Negro* (1938). His lessons explain how so many of the African American's cultural roots were severed or diluted. When they share with their peers such wisdom, it is amazing how encouraging everyone can be. To hear people who overcame the negative conditions around them gives hope.

It is a real gift for all of us to understand African American people among whom less than one child out of every hundred was born out of wedlock in 1900, as verified by Paula Giddings in *When and Where I Enter: The Impact of Black Women on Race and Sex in America*. Likewise, it is equally important that we have a grasp on the Hispanic American journey into this country through the reflections by Virligio Elizondo in *The Future Is Mestizo: Life Where Cultures Meet* (1998, and re-printed in 2000).

Why is this important? It is because we live in a pluralistic society where the barriers among us are about as cruel as what people before us had to endure. It is sad to be aware of how the beauty of people's history was cut. But only when the situation calls for such nurturing of the values of which they are deprived, does it relate to their lives. If it is given before it is wanted, it is nice information that makes little-to-no impact on their coming to be proud of their people, themselves, and their future. It makes the "giver" feel good, but will probably do little for the "receiver."

Sister Rosalie, a Mexican American, grew up in a town that was prejudiced against her culture. As a result, her family was not treated respectfully. But her mother had instilled a sense of cultural value in her children by reminding them that they were "persons first," who just happened to be Mexican.

Rosalie's Mom's focus on the last four letters of "Mexican (I-Can)" was a reminder that cultural ignorance was no reflection on their gifts or ability to be responsible for their own lives and outcomes.

Here, Sister Rosalie shares Maria's story to underscore the necessity of discovering cultural confidence in a group setting:

"Maria was a darker-skinned Mexican girl whose father gave her a hard time because of her complexion. He would put her down, saying things like, 'I do not know who your father is.' Maria, the eldest child in the family, wound up treating her brothers and sisters the way she had been treated by her father.

"In the group, she confessed that she had never shared this personal story before. A young man in the group, who happened to be a light-skinned Mexican, said that his parents discussed the issue often and he had come to the conclusion that skin color does not matter. 'You are a person, and everyone's special,' he said.

"Well, about a month later we invited the girl and a few other young people to one of our board meetings. She was asked what difference Life Directions had made in her life. Maria said that her mother had just told her that when they visit Mexico again her cousins will not recognize her.

"'They are used to me not being very nice and I have changed so much,' Maria told us. After that experience of sharing her feelings, she became more involved with her church, got involved with its youth group, and had completely changed the way she was interacting with her brothers and sisters.

"Maria was able to let go of the weight that determined the negative way she felt about herself. It was not that anything dramatic had happened. She was just able to share her feelings in a group that, except for the light-skinned Mexican boy, did not challenge; they just received what she shared."

In *Man's Search for Meaning*, author Victor Frankl defined this form of existential analysis as "logo therapy." It was this discipline that helped him survive the Nazi concentration camps and sustain the mental freedom to belong to a Power Greater Than Himself. The unconditional love relationship with his wife served as the energy that touches eternity into time.

Most importantly, Victor got in touch with the "why" of his actions. He came to the conclusion that, even under the worst conditions, he wanted to survive because of the unconditional love of his wife. He knew he had to endure whatever atrocity just to survive.

Knowing the *why* of all the things we put up with in order to "be there" for the young people has energized us to navigate rough and unexplored terrain in public schools. When we went into the public schools, we knew *why* we wanted to be there—to wake up young people before it is too late. It is a privilege to know how many young people see with hope and positive energy and are alive because of it.

PARABLE OF THE BASKETBALL GAME

I told some basketball players that I could make basketball boring. They said it could not be done. I brought them down to the gym. They broke into two teams. I gave them the ball and said "start playing." They asked me about the hoop. I said the game is basketball. "I gave you a ball, so play. And do not use one hand but two to dribble. Pass with your foot. And the goal is the square outlined on the wall."

"So what is your point?" they asked me.

I wanted to know if it was boring. They said they never had a chance to play. I said, "Since you know the game and you know what makes it work, you keep the rules and enjoy it. When it comes to what you need to make it in life, if you do not have a 'hoop' and no one tells you the 'rules', you may never enjoy life."

1. What made the game boring would be *not* having a goal. What does this say about not having a plan for your future?

2. When you want to get better at the game, having a coach with experience is a real value. He does not need to play himself to know what works. Where do you find such a "coach" for your future?

3. It is great if you have someone who knows the game and you can learn from him or her. What is this say about having a peer mentor?

CHAPTER TEN
"IT AIN'T OVER 'TIL IT'S OVER"

The two towers of New York, the two cities of Chicago and Detroit—we believe there is a lesson to be learned that can rise up to be seen, if forgiving becomes part of how we remember what happened.

General George Marshall was in charge of the plan to carefully rebuild Europe after World War II. Prime Minister Benazir Bhutto of Pakistan wrote her book to promote *"Reconciliation,"* not just for her country but for the world. When she read what the General said, she heard what is true of any country with urban decay. The world situation was very fragile and serious. The complexity was difficult for Marshall to describe to people in the United States, especially those who were distant from the post-war realities. He did not know how to share the situation in a way that others could comprehend the plight and consequent reactions of long-suffering peoples. Marshall failed to connect rebuilding Europe and addressing the needs of long-suffering people with an international effort to promote peace around the world.

Is it time to announce the Marshall Plan for the cities devastated by the "war within" that began in the '60s? Rather than Marshall Law, we need to gently and humbly engage with the people in the midst of their pain with a Marshall Plan for the United States cities in poverty.

The issues Prime Minister Bhutto saw as essential to the rebuilding out of poverty and decay were two-fold. The first is public education, and the second is economic opportunity for people to become part of the middle class. Benazir Bhutto was assassinated in 2008, one month after publishing her book. I am grateful for her call to hope.

Many people responded to the 9/11 tragedy by declaring a "war on terror." What would happen if we took time to reflect upon the "war on values" that is happening as we look at people within our own communities? We tend to separate due to prejudice, and make decisions that continue the war without knowing it. I pray we wake up before others die.

It can be done with the people themselves being seen as integral to the solution. We need to know what we do not know. What has it been like with the world as we know it collapsing street-by-street? What do we want for our children's children, and what do we have to contribute to make that possible?

We believe it is time to learn the lesson from using violence to stop violence, on the one hand, and solutions designed by those who do not know "the plight and consequent reactions of the long-suffering peoples," on the other. The lesson can be learned by those who believe in hope against hope, as Abraham did (Romans 4:18). I am aware of what happens to the prophet who explains the parables, especially if the prophet is speaking with purified lips sent to a people being destroyed, as Isaiah was sent (6:1-13). I hope it is time to explain the parable to those who want to follow the Person who was before Abraham (John 8), and ended His human life as a slave led to the cross (Philippians 2:5-11).

If it is not time, then we will have written down the vision that will come in its time. "It may seem slow in coming, but wait for it; it will certainly take place, and it will not be delayed" (Habakkuk 2:3). As we wait, it is good to hope against hope with the old dreaming dreams, and the young seeing visions (Acts 2:17). It is all about remembering "unless the Lord builds the house" (Psalms 127), "even if a mother forgets her child" (Isaiah 49:15), "if you are unfaithful, I will be faithful, I cannot deny myself" (2 Timothy 2:13), "with the Lord there is mercy and fullness of redemption" (Psalms 130), "to renew the face of the earth" (Psalms 104).

The separation of Church and State has forged a chasm that is destroying the children. It is as if each side is unintentionally against the other, rather than bringing the best out of each other. After forty years of living in the middle of this chasm, I have come to discover the meaning of "the salt of the earth" remembered by Matthew, the tax collector (Matthew 5:14). We are meant to be sent into the whole world and not into separate worlds. We are meant to bring peace through forgiving for all to live.

Many people of all faith communities, and people of good will who belong to no group of believers, know what is needed to get to the cause of violence and respond peacefully. We carried on conversation circles with people of other world religions. As we shared, it was enriching and enlightening to hear various ways to know justice and peace and joy. We hold the values in common. Hearing how we embraced it differently was a gift we gave to each other.

In the way we see as Christians seeking peace, we know an unconditional love sent the Son into the world *not* to condemn (John 3:16). We know his name as Jesus who breathes forgiving in the midst of a very violent death (Luke 23:34). We remember earlier in the same book He spoke of His Father in a parable of forgiving, that the Father wanted the separation between the two brothers to be bridged (Luke 15:11-32).

We remember Saul, who was killing those following this way but was "blinded" and was given back his sight (Acts 9). We know he became, by the end his life, an Ambassador of Reconciliation (2 Corinthians 5:15-20). We believe that Jesus' death gave birth to Jews and Gentiles coming together in one Spirit – those close and those far away built together (Ephesians 2:22).

As the Islamic community shared, it became clear that forgiving was their way to peace and harmony. The Buddhist tradition was given as a way to empty ourselves of desires that are destructive of life. People from Alcoholic Anonymous were clear on the purpose of their twelve-step program and focused on the fifth step: forgiving. We were grateful to have heard the goodness within those of us who made the time to share. We complimented each other in each tradition's way to promote peace through forgiving.

As I mentioned, while writing this book, I went to a desert in the Middle East to be in silence. I come from a faith-based tradition with the importance of being contemplative to listen (Hosea 2:14). I was with a faith community who values the same way to find the truth. I was conscious of the political and economic issues the Middle East represents. I was conscious of the violence that is potentially present. I was aware of the people who were part of 9/11 who had grown up in this part of the world. I asked myself the question, "Is the separation of Church and State, as we are living it, becoming an obstacle to bringing peace forward?"

Life Directions was born out of the issue of violence. We began our work in 1970s crossing the Ambassador Bridge between the U.S. and Canada for our focus: LIFE retreats. We began when the Middle East oil embargo was a defining event that would involve people from the Middle East coming to Detroit. What better place than the Middle East to write my reflections on our work to share the cause of violence and how it can be healed.

What a surprise when I found out that Francis of Assisi came in the thirteenth century to meet with the Muslim Sultan. From their meeting, Francis was given the freedom to share his faith. And from Francis's spirit comes the prayer, "make me an instrument of your peace." The gentle and humble call in the prayer is to understand more than be understood. I wonder if we take time to understand why hate is deep in the heart of some. Could it be the result of backing dictators, when it's in our self-interest? Could it be a more expansive reason—the result of colonialism that made people hide to survive? What healing is needed to set a person or a people free of such oppression? The solution is breathing forgiving, especially if we represent the person or group controlling the lives of others.

As I read Benazir Bhutto's work, I was amazed to read that her recommendation for reconciliation in the United States would be young adult professionals, who believe in reconciliation, breaking down barriers and building bridges among young adult Muslims, Christians, Jews, and Hindus. She believed such an action might begin dismantling the "global war on terror" that has had a ripple impact on one hundred million Muslims who saw it as a global war on Islam.

Is it time to say that the reason for violence is violence? The reason for killing is killing? Martin Buber, in 1923, said that if we approach people as objects, we are going to go to war again. He was a German Jew. He wrote his little work called "I-Thou" (in German "Ich und Du"), stressing we are all equal with one another. Imagine world powers seeing no one as the enemy but only a friend that they are forgiving.

When I heard President Obama speak after the Newtown tragedy, I wondered if the time had come. When he shared how we seem so powerless, I thought of what Jesus said to Paul: "When you are weak, I am strong." (2 Cor 12:7-10). For me, the answer was, "Yes, we are powerless. To accept our powerlessness is a way to freedom for all."

It will happen when we come to understand that what our grandchildren want is peace for all, not just for those we like, but for those who are seen as our enemies. This intuition is the truth that will set us free from violence and will change the rest of our lives. It takes hope against hope to believe what Annie sang: "Tomorrow! Tomorrow! I love you…You're always a day away."

Looking for Jedidiah

Most people in large urban settings, like Chicago or Detroit, are aware the educational system is not working for children. We see the closing of public schools and the opening of charter schools. This follows in the wake of the closing of private, faith-based schools. People who are faith-based are aware that organized religion isn't working for young people. I was with youth pastors whose salaries depended upon young people staying in church. After the young people grew up, the majority moved on from their faith community.

Is it time to see the divisions among peoples causing the falling apart of systems of service and support? Whenever a solution saves those who have an interest in it, and it does not look to the common good to be open to find ways to serve everyone, it will divide the "haves" from the "have-nots." The "haves" will say they are taking responsibility for their lives. The "have-nots" will say they are doing the best they can with what they have. Both may be right, and both may be wrong.

It will call for the Wisdom of Solomon, named Jedidiah (2 Samuel 12:25), to bring both sides to see that the other is right, and that the other is the only one positioned to face what is wrong within themselves. When one side says the other is wrong, it does not work. It creates a negative energy that will explode—sometimes literally—especially when one side is doing well and the other side cannot meet their needs for themselves, their children, or their grandchildren.

Luke Skywalker was looking for his Jedidiah. He went to a deserted planet and left his ship which began to sink. When an elder asked what he was looking for, Luke told him he was seeking the Jedi. With that, the old creature used "the force" to lift the ship out of the quicksand. Luke could not believe he could ever do what the Jedi Master had just accomplished. That is exactly why he could not, Obi-Wan Kenobi replied, because Luke did not believe.

Is it time to learn from the first One who had the "weapons of mass destruction" in the Middle East? He told his first in command, "All who take the sword will die by the sword... Do not you know ... I could call for help... and have twelve armies of angels?" It is beyond the way the world judges. He knew that (Matthew 16:23).

With all the nuclear weapons on the planet that cannot keep the peace, are we ready to think "out of box" and "out of this world?"

Is it time? The walk begins with one step at a time, one person at a time, remembering the Person who kept the energy of forgiving alive through a dozen cowards who denied, betrayed and ran away, all because of fear.

I am from Missouri, the "Show Me State." What you do is what you mean by what you say. What many have done tells me that forgiving is false to them. It does not work for them.

With this mindset, FEAR becomes the acronym for "False Expectations Appearing Real," but when you believe it is true—as did Nez Perce Chief Joseph; Hindu Mahatma Gandhi; the leader of the Civil Rights Movement, Dr. Martin Luther King, Jr.; the leader of American Farm Workers, Cesar Chavez; El Salvador's Archbishop, Oscar Romero; Pakistan's Prime Minister, Benazir Bhutto; and Deacon Stephen, when he forgave Saul to be transformed—then FEAR becomes "Forgiving Excelling Always Redeeming."

Let's see what we mean by what we say. Let's see what we do.

When the twin towers collapsed, "God Bless America" was put up on a South Side Chicago school building. Our coins are inscribed with "In God We Trust." I know what we *say*, but I will know what we mean by what we do. When we do what we do, do we trust God the way God wants us to trust? Does God agree with the way our government spends money? I assume we do not want to reprint the money to say "In *Us* God Is to Trust."

I know some people want to take the word "God" off our currency. I suggest that if we found a way to put God on money and we are told by the Master that we cannot serve God *and* money, what is the reason we print His name on our currency? Would it be possible to use the same reason to build bridges to promote peace-building through forgiving? This is what the Lord's Prayer says we want to do, before it is too late for our children.

Is it time? What we do will tell us and others what we mean by what we say.

Awareness of the Three IQs

Is it time to look at the marathon as a better way to run the race rather than to use the sprint approach to life? The United States ranks eighth in the world for young people entering college. We are the second to last in developed countries for those completing college. The dropout rate from college, not to mention the fifty percent dropout rate from high school among those in poverty areas who sign up in ninth grade, is happening even though we are more employable if we stay in school.

The fast-track approach to solving problems focuses on the immediate proof of increasing grades. It does not work for the long run. In fact, it may actually encourage an addictive way of life that a developed country like the United States faces. We have a choice, because we have more than we need to survive. The IQ approach to stopping what people are doing by saying "no" is heard in the mind, but not in the soul of people. To say "no to..." is not heard spiritually and often encourages emotional irresponsibility. It is a form of banking which shows the weakness of learning that is not built on positive life experiences. We can waste not just our resources but ourselves.

To be aware of the growth of the three IQs is to be aware of the whole person. To perceive their interrelationship, and how they are impacted by their peers and their elders, is to be ready to prudently encourage a moderate way to move. We gradually walk with a person or group toward a maturity that makes them want to find peace-building in the face of conflicts of values or needs. The conflicts of values call for unconditional love to accept what we cannot change. The conflicts of needs encourage all people to want everyone to have what will make living possible. Live simply so all can simply live.

IQ (*intelligence quotient*) measures the "Conscious" capacity to know. EQ (emotional *quotient*) expands the "Conscientious" growing in understanding. SQ (spiritual *quotient*) forms the "Conscience", moving toward wisdom. As we develop our IQ and our heartfelt EQ, it is the soul-filled SQ that draws a person to want to be for others. It makes it possible for a people to want to be for everyone, against no one.

The Joy of Riding

What happens when the conscience is maturing toward the common good for all? Everyone is seen with the dignity that acceptance encourages to overcome either/or and seek the wisdom needed for both/and ways of thinking. To awaken people to their IQs to the common good, a question like this helps: "Who is making money on you?" As a consumer, whoever is producing what I want is making money on me. This is true for what is essential and for what is not necessary — be it healthy or not.

To focus our EQ on the common good, a question might be: "Who is receiving money *from* you?" This opens up to people we care about to looking at the taxes we pay and the people who depend on us.

To invite us to listen to our SQ may be: "What can you not live without, but money cannot buy?" This draws people to see something beyond their control. It is at this level when we see what is beyond being bought and sold. We want to encourage young people to influence what matters to them that is priceless: their love for others and for God. They may then want to reexamine where and how we spend our money personally and as a people.

As the SQ becomes the center of what matters most, there are three "Ds" that are important to know: Discipline, Desire, and Destination. To the extent these three dimensions are not in harmony, we stay at the surface and rarely engage anything of substance. For IQ, the "Discipline" to learn is as good as the person whom we follow, a guide toward the truth we are seeking. For the EQ, the "Desire" to love wants another to join, someone whose love is unconditional. It is as healthy as the relationship is mutually growing. For the SQ, the "Destination" is to let go and be free to walk. As we know why we are on this quest, we will know how to have a steady step. If we feel too weak, this is where the elder encourages us to be patient.

An analogy sometimes makes it easier to see. Growth in all three arenas is like learning how to ride a bicycle. When we start, training wheels can be very helpful. As we get a sense of balance, we can take off the training wheels and go on our own. We may fall a few times, but eventually we'll find our way to keep our balance. It will come through practice. It is then we can encourage others to enjoy riding the bike. If they do not know how, we will teach them so that they can know the joy of riding.

Balance Within and Among

We gradually became aware of what is possible in high school and their feeder middle schools. We have done our Peer Motivation Program in thirty-one high schools and our Peer Mentor Program in forty-seven high schools/middle schools, and their communities in six states. Based on the boundaries within which we were to work, we saw the powerful impact that being responsible for ourselves had, as peers would challenge peers to know they are victims because they want to be. The results of such a discovery made a powerful impact on young people's EQ. If they see negative, they respond negatively. If they change how they see, and if they learn how to sustain their vision, they can make it.

When we engaged young adults from eighteen years of age and

older in all the communities in which we worked, we would invite a way of connecting with their Power Greater Than Human through the inductive process among diverse strangers with mixed cultural and faith communities and with an equal balance in genders.

We designed the context for mutual interaction with a profound sensitivity to integrity through personal space for reflecting and interactive space for acting. The content came from the people themselves as they shared their varied experiences and choices they had made.

The convergence with elders and people of wisdom throughout history would be shared as input calling everyone to see models of excellence. The twin values of justice and peace would be the guide for choosing who and what to present. The ending of any event encouraged self-control and a way of being intimate that would make sense in the ordinary settings in which they lived and worked.

Balance within me, and among each other, is a lifelong quest. In articulating the paradigm of "victim-persecutor-rescuer," we were aware we were using a number of well-known leaders of young people in their teens and young adults in their twenties who relate to them. Two prominent people whose work we studied were Merton Strommen, the founder of the Search Institute in Minneapolis, Minnesota; and Bill Gotthard, the founder of the Institute in Basic Life Principles in Oak Brook, Illinois. Merton's work, *Five Cries of Youth*, and Bill's Seminar of *Seven Basic Life Principles* spoke to issues we discovered as we began our work in Detroit in 1973.

To sustain the mission to change the paradigm of victim-persecutor-rescuer to self-responsible, balanced partnerships, calls for resources. In a capitalistic system, this means we need people who reverence our vision and respect our mission to lend resources to sustain a core team. This team would develop and organize self-supported people who are spiritually rooted and have a passion to inspire their peers to be aware of the journey to receive and give unconditional forgiving--one of the most challenging expressions of unconditional love.

Building bridges across the chasm between the Church and State systems that are maintaining faith communities and public life calls for patient enthusiasm. Faith communities are at their best when they nurture values with spiritual energy, such as, hope, encouragement and enthusiasm. The public systems are at their best when they provide for the needs of the people who depend on them, such as jobs, housing and education. Both faith communities and public systems work well when the two people who conceive a child raise the child unconditionally. When unconditional love between two people is not present or is rejected by the child, both systems weaken and can often make things worse.

Meeting the real need for unconditional love is what Life Directions has been dedicated to encourage. Our work depends upon people to want to inspire their peers to grow into unconditional love through unconditional forgiving.

We looked at various faith-based efforts that would ignite young adults to want to be mission-driven and give one to two years of their lives to inspiring teens at risk in urban and suburban settings. Some denominations had youth pastors who had strong followings. There were movement-type approaches that called young people to life-changing "mountain-top" experiences.

What we found was usually very intense and having powerful impacts on people. How long and how sustainable the "awakening" would be was our reflective quest. We would come together as a team to look at what was done, why it was done, and what happens when it is all over. We wanted to ensure that our impact on young adults from eighteen to thirty-five years of age would encourage a discipline that would be self-sustaining and not dependent upon the event or leader that began the work. We wanted to ensure that *we* would decrease and the Power Greater Than Human would increase.

We knew what we did not want to do. We did not want to explore with participants their journey of discovery of how the Power Greater Than Human was calling them to be free and excellent without the energy that only comes from the Creator. We were so clear that we are not in control of the culture or creed of any persons. We saw the culture as the receiving side of creation, and the creed as the giving side of the Creator. This was true for us and it was a spiritual value that would let go and let what only immortality can draw us to become.

Our awareness of most of what we understood from going to seminars and workshops and studying interdisciplinary resources was that the outcome was to result in someone making a choice or joining a group to indicate the work was successful. Outcomes like graduating from high school, going to college, and getting a job was the manner in which our Peer Motivation and Peer Mentor Programs would be evaluated. They were either explicitly asked in a third-party evaluation or were implicitly wanted by a donor or an administrator. Outcomes like joining or returning to a faith community, marrying and staying faithful, holding certain positions on issues of morality, was a set of results that some thought we had in mind. Since some of us were ministers within the Roman Catholic Church, this was especially a question that would be in the minds of some. I would bring it up to others, as I became aware of the hesitation of some to ask me directly.

When people observe us and judge us based on what they see as "right" for young people, we encourage them to be aware of what *they* are doing. It is a temptation of people who have power, prestige, or popularity to want to perpetuate what gives them value. If people are open to putting on the glasses we call the Hebrew and Christian Scriptures, we invite them to open to Isaiah 58: 6-9 and Matthew 4: 1-11. If people are open to the Qur'an, we encourage them to turn to The Cow II., 183,184,185.

The importance of fasting relates to doing justice for all people and nurturing peace through each other. It may free you to be aware that the tempter was called an accuser, which is the way to blame, shame, and defame. It is a way to encourage violence in relationship to authority, whose purpose is to encourage life, and to community, whose purpose is to sustain life.

In the history of peace-building, the discipline of fasting has been essential. To practice losing that to which I feel I have a right to have is to ready me to yield to those who will take what I have. When it is happening, I will have the energy to breathe forgiving for their sake, even till my last breath. Fasting is the path to balance and to joy that lasts. I often fast when I am getting ready to work with young people who are dealing with the result of violence.

The most challenging part of our mission at Life Directions is to ensure that no one is responsible *for* anyone else, but that everyone is responsible *to* everyone else. In Chapter Two I wrote about the pimp who pushed me down a flight of stairs. I looked up and told the young man that I felt sorry for what he had done to himself, not to me. Yes, he had violated me, but I had managed to control any violent reaction from me.

What I did not share was that fasting ahead of time gave me the energy to be in control, if I were to be denied what I value. It worked at the bottom of the staircase. It is a simple principle; if I do not hit back, the violence loses momentum. This gives me even more reason to want to reach potentially violent people before it is too late for them.

The temptation of a leader is to build a dependency upon the person. Usually it is a charismatic leader. In politics we elect; in faith we are "called." The issue of accountability is the core matter. To whom is the charismatic leader accountable, and will the faith-based person decrease so that the One who called him or her can increase?

Youth and the young adults working in both Church and State

arenas are most vulnerable when the person they are leading is not responsible for their lives, choices or their consequences. Arcadio Gastelum, the Pascua Yaqui Chief living on his reservation in Arizona, gave a challenge that was the strongest one that I ever heard in my life. Twenty people in his tribe witnessed a need for their drug counselor to be retained. "She keeps us sober," was their theme. The Yaqui Chief responded: "You have explained why she must go. It is better for each of us to depend on ourselves and seek the power to do so from the Great Spirit."

An Ambassador of Forgiving and Understanding Addictions

Avoiding being responsible is another aspect of a spiritual anorexic, as we have experienced it. It often begins with being addicted to sexual activity, drinking, or drugs, as I mentioned before. These are three superficial addictions. They lead to three more addictions that are more substantive: gossip and personality assassination, gambling and reckless actions, and homicide. The end result of all of them is to take one's own life. When the sequence intensifies, the addictions collide and give an even greater thrill.

To invite young adults to discover a way to break this violent path, we encourage people to want to be self-responsible. We see a retreat experience that gives people space to listen to their past, let go of whatever is controlling them and look to the joy that developing their talents can do for them and for others.

Falling in love is the common way that awakens the joy of living with purpose. When this way of loving is more than intensity, there is found the intimacy of long-lasting commitments. There will be intense moments as the energy of unconditional love brings us back to life. A friendship that is based on mutual respect and desire to encourage each other to be our best has a similar impact.

We encourage young adults to become ambassadors of forgiving to see a way of living where no one can take away our joy but ourselves.

Such ambassadors understand a healthy way to enjoy life and the self-defeating path of addictions. Human sexuality is the celebration of unconditional love. Drinking alcohol is a way to share our joy. Drugs are a way to heal and manage mortality's pain. Seeing talents as the matching of peace builders is inventive. Risk-taking, to be excellent, is discovery. Defending is prudent courage. These can be discovered and lived by those who take the time.

Is it time to build character? Do we want to build people who are fair, generous, and have integrity? Do we want to encourage effort, diligence, and perseverance? This will nurture hope for the future of our children's children. The importance of justice will be wanted to treat all with equal respect. Its witness will be the unconditional love that remains at the end of the day.

When we began in October 1973, I realize now that I looked for three needs to ready myself to do the mission for which I was sent. My first need was met by Redemptorists who sent me--a place with resources to begin. The second need was to define the people to whom I am being sent--dropouts from faith communities and public schools. They were all around me. The third need was to build a team to do the mission.

When I met Fr. Alex Steinmiller, I was looking for a retreat house for the people I wanted to wake up to the spiritual life and its challenge to live for values that money cannot buy or control. Alexander and Judith MacDonald's immediate need was for their children who were to go into public high schools. When we first met, Sister Rosalie Esquerra was working with a federal program seeking to keep minorities in school.

All of us had a similar feeling of restlessness. We were all searching. It was and continues to be true. When a person hears of the real need to touch the cause of broken marriages and families, communities and countries, there is a spark that can ignite a fire. What we found that works is what we now see as important to put in place to sustain the mission. It takes an inspired team of people to make a commitment to stay the course together.

The decision to be in the race for the long run is why we kept our journals and why we were aware of what increased funding can do. It can fund us to fail, if we are not clear on the mission. It almost did. But our roots made it possible to learn from our failure.

Over the years, we have developed ways to select and train staff and volunteers. We have built ways to bring credibility to what we do through third-party evaluations. We have expanded and replicated our work when resources made it possible. We also have contracted our efforts as support diminished.

Cutting back was painful. Faith-based communities had to close their services. Cities faced bankruptcy. We have kept our balance with our roots in an inclusive spirituality that respects all cultures and creeds among people of good will. We know how to measure our growth within ourselves and among those with whom we work by seeing the value of self-responsibility and balanced relationships among youth and young adults.

The message is not meant just for those with whom we directly engage. This was the reason Peter Raskob presented our vision and mission to the foundation of which he was a member. We sense we have an insight to get to the cause of the violence that happened on 9/11. Because of this truth, we are aware of two inter-related values: keep our feet on the ground and our face to the sun. We pray for the spirit of unconditional surrender to the "Lord of the Dance" who loves us so much that He sent His only begotten Son (John 3:16). May what we have discovered be part of the "play book" for those seeking to find a way to build peace one person at a time.

Looking at the team that has been on the enterprise called "Life Directions" may inspire others to do the same. A charismatic leader has a place but is only one of five talents needed. The complement of talents made up our team for the long run. We needed a person to make sure we have all we need; a person to be clear on the direction needed, knowing the devil is in the detail; a person who listens and has the healing touch; and a person who sees the implications of both choices and more. Then if the mission is of God's people, the vision will grow in its own way.

We followed the Word of Life's way to know when someone's word meant commitment. The parable was the Master's way to discern who is and who is not totally committed. In the Book of Judges, Gideon had 30,000 soldiers but only 300 were willing to be faithful to death (Judges 7:7).

In Jesus' parable of the sower (Matthew 13:3-9), the sower seems to have been blind, hearing how he just threw the seed, but then listen further:

The foot path is created by the crowd who loves "sizzle" but not "substance"; they blow with the wind. The rocky ground is for the curious who loves the leader, but continues to look for more leaders before leaving. The thorny bush is the way of the follower who wants to commit, but cannot say "no" in order to say "yes." The rich soil is the leader who makes a commitment and goes one step further by challenging fellow followers to do what they say and say what they do.

Usually it takes one hundred people in the crowd to gain ten committed people. We discovered this formula by reflecting on Matthew 13: 16-23 and seeing our story through the prism of meaning that we called *The Word of Life*.

From our past, the five of us drew what we had received from our families. It continues to fashion a fabric of our future together. Our way to reflect upon our experience surfaced our choices for action. It is in the listening to our past that the values that are life-giving for the future come forth. We constantly are thankful for the patience and gentleness that sustained us. We seek to awaken that value among those with whom we work.

If You Want Peace, Work for Justice

Understanding a three-fold IQ as part of the integrity of a mature person was essential to being centered and focused on our mission.

We wanted IQ, the mental exercise that knows what is to be known. Each of us wanted to do our best to know the situation. There is no room to be naïve when engaging issues of violence and poverty.

We wanted EQ, the emotional maturing to be aware of what we see is the place to begin to be aware of the spirit surrounding what we know.

We wanted SQ, our spiritual awakening that the wisdom of the Jedi would bring us beyond our limits through freedom flowing from the power that chose us to be free. Such integrity would guide us to face our fear of risk-taking. It would encourage us to let go as we open to the "not-yet" that is beyond our lifetime.

The team will develop their ability to discern what to do to support and spread the mission. With the gentleness and humility essential to surrender unconditionally, they will seek to do God's will for the people. Their mission will work to bring life to all involved, including the team itself.

Each person's talents will be the value-added to others. We identified and tested the importance of five styles of influencing others to sustain any initiative where walking is to create the path. All are equally important. All styles are needed so that the team has what it needs to do what it does best.

The five ways to influence each other and others are the

following:

1: Maintain the foundation; 2: Give clear direction; 3: Receive each person with respect; 4: Attract people to want to see more; 5: ensure lessons learned center on the core values of the mission itself.

To initiate the team itself, the influencing "style" that is most important is the fourth: "attract and recruit others to follow." The next essential style to sustaining our balance is number five: "ensure lessons learned are centered on the core values of the mission." The importance of the first style of maintaining the foundation will make it possible for the other two--giving direction and receiving each person--to be sustainable.

The answer to our succession plan will lie in the building of a team that will have its own life. May what God did with the five of us encourage those who want to run the marathon. It will take people of solitude to encourage conversations seeking partners for the journey to bring values back through people who want to "pay it forward." How wonderful when our stories become His-story.

Telling Our Story Made Our Team Work

Born in the summer of 1942 in St. Louis, I grew up in many neighborhoods. Every five years we would move from the south side to the north side of the city, then to a little suburb only to move again into a more middle class community. When I left to start my journey toward seeking my mission in life, I left home to go to high school in another community of St. Louis County. This closed, and I went with the seminary to Wisconsin. I took a year away to discover if I was meant for the Redemptorists. It was a mutual time of testing, called "Discernment of the Spirits." When I left there to return to Wisconsin, it was in the middle of a major shift in our understanding of our global tradition as Catholic Christians in the world. Vietnam was escalating, and constant unrest was capturing the news. The year before I was to be ordained, I went to New York to complete my studies. What I did not know was that I was being trained to find my center within myself. I was also being trained to seek people whose actions would tell me what they meant by what they said. After five years of doing the work of a Redemptorist priest, I went into solitude to listen to the lessons of my life journey of thirty-one years. It was then that I discovered what has become my life work.

What I discovered was that I was trained in survival and in trusting my instincts. I came to Detroit in October 1973. Discovering Fr. Alex was possible because of how I was trained. He wanted to move into the unknown. He wanted to find a way to connect with people on the margins of society. He wanted to take our faith community's challenge seriously. "If you want peace, work for justice" (Pope Paul VI). He wanted to move out of retreat ministry into the streets. I wanted to find a retreat center for young people on the streets. We met and forged a relationship built on mission. The less we were accepted by the systems, the more we threatened to stay and find a way to get to the cause of self-destructive choices. Both of us had similar stories. The power of our stories is not what happened but what we did with what we were given.

In meeting Sister Rosalie we were to enter a life journey that was very different from what we had known. She grew up in Kingman Arizona—known for Andy Devine and Route 66. It was a small community with one traffic light, as she tells her story. She was a stay-at-home daughter, helping to raise her brothers and sisters. She went to the Adrian Dominican Motherhouse in Michigan, attracted by the "nuns who taught me." Her career in teaching was with first-graders in Detroit and along the Arizona border with Mexicans and Mexican Americans primarily. Her journey as a person within the school system ended in Las Vegas, Nevada. When she first told me her story, she was working to keep minority students in school. She was passionate about those left behind by the system. Her skill with the school system and her talent to help first-graders to see their potential was such a gift for us, as those who knew faith-based systems.

Alexander and Judith were dedicated to their children and to their faith community. Alexander was in our Redemptorist seminary for a short time, finished high school in Detroit, went to the army, and came home to Chrysler. Judith was in his class in high school, tested the convent, went to school to be a nurse, and married Alexander in 1963, the same year Fr. Alex and I took our vows. They were steeped in the challenges of raising their children in a community that was under major shifts. His understanding of factory life with her experience as a triage nurse was an amazing gift to be brought together with the three of us.

Our common ground was "those left behind, as people moved away and the systems to serve the most at-risk were closing." We had a common faith-life and found ourselves sharing a common understanding that diversity of cultures is a joy that makes diversity of creeds make sense. We also found out that we all had two parents who married before starting their families. All of our parents had raised six or more children. We were aware of our roots. We knew that the journey of life is a marathon and not a sprint.

Stopping to remember, it is no surprise to us that we have stayed together for forty years. And we can honestly say that each of our stories is the way in which we conceived, and have brought to maturity, the mission that began in the basement of "A & J's" home, as we affectionately called the MacDonald's home on Cavalry Street in southwest Detroit.

Yogi Berra, a fellow St. Louisan, is known for pithy one-liners. The one that our team of five has always held to be true is, "it ain't over till it's over." Many times it seemed to be over. We would then come together to reflect upon the choices facing us. We would put before us the statue of "the child in the hand" from Isaiah 49:15. We'd pause to pray, "If a mother were to forget her child, I would never forget you. I have carved you in the palm of my hand." Then another one-liner would break us out of our paralysis: "There is a fork in the road. Take it."

We draw from our story some lessons learned that we hope will encourage you to believe in your own story and discover the talents you have that are needed for those who are discouraged and looking for meaning out of loss and violence and emptiness.

First Insight: *Remembering Is a Way to Find the Message within the Mess*

We listened to our lives, as we shared what happened to us before we met. We found threads that would weave our experiences together. But to find the message, we needed to go to our roots in family and faith.

We needed to journal apart from each other and focus on how we felt about what we heard. We would write ahead of time. Then we would meet and share. It is amazing how the spirit surfaces what it means to be poor in spirit and rich in mercy.

For this reason, we are grateful for parents and elders who teach how to be aware: Boredom can awaken wisdom. "Sizzle" may have no substance. Yielding to the passive/aggressive keeps distance. Listen to what *isn't* said, for more may be heard that way. Chaos is the call of self-control within. Life is more right-and-left and not right-and-wrong--open to both/and more than an either/or way of judging each other.

Second Insight: *Keep Track of What Does not Work and Be Thankful for the Lesson Learned*

This insight kept us from going in directions we thought would be the way to go. We wanted to prepare those under eighteen years of age to want to come to our focus: LIFE retreat. We had experience with some young people fifteen to seventeen years of age doing well, so we designed a retreat called "Life Journey." It was very inactive and lightly encouraged spiritual ways of thinking and praying. The discipline was off-the-wall, literally. We were not prepared to "police" the place. We got through our attempt. What a lesson learned without much fall-out!

Then we thought we would prepare people over thirty-five years of age to be the team people to maintain our ongoing growth for young adults from eighteen to thirty-five years of age. In the middle of the weekend we became aware that we had created a group of advisors who knew what was needed but did not want to be part of delivering it. It was good for those who came, but never would translate into action for those for whom it was meant to serve.

Sister Rosalie told us a story of the donkey that would not move. The donkey was a very obedient donkey for her preacher. She would take him from town to town, till one day she would not move. The preacher pushed and pulled, swatted the donkey, and put some food out in front of her to get her to walk. Nothing worked. A person came by and asked what was happening. The preacher explained. The person said, "I just came from the town where you want to go. They heard about a preacher coming. They cannot wait to beat him up and send him on his way." The moral of the story: do not kick the donkey.

Third Insight: *Truth Depends on Relationships Among Messengers*

The more people committed to the same mission are different, the greater the opportunity to expand our mission and be ready to communicate with others, especially those different from ourselves. Bringing values to life within the public school system has its own set of obstacles, but having people with different talents and personalities made the work much richer.

There was a perception that we would *teach* values, more than awaken them from within each other. Our beginnings were the year of Watergate's deception and *Roe vs. Wade*. People who wanted abortion did not trust people from a faith community who opposed it.

We discovered that we were not worthy of trust among young people by those responsible for the system. Those in authority wondered what we would teach. We sensed they were seeking to test us. We knew it would take time. As we stayed consistent with our message, trust built. They came to trust us.

Fourth Insight: *The Leader Draws Sight from the Source That Sends*

Each person, who is to awaken others to be responsible for themselves, needs to be responsible to someone else. We knew that we would be measured by the choices the people for whom we worked would make. Would they complete high school? Would they go to college and complete it? Would they get a job and responsibly raise a family?

I remember the day after the Rodney King beating, I was to go into Wendell Phillips High School on Chicago's south side. I had just filled the position of a program director, who was an African American minister within my denomination. We drove up to the school. He refused to get out and go in with me; he told me he did not want to be killed. The students were all African American. I reminded him that he had always preached that young African American men needed role models. He blew it off; I went in alone. I told the young people, "You kill me, and people like me make lots of money on the news story. I become a hero for many, a martyr to remember. You all go through the emergency room at Provident Hospital and then to jail. I am supposed to be scared of you. You are supposed to think I am stupid. It is our choice. I am here. What do you want to do?"

I freely taught that each young person was responsible for his choices and not the media. I used this opportunity to wake them up to this value. I knew it would work. And they knew I believed in them. What they did not know, since it was against the law to say it, I remembered I was sent by someone whom I believe rose from the dead. If we did not believe, we would not do what we were doing.

Fifth Insight: *It is Finding the Mystery Hidden Beneath the Problems We Are Seeking to Solve*

We are constantly hearing of and responding to problems. We are asked how to solve the housing crisis, health care, education, employment--the list continues. We share what we think and we listen to what others hold to be true. It is a way of life, like violence is news. What is hopeful does not come from such ways of talking and remembering. It comes from seeing each person as a unique gift for all.

There is something deeper. Every time I hear, "Why does not the news media tell the good news?" I remember why. The Good News is Life out of Death. The media does not take away my joy. I see every young person as a mystery to be discovered. I pray to ensure the negative on the outside does not hide the beauty within.

I was asked once by a newspaper reporter in Detroit, "Father John, White people in the suburbs take care of their property. Black people in the city do not. What is wrong?"

Fortunately I remembered a former broadcast journalist who told me, "News is all about breaking the fifth, sixth, and seventh commandments. If you have a role in society where you are perceived as above such actions, it is even better news. It is all about Nielsen ratings."

"I live in the city," I answered, with a deliberate pause for effect. "I know young people who are being encouraged by the Grand Am Club to stop the fires on Devil's Night." I avoided the shame, blame, and defame trap. I silently breathed peace during the rest of the interview, remembering my "why"—the young people with whom I work. I would put up with any "how."

Sixth Insight: *If It Took Since the 1950s to Create Chaos, It Will Take Lots of Time to Find Community*

Someone once asked me, "Father, have you read this book about gangs?"

I responded, "No, I do not have time. I am *doing* the book. Hope you do not think once you read it anything has changed."

What I meant was that I needed to do enough so that I would learn from other's experience relating to me, as I learned from my dad, though it was years after I had the experience to appreciate it.

One night at supper, my brothers and I were having fun at my mom's expense. I do not remember what we were doing. But I do remember my father standing up and saying, "Sons, you won the battle by making fun of my wife. But you lost the war. You can now leave." It got really quiet. We all got up and walked out the back door. It seemed forever before the screen door opened. "My wife wants you back. Someday I hope you remember she is the center of my life, and then I hope you find someone to be the same for you."

What a lesson in unconditional love, which I am still learning. We found that the way to walk with young people and young adults is to follow the "law of gradualness." We hold up an ideal and know it takes time to grow. We hold up the value of forgiving when others speak of violence. When we find people who are in an entitlement way of thinking and others would want to begin with self-interest, we speak of life as a gift for which we are thankful. We share that each of us is part of the common good meant to be on the holy ground of the common good. We do not denounce or announce; we just share what is understandable to the person or group to whom we are sent.

Seventh Insight: *The Enemy Is the Friend That I Am Forgiving*

When I read James W. Douglass' *JFK and the Unspeakable*, I could accept the thesis that his death could have been a plot. When I hear the rich getting richer and "those living in an environment of poverty" getting poorer, it is not too difficult to agree with that. When I would listen at funerals about the young man in the casket who was killed, I would hear how God must have wanted him, or he would not be dead. To see what is wrong usually leads to talking about the wrong-doers: the person or the system. What is sad is that it does not lead to taking responsibility to become part of the solution.

I remember, as a teenager coming home from school one day, I told my mom that I was screwed up because she did not raise me right. She was making chili, barefoot and stirring the pot. Without looking up, she said, "Burn your behind, you sit on your own blister."

Change begins in me. "Would I forgive my mom or not if I saw her *not* doing what I needed?" It is my choice. Do I forgive others whom I believe have wronged me? It is my decision. And if I forgive, am I not free to be reconciled with the other?

Along the way there have been moments where I made some serious mistakes. It was sometimes difficult for me to see the wrong, and sometimes I meant to do what I did. I discovered something very important to me, when I wronged people who were close to me. Some would refuse to forgive me when I would ask forgiveness. Others would explain it away as if it did not matter. Only those who accepted me as being forgiven, and would remember what happened as being forgiven, were free to walk with me. The others would leave our work eventually. They would want to be within our team of fallen people seeking to support each other to be excellent.

Eighth Insight: *The One Who Does What is Right May Not Get a Crowd*

Supporting something that is not popular, like Branch Rickey did when he had Jackie Robinson be silent as he faced racism, makes for a good story—but only if it works. I was told to remember that success has a thousand fathers, and failure is an orphan. A statement like "people without a vision perish" is good to hear, but it is quite a different sound when I am alone.

To keep on keeping on demands teamwork committed to a dream that will come forward forty years after those who began the journey. This was true for Moses leading people out of slavery. Why do we think it may be different in leading people out of slavery by a different name? I once read a letter attributed to Barnabas. He supported the first followers of "the Way." When I reflected on Barnabas' way of responding to violence against Christians, I too wanted to encourage young adults to develop a spirit of reverence and perseverance through self-control. Provided we hold fast to these virtues and support each other in prayer, wisdom and understanding, knowledge and insight will make sure we never lose our joy.

I remember driving home after I was ordained a priest. My dad looked over at me and said, "Son, you do not need to live the values you professed. Lots of people do not. You can enjoy the good life and forget about 'those living in an environment of poverty'. No need to tell me what you will do. What you will do will tell you what you meant by what you said."

Ninth Insight: *As Rescuers Are Burning Out, the Self-Responsible Are Getting Fired Up*

The "haves" and the "have-nots" is a way to see life for most people. You are either one or the other. Depending on what you are analyzing you can have or not have money, talent, job, home, education, opportunities, health, and so forth. When this is the way in which we analyze, we can easily fall into the trap of seeing victims who need rescuers and who have nothing to give themselves.

What happens if everyone on all sides of every condition is self-responsible for the talent that each of us has and if the "haves" and the "have-nots" share with each other? What happens if everyone sees the joy of giving and receiving talents among people who are all part of the same world? What happens if everyone wants the richness of diversity to include all of creation? What happens is the paradigm shifts and equity and equality are bound together with a common destiny.

The place to begin is not with the victims hearing about the perpetrators. The place to begin is not with people with resources not being involved. The place to be is to challenge the rescuers, who want to be messiahs, to bring "the haves" and the "have-nots" together. To keep this spirit alive as a work-in-progress is to remember that wisdom moves each of us to want to live our "spark," our talent. This was seeded when we were not yet born.

Tenth Insight: *"Not Yet" But It is About to Come to Light*

Our journey continues. It is part of a journey into hope that lies within the mystery of each person. We are still seeking the answer to the way to have a succession plan, knowing that the stories of thousands are more than enough. We are still searching for the cause of violence, as we breathe forgiving. We are still knocking on the door to feed the hungry who are anorexics to values and inclusive spirituality.

To remember what came from what began with Melchisedek is to take time to listen to the few who want to make a difference. Abram became Abraham and began a community where two percent wanted to follow him. He left his work to Isaac to continue the vision.

Moses wanted to bring the people out of slavery with the Golden Calf distracting people from the mission. Jesus influenced thousands with his action plan but his life ended with only a few at his funeral. The key to succession planning is to know most works of importance happen after it is all over.

Do we imagine a world that is free from violence? Our insight at Life Directions revolves around choosing forgiving as a way to come out of violence to make peace possible. Our faith tells us that this is the way to move from the paradigm of violence to the paradigm of forgiving.

It is About Just Doing It!

I pray that more people remember why we began our work. Let the "why" sustain you as you endure your "how." We have called this discipline "logo praxis." It has made all the difference to us. When asked "why" we are hopeful for the mission, we remember the children's children and respond "why not?"

Isaiah 49:15 encourages us in our quest to know that time is a precious gift; As my father taught me, "it is only just a minute, sixty seconds in it, forced upon us, cannot refuse it, did not seek it, did not choose it, give account if we abuse it, just a tiny little minute. But eternity is in it." Enjoy the journey!

THE PARABLE OF THE LOST PLANE

"Twenty six countries are searching for any sign of the 777 plane that disappeared in the middle the night. The best and most expert people are seeking to find indicators of where to look--for a crash, for a hijack...for whatever. Why is a 777 plane so internationally important? So similar to the twin towers is the fear that it could easily happen to any country, anyone and anywhere. Because of human nature, we are all vulnerable. Is it time to discover how our way of seeing perfection as symbolized by 777 needs to be viewed the same way as we look at 666, which happens just before 777?

Seven is the strongest number that cannot be divided. Six is the weakest number, divisible by two. Is it time to respond to weakness and wrong in a way that embraces the fearful, encourages the hopeless? Is it time to believe "In God We Trust?"

1. Why do you think 777 are the numbers used to win at casinos?

2. What do you want to teach your children and your children's children as ways to believe in life beyond what money can give?

3. What does the fear generated from accidents and the thrill surrounding sports have in common?

It will take a team of people who have the energy of youth, the knowledge of mentors and the wisdom of the elders to know how to be understood in responding.

Life is more than chance. Our purpose lives within what sparks creativity for the sake of others.

1. Money is but a means to express the priceless gift of unconditional love.

2. Such love casts out fear when our enemy is the friend we are forgiving and we do not want anyone to lose.

CONCLUSION
NOW WHAT?

The cure to violence is hidden in plain sight. Central to every world religion are peace, healing and joy. Our life's work is to lift up the truth that will set us free so that all people may live. The cure is *forgiving unconditionally*. It is the hallmark of the Master who taught his disciples how to pray "forgive us as we forgive others." The only sin that cannot be forgiven according to the Christian GPS is the sin against the Holy Spirit (Matthew 12:32). Is this not the sin of *not forgiving*, breathing as the one who taught us how to pray, "Father, forgive them; they do not know what they are doing"?

We knew why we needed to be hidden. Being from Missouri, the "Show Me" state, I am focused on what we do to know what we mean. I saw that the Word that came to speak was silent ninety percent of His time on earth. When He broke the silence at twelve years of age, he was "grounded," as I saw it (Luke 2:51). When He spoke for the first time in His home town at the age of thirty, He was rejected (Luke 4:24). He lived only three more years.

I knew from the way I was treated in public that what I learned in school, and what I heard Gandhi say, was right. Christians and its leaders have treated each other and others at times outside the spirit of the Gospel.

I thought it best to follow my Provincial and Nike Tennis shoes and "Just do it!" Who would have believed me if I were to say that we Christians are "lovers of freedom?" We want all people to come to decisions following their conscience and in light of truth found in relationships centered on the Creator, govern their activities with a sense of responsibility, and strive after what is right, always willing to join with others in cooperative effort.

I was taught to bring forth new things that are in harmony with the things that are old, but I was staring at the spirit of competition among religions and among educational institutions. Most everyone was focused on defending the independent systems. In Detroit alone we had, at one time, more than 800 churches. No way would what we have in common, "forgiving and being forgiven," be the common ground for discovering how to bring the cure into the cause.

Given the first response from public school principals and the reaction of U.S. citizens to the "Mondale Law" introduced in 1974, we sensed it would be better *to just do it*. We knew "why" we wanted to be with "those living in an environment of poverty" caught up in a climate of violence.

I was taught to respect each person's conscience and to refrain from any manner of action that might seem to carry a hint of coercion or of a kind of persuasion that is dishonorable or unworthy, especially when dealing with poor people.

People were telling me, "Father, you have to tell them to be…." The focus was on banking information (IQ). But I remember my answer to my mother, when she asked me how many times she had told me something. (See Parable at the end of Chapter Five). I answered "thirty-eight times" and she corrected me for speaking back. Later I found out she thought if I knew what she said I would obey. How many times have we heard the Ten Commandments? Knowledge of what is wrong is good. But to say "no" is a decision of the will. It calls for the wisdom to do what it right, even when we do not feel like it. The key to the success of Life Directions for forty years has been our ability to stay together--spiritually, emotionally and operationally. How did a group of like-minded but drastically diverse individuals navigate opportunities and overcome monumental challenges? An insight into the answer, of course, can be found in the parable of the rope around the glacier.

Imagine if the Titanic and the glacier had stayed together. The Titanic, built in Belfast, Northern Ireland, was believed to be the boat that could never sink. When it went on its maiden voyage, its passengers were enjoying themselves without a care in the world. Then on the evening of April 14, 1912, it hit a glacier. Panic set in; lives were lost at sea. Some, in life boats, were saved to tell the story of what happened. If only no one had been lost, what a joy there would have been around the world. This outcome could well have been possible, if only the people on the boat had worked together, taken the rope used for the anchor, and wrapped it around the glacier. If only the glacier would not have been seen as the one from whom to separate but to whom we would do good while experiencing persecution.

Dedication to the spiritual core of our mission is the rope that has tethered us to the glacier. It was and is the anchor that got us through the "whys" of our journey.

We knew *why* we wanted to be with young people in public schools. This is the way we are in our pluralistic society. What better place to do "forgiving" as the cure to violence than when we are all together: the good, the bad, and all in-between. We saw no value in separating people. Since our GPS said it is not in our power to separate creation (Matthew 13:30), the authority to do so is with the Creator.

We knew *why* we wanted to be with young adults with whom we could legally deepen the cure to "violence." Based on what we do as a country, nuclear threat is essential to keeping the peace—peace through strength. I read Douglass' *JFK and the Unspeakable.* The conversation that looked to disarmament, that never surfaced while he was alive, was what I had sensed would happen if ever we were known for promoting trust through forgiving as the cure to the fear of violence.

The author told of the communication among Nikita Khrushchev, John F. Kennedy, and Pope John XXIII when they were exploring ways to disarm for the sake of peace. Pope John published his work, called *Peace on Earth,* in April 1963. He died in June. JFK was assassinated in November, and Khrushchev was removed in early 1964.

We knew *why* we wanted the Life Circles for young adults and elders. In 1939, a religious leader said that "nothing is lost by peace; everything is lost by war." The United Nations was founded in June 1945. Bobby Kennedy, author of *The Enemy Within* (1960) cautioned that: the "victims of violence are black and white, rich and poor, young and old, famous and unknown." Sadly, he was assassinated just two months after making that statement.

I studied Pope John XXIII's insight that nuclear arms in economically more developed countries involve a vast outlay of intellectual and material resources that saddles people with a great burden and leaves others lacking what they need. Only young adults who are determining their way of life and work are positioned to change what they can. They are in the best position to do so. We believe young adults know from their experience in growing up in our country that to claim one's rights and ignore one's duties is like building the house with one hand and tearing it down with the other.

We know *why* we wanted to hold up "forgiving" in the way the Master did. He was hit on the cheek (Matthew 5:39-41). I know from study that this response is the way to shame the violent. But I thought it best to "just do it."

On retreats, I ask someone to hit me on the right cheek. I then ask, "When did the Master get hit on the cheek? It was when he was before the spiritual leader. Yet, he turned the other cheek (John 18:23). He confronted the violent assertively. When I am hit, I am in control of my response. When violence leads to killing, knowing that the violent are addicted and are close to self-destruction, to kill in response does not stop the killing."

Marietta Jaeger's book, *The Lost Child*, speaks of her journey. She went from wanting to kill the man who mutilated her daughter in Montana, to forgiving him. Jaeger desired to meet the killer in prison. She did not make it in time because he took his own life. I recall how she shared the experience of actually going into his jail cell. It was extremely dark and dreary. She sat there and imaged the man's presence with her. She forgave and blessed him. I remember her explaining how "a light" or "brightness" took over the jail cell, replacing the darkness.

We know *why* we do the mission of Life Directions. "If a mother would forget her child, I would not forget you" (Isaiah 49:15). I referred to Giddings' work, "*When and Where I Enter, to* explore the beauty of married love's way of birthing and raising African American children at the turn of the twentieth century. What would the book say about the beginning of the twenty-first century with 9/11?

We know that everything works together for the good of all. As I began to write this book, Alexander MacDonald started to have a health challenge. He gradually weakened and was unable to speak. He knew I was writing our story. He was grateful. He wanted us to give to the next generation what we had discovered: forgiving is unconditional love's response to violence. He told us he was offering up his suffering for Life Directions.

He passed on as we were completing the writing. A man of integrity to the end, Alexander encouraged us to give to our children's children what we had discovered. What a great way to end his life direction: wanting to give what he could, his prayers, for what had been integral to his beginning.

Our hope is to plant the seeds of forgiving within the same soil seething in selfishness, knowing that the selfless will live in FEAR that leads to freedom, because it means "Forgiving Excels Always Redeeming." The flower we use to symbolize our mission is the forget-me-not. Whenever forgiving is a challenge, we ask each other to give us a forget-me-not to remember that nothing is lost by forgiving, and nothing is gained by refusing.

Three men taught me an invaluable lesson by making me face hate and the refusal to forgive. Their denying me forgiveness opened me to see the difference between forgiving and reconciling. One was within my personal life; another was from a fellow priest; the third was from a person with whom I worked. What I did or did not do was not the issue.

The issue was that I was given awareness for which I am thankful. Recently, one of them told me he forgave me after fifteen years. The other came to an event to be with me, and his presence was how he spoke. The other, I pray for him. It was so violent, but not toward me as much as toward himself.

Eve would not have wanted capital punishment for her son Cain. Abraham would have gained so much more if only Isaac and Ishmael would have both been free together. Solomon's wisdom was best expressed when the truthful mother was found after ensuring the king not to give her only half a child.

The Master would have wanted both thieves to steal heaven. I believe he would have wanted Judas in the upper room with the other eleven. He would not refuse him forgiveness. The only reason Jesus could not forgive Judas was because Judas could not forgive himself.

Recent research says that people who take their own life are mentally ill. Knowing the research on addictions, is it time to find a different solution to the problem of violence? We will, if we remember *why*--practice *unconditional love through forgiving*. We are our brothers' keepers. That is *why*. Or do we disagree and want to continue to live the question as Cain did? Are we "able" to change?

Our *why* is the road less travelled. With our spiritual GPS, we are constantly recalculating. I wish to end with one of the more insightful parables that sustain us. I alluded to it before, but the richness that is within the "seed," is constantly unfolding. We do what we remember, and that is how we remember what to do.

"The sower went out to sow some seed" (Matthew 13:3b). When we take time to reflect upon what happens to the "seed," it keeps us aware of the importance of waiting to see what people do with what they receive. Maybe that is why we in Missouri say, "Let's wait. What they do will tell us what they meant by what they said."

For me, the sower seems to have been blind. He was just throwing the seed without consciously ensuring the ground was ready to receive it. I think of all the people our work has touched. We have shared insights and actions, planning and training, teaching and organizing, preaching and directing, fundraising and marketing. We have thrown out a lot of "seed."

What a gift we have received to know the Master of Life explained why most of what was scattered would not take root. "Their minds are dull, and they have stopped up their ears and have closed their eyes. Otherwise, their eyes would see, their ears would hear, their minds would understand, and they would turn to me, says God, and I would heal them" (Matthew 13:15).

We know the reason; it is all about control. It is all about building spiritual cholesterol conditional forgiving, not wanting our enemy to be our friend. We want to receive that which gives us what we want to be free, but we do not want to bring this same freedom to people we do not know and do not know us. We know the reason such a vision is not seen, such a mission is not heard. We do not freely give the forgiving we so much want to receive. We have a hardened heart toward those whom we do not love, as we want God to love us.

"Some seeds fell on the footpath." Many people whom we touch may blow off what we have given. We were talking to the self-interest crowd. They were polite but moved on, as if we had never been there. I remember Judith and Alexander being told by more than fifty people that they were coming to a meeting to hear more about our work.

When they told me about the expected large gathering, we set up forty chairs. Four people came, including the three of us. This is where we began to think it would take asking a hundred people to have ten come, and it hasn't failed us yet. We do not get burned out because we remember what He did and we do what we remember. We keep on giving.

"Some seed fell on rocky ground." When the "ten" we had wanted came to a gathering, we found that most people who hear the message get really excited to know "something's being done." They cheer us on, clap, and tell us how proud they are for what we are doing. They admire us and tell us to keep on going and do not give up. They even ask when they can hear more.

I remember Dr. Leo Rasca telling me of the ten "conversation meetings" he had where an average of twelve people came with six people signing up for the follow-up meeting. Out of the sixty who said they were coming, twelve did. I was grateful that Alexander and Judith helped me see what to expect.

"Some seed fell among thorns." We listen to people say "yes" to what they hear. They want to follow our way of building peer-to-peer groups that will support the work of promoting peace-building to reduce violence.

We share manuals and workbooks with action plans for eighth-to-twelfth-graders. We do the work in the schools and in the communities. We build gardens, create murals and plan activities for people to mix with people of other cultures. We put together gatherings for young adults and adults who want to deepen their knowledge and skills to contact and recruit others, present programs and work with those who come. I remember us buying the food for the twenty who signed up for training and giving the food away to the five who kept their word. We called the fifteen others, and it must have sounded like what the Master heard from people who said they would follow him (Luke 9:57-62). When this happens, it always hurts, and it is quite a consolation to have the GPS recalculate and keep us moving.

"Some seeds fell on rich soil." When this happens, the power of the few becomes such a source of encouragement and hope. We see unconditional forgiving getting to the cause of violence. I now know what it must have been like for the Master when one came back and it was a foreigner, and to think the Master had cured them of a terminal disease. I now know what Gideon found out: 20,000 soldiers will probably produce 300 people who are totally committed.

We believe that the few will feed the many, if we give what we have and are willing to let God do what only God can do. We do not know how the resources will come. We do not know who the participants will be. We do not know where we will build up partners for peace-building. We do not know when the young people will be hungry for values and not violence, or when the young adults will be thirsty for reconciliation and not retaliation, or when adults will be willing to respond to the need to show how love overcomes fear (1 John 4:16-18).

We know what we do not know. But this we know, "God, who began this good work in you, will carry it on until it is finished (Philippians 1:6).

May I speak in the name of the co-founders as I say, "Thank you" to each person who says "yes" and means it, every donor who believes in the vision, every participant who trusts their peers, and every young person who wants to give peace a chance?

Fr. Alex and I went to see two films early in our relationship that captures our spark so well. *To Kill a Mockingbird* (1962) raised the issue of violence. *One Flew Over the Cuckoo's Nest* (1975) let us know what to expect. Like Scout in *Mockingbird*, we remember many young people "see what we older folks are doing." Like Nurse Ratchet in *Cuckoo's Nest*, we remember many are part of the system that keeps violence festering. To these we say, "Father, forgive them, they *do not* know what they are doing."

But we do, and we are entrusted with the challenge to do what we can, wait for what we cannot do, and then enjoy those who do more than we could have ever asked or imagined.

ABOUT THE AUTHORS

Rev. John E. Phelps, C.Ss.R.

President and Chief Executive Officer

Father John Phelps is the President and C.E.O. of Life Directions, which he co-founded in 1973 with four other concerned Detroit citizens, Fr. Alex Steinmiller, C.P.; Sister Rosalie Esquerra, O.P.; Alexander and Judith MacDonald. He is a Roman Catholic priest, ordained in 1968, and belongs to a religious community of men called the Redemptorist Congregation. Fr. Phelps' primary work is among young adults (thirteen to thirty-five years of age), with a priority on those on the verge of dropping out of school and into self-destructive life choices. He is especially focused on those who come from families below or near the poverty line.

Among his many academic achievements, Fr. Phelps holds a Bachelor of Philosophy Degree with a minor in Psychology, Master of Arts Degree in Religious Education, and a Master of Divinity Degree. In 1999, he completed a four-day Executive Training course offered by the Gallup Organization in Lincoln, Nebraska.

From 2005 to 2007, Fr. Phelps served as Pastor of St. Alphonsus "Rock" Church in St. Louis, Missouri and President of Nativity-Miguel Middle School in St. Louis, serving 350 pre-school to eighth grade students. In 2009, he returned to Life Directions as full-time CEO.

Fr. Phelps is a renowned preacher and lecturer. He has led hundreds of workshops in cities, colleges, and universities throughout the United States and abroad. In 1990, Fr. Phelps was invited to bring Life Directions to Chicago. In partnership with the co-founders, in 1993 he established Life Directions USA as a not-for-profit organization incorporated in the State of Illinois and doing business in four additional states.

Additionally, his work had led him to be highly sought after as a consultant on issues concerning at-risk youth. He has served with various ecumenical organizations, church groups, corporations and educational institutions that are striving to place a priority on developing inclusive partnerships among people of diverse backgrounds and economic differences.

With Fr. Phelps' leadership, Life Directions has been working for over forty years to promote the powerful dynamic of *Peers Inspiring Peers Through Forgiving.*

Fr. Alex Steinmiller, C.P.

<u>President, Holy Family Cristo Rey Catholic High School, Birmingham, Alabama</u>

Fr. Alex Steinmiller is a Catholic priest and belongs to a community of missionaries known as the Passionists, which works with the poor and marginated in fifty-eight countries.

The Passionists have been located in Ensley, Alabama, at Holy Family Parish and schools since 1936. They built the Holy Family Community Hospital which accommodated black families and hired black doctors and nurses during segregation days. The parish has a middle school.

Fr. Steinmiller is the president of Holy Family Cristo Rey Catholic High School. The school includes 171 students from families who cannot afford a college preparatory education. Every student works their way through high school in the Corporate Internship Program. In this program, students contribute to their tuition by holding a once-a-week, entry level, corporate job. The school is in its fifth year of operation. While the school boasts that one hundred percent of all grads are accepted into college, the first full four-year class of graduates has eighty-seven percent of the students still attending college.

Fr. Steinmiller spent thirty years developing programs with at-risk young adults, thirteen to thirty years of age in Detroit and San Antonio. He co-founded Life Directions, which continues into its fortieth year of work in Chicago and Detroit.

He holds a Master's Degree in Divinity from the Catholic Theological Union at Chicago. He has done extensive work in the area of breaking the cycle of poverty, non-violence, and male spirituality.

Rosalie Arcelia Esquerra, O.P.

Co-founder of Life Directions and Director of Life Directions' Training Center

As a Director of Life Directions, Sister Rosalie Esquerra has co-designed and implemented Focus LIFE Volunteer Training and Development and three other programs: Peer Mentor, Peer Motivation, and Neighborhood Enrichment. She has co-authored manuals and workbooks for staff and volunteers from a multi-cultural and bi-lingual perspective. Additionally, in 2001, she became the Director of the National Training Center for Life Directions.

Born in Kingman, Arizona, Sister Rosalie (as she is affectionately known) has been a member of the Adrian Dominican Sisters since 1955. She holds a Master's degree in Education; a Bachelor's in Philosophy and has been certified as a conflict mediator, youth and parent effectiveness instructor and as a third-party conflict manager.

As a teacher and principal, from 1957-1974, Sister Rosalie created a positive and supportive climate for learning. She holds specific interest in children in need of special attention--academic, emotional, and spiritual. As a coordinator of the Title VII project (1974-1976, LASED Detroit), she directed a team responsible to ready parents to advocate for their children for bi-lingual education in the midst of the desegregation crisis. Impact accomplished needed changes with parent involvement that continues in southwest Detroit.

Sister Rosalie, a Mexican American, is bi-lingual with the abilities to read, write and speak Spanish and English. In 1974, she was involved with Hispanics as a partner in the Archdiocese of Detroit's creation of its first Hispanic office. She has given numerous workshops in Spanish on communication skills, assertiveness, conflict Management, and cultural awareness. She has also led retreats and parish missions in Spanish. In 1995, she initiated Life Directions within the Native American community of Arizona

Among her numerous recognitions, Sister Rosalie is the recipient of the "Citizenship Award" from Detroit Public Schools for her outstanding contributions to children, schools and community (1974). She has received numerous other recognitions, proclamations and special tributes for her educational and community service.

Alexander and Judith MacDonald

Co-founders of Life Directions

Alexander MacDonald, who passed away in September 2013, celebrated his fifty year wedding anniversary with Judith May 4 of this year. They have eight children, twenty grandchildren, and two great grandchildren. Alexander was born in Nova Scotia. He came to the United States when he was ten years old. He graduated from Holy Redeemer High School and served in the U.S. Army Reserves for six years. He worked at Harper Hospital as an OR technician. As a technician, he worked on some of Dr. Forest Dewey Dodrill's heart cases. Dr. Dodrill was famous for performing the first successful open heart operation in the world. Alexander attended Sacred Heart Seminary for five years and received a Certificate in Pastoral Ministry. Alexander went to work for Chrysler in 1965. He attended Chrysler Institute and received certifications in the following studies: Professionalism in Management, Public Speaking, "Rubenstein's Problem Solving" and Professional in Management Phase II. Alexander retired in 2000. In the formative years of Life Directions, he helped build the leadership of adults to work with young adults and conducted groups of young adults with the focus on Peers inspiring Peers to forgive. He took many leadership roles in his parish, St. Gabriel. He served as Chairperson of the Parish Council and as a pastoral Minister, he prepared couples for marriage and baptisms. Along with his wife, Alexander co-chaired the Archdiocesan Endowment Campaign for "Stewards for Tomorrow" in their parish.

Judith MacDonald graduated from Holy Redeemer High School and McAuley School of Practical Nursing. She continued her education at Schoolcraft College and Sacred Heart Seminary. She served in various capacities in Life Directions, as administrator, manager of personnel, finances marketing and public relations. Judith conducted groups for leadership--among adults and young adults in the neighborhoods. She served as Life Directions' focus:

Life Directions: Raising Hope, Building Peace

Life first chairperson of the Board of Trustees and on Our Lady of Mercy High School's first Board of Trustees. Judith was a member on several parish councils. She retired from Detroit Receiving Hospital, Trauma Center, where she worked as a Medical Licensed Practical Nurse (MLPN).   Presently, Judith is a corporate member of Life Directions, serving as the Vice President of Mission Effectiveness.

GRATITUDE

To be grateful for completing this work is to be aware of the thousands of stories that weave a quilt of life that is yet to be told. We want to thank the young people and young adults whose courage continues to encourage us to stay the course on our journey as peace-builders.

We want to thank our religious congregations: the Redemptorists, the Passionists and the Adrian Dominicans. We also want to thank the Capuchin Community of Detroit for their hospitality and support; Sr. Gail Trippett, a Sister of St. Joseph of Carondelet, for her tireless review of the drafts that were both corrective and encouraging; and Fr. Gerry Kleba of the Archdiocese of St. Louis for his insightful review that called us to ensure the stories of those we touched showed the results of our pursuit to getting to the cause of violence.

We want to thank the faculties and administrators whose collaboration made it possible for the young people to discover their "sparks" and inspire their peers to find theirs as well.

To our Board of Directors and Boards of Trustees that support the mission, we are grateful for their generating the resources for this work.

We want to thank Sylvester Brown, Jr. for his counsel and sensitive complementary, with his expert way of crafting our journey after studying our journals handwritten from 1973 on.

We want to thank our Administrative Assistant, Bonnie Remenapp, and our Project Director, Van Bensett for their encouragement and support.

We want to thank the people of the Middle East who were so encouraging of me throughout my writing of our story and for donating funds to support the underwriting for this work. We thank Larry Tokarski for his consistent belief in our mission and for his generous matching gift to make it possible to complete our work in a timely way.

Finally, we want to thank Annette Howard, whose desire to "write her story" inspired us to do what we needed to do to tell "our story;" to Pat Trainor, Tom Howard, Dr. Leo Rasca-Hidalgo, Karen Kerrigan, Donna Cruz, Rory Calhoun, Ricardo and Myra Larios, and all those who helped us remember.

WORKS CITED

Chapter One
The Confessions of St. Augustine by St. Augustine of Hippo (between AD 397-AD 398)
Life Code: The New Rules for Winning in the Real World by Dr. Phil McGraw (2013)
The Third Wave by Alvin Toffler (1984)
How Children Succeed, Tough, Paul (2013)

Chapter Three
Slavery by Another Name: The Re-Enslavement of Black Americans from the Civil War to World War II by Douglas A. Blackmon (2009)

Chapter Seven
The Road Not Taken by Robert Frost (poem, published in 1916)
The Farther Reaches of Human Nature by Abraham H. Maslow (1973)
People of the Lie: The Hope for Healing Human Evil by M. Scott Peck (1998)
The Different Drum: Community Making and Peace by M. Scott Peck (1998)

Chapter Eight
The War Prayer by Mark Twain (Written during the Philippine-American War in the first decade of the twentieth century/Source: Amazon Books)
When Society Becomes an Addict by Ann Wilson Schaef (1988)
Pedagogy of the Oppressed by Paulo Freire (first published in Portuguese in 1968/ translated into English by Myra Ramos and re-published in 1970/Source: Amazon Books)
Fundamental Moral Attitudes by Dietrich von Hildebrand (Essay Index Reprint Series/Hardcover 1977)
Strength to Love by Martin Luther King Jr. (4th Printing edition (1968/Source: Amazon Books)
U.S. Catholic Bishops' Statement to the Native American People (May 1974)

Chapter Nine
Out of the Shadows: Understanding Sexual Addiction by Patrick J. Carnes Ph.D. (Paperback edition 2001)
The Mis-Education of the Negro by Carter G. Woodson (Originally published in 1938)
When and Where I Enter: The Impact of Black Women on Race and Sex in America by Paula Giddings (1985)
The Future is Mestizo: Life Where Cultures Meet, by Virgilio Elizondo (Revised Paperback Edition 2000)
Man's Search for Meaning by Victor Frankl (Revised, updated Pocket Books edition 1997/Source Amazon Books)

Chapter Ten
Reconciliation: Islam, Democracy, and the West by Benazir Bhutto (Paperback edition 2008)
I-Thou ("Ich und Du" German translation) by Martin Buber (1st edition 1971)
Five Cries of Youth by Merton P. Strommen (Revised edition 1988
Seven Basic Life Principles – Seminar by Bill Gothard
JFK and the Unspeakable by James W. Douglass (2009)

Conclusion
Peace on Earth (Pacem in Terris): Encyclical Letter by His Holiness Pope John XXIII (1963)
The Enemy Within: The McClellan Committee's Crusade against Jimmy Hoffa and Corrupt Labor Unions by Robert F. Kennedy (1960)
The Lost Child by Marietta Jaeger (1983)

Made in the USA
Charleston, SC
09 February 2015

3844329IR00174